A New Day in the Delta

TREASURE
COAST

LITERARY
SOCIETY

Sponsored By:

A New Day
in the Delta

Inventing School Desegregation
As You Go

David W. Beckwith

THE UNIVERSITY OF ALABAMA PRESS
Tuscaloosa

Typeface:AGaramond

∞

The paper on which this book is printed meets the minimum requirements of
American National Standard for Information Sciences–Permanence of Paper
for Printed Library Materials, ANSI Z39.48-1984.

Library of Congress Cataloging-in-Publication Data

Beckwith, David W.
A new day in the Delta : inventing school desegregation as you go /
David W. Beckwith.
p.   cm.
ISBN 978-0-8173-1633-4 (cloth : alk. paper) — ISBN 978-0-8173-8110-3
(electronic) 1. Beckwith, David W. 2. Teachers—United States—Biography.
3. Teachers, White—Mississippi—Leland. 4. Faculty integration—
Mississippi—Leland. I. Title.
LA2317.B34B43 2009
371.10092--dc22
[B]
2008025567

Acknowledgments

I would like to dedicate this book to my wife, Nancy, who I am sure is jumping for joy now that this project has finally come to a conclusion, and to thank her from the bottom of my heart for her help in editing the manuscript. She spent many, many hours slaving over this book to make sure things were correct. This is the latest attestation to a wonderful lifelong partnership. I also thank my brother Bill, my technical guru daughter Aimee, and my friends Lollie Morgan, Bobbie and John Danise, Sheila Small, Henri Sue and Jimmy Bynum, Tameika Jackson, Carolyn Perkins Gibson, Annie Taylor Paden, Ron and Sherry Seher, and Stephanie Park, who have been both helpful and supportive at times when I needed both. A very special thanks to Caldwell M. Bibbs for the values he imparted as an educator and a friend.

A New Day in the Delta

Introduction

The year was 1969. Richard Nixon had been inaugurated as the thirty-seventh president of the United States. Neil Armstrong and Buzz Aldrin walked on the moon. Young people gathered for four rain-soaked days outside Woodstock, New York, for sex, drugs, and rock and roll. The world was introduced to *The Godfather* and sang with Simon and Garfunkel about the naughty Mrs. Robinson. We lost another venerated president, Dwight D. Eisenhower. Texas was the national college football champion. Joe Namath and the New York Jets astounded the country by defeating the favored Baltimore Colts in the Super Bowl. Ted Kennedy was disgraced in an automobile accident known as Chappaquiddick. Hurricane Camille ravaged the Mississippi Gulf Coast.

Different kinds of storms brewed as protest went into high gear over our unpopular involvement in Vietnam, and civil rights groups moved toward another conflict—the final desegregation of America's public schools. This upheaval in social change was brought about with all the delicacy of a wrecking ball.

I wasn't a social activist. I was merely a young man just graduating from college who desperately needed a job and was thrown into the middle of one of the greatest social movements in post–World War II America. As in any period of change and stress, there were heroes and villains on both sides.

Human reactions to life-changing events are influenced by our roots—the culture to which we are exposed. While the life-changing events described in this book took place throughout our nation, the human reaction was profoundly different in the South. The people of the South, with their strong regional identity, struggled for many years over the issue of integration. The history of the issue of integration in the South is wrought with hatred and violence.

It is not the purpose of this book to condemn or condone the human reactions to this watershed event in the South, and more specifically in the Mississippi Delta. Rather, through exposure to some unique aspects of southern culture, the reader will acquire a better understanding of southerners and the perceptions that motivated them. For example, southern politicians justified segregation for many decades with the use of the concept "separate but equal." Most white southerners knew that equality didn't exist, but until they felt a direct impact on themselves or their families, they repressed the reality and found it easy to live with the illusion of parity.

As a child born and raised in the Delta, I was taught at a tender age most of the things that distinguish the South from other areas of the nation. It was never troublesome to me to hear others say that people from the South talked funny. From our perspective, so did outsiders; they not only talked funny but talked really fast.

The South has frequently been referred to as the "Bible Belt" because of the significance of religion in the lives of most southern families. In many rural southern communities, religion is the focal point and social center of family life. Social events and church services always included music. The South was the birthplace of many musical styles, such as rock and roll, bluegrass, blues, jazz, rhythm and blues, and zydeco. Southern food has long been considered delicious, though in some cases local delicacies such as grits and catfish were mysterious to outsiders. More often than not, these foods' common denominator was that they were fattening.

Also unique to southern culture is the southern way of speaking. For example, the designation "lady" is often used instead of "woman." One knows that beauty can fade and wealth can diminish, but character is a lasting legacy. In the South, being referred to as a "lady" means that one possesses all the requisite manners, and it is perhaps the highest compliment a woman can receive. The reader will find southern colloquialisms throughout these pages.

This book is based on a diary I kept during 1969 and 1970. It is written from the point of view of a multigenerational white, southern "insider." I filled out the dialogue in order to add impact to crucial scenes. Characters are portrayed as I perceived them. As is often human nature, I am sure that some people's perceptions of themselves differ. Racial epithets used in the book are not meant to demean any group. They were, however, used during this period and add historical authenticity.

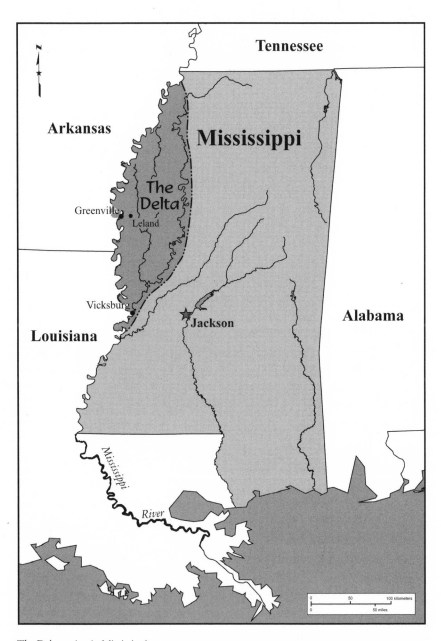

The Delta region in Mississippi

1

The day had started badly. Most of my days recently seemed to start badly. Each began with a series of skirmishes that more often than not escalated into battles which then, if not checked, became mini-wars. There was seldom a clear-cut victory in these conflicts. Things sure had changed since I was a student, I mused. My teachers weren't always respected, but, by God, they ruled. They were the lords; we students were the serfs. My secret thoughts of rebellion had always been fleeting and had never been verbalized. After all, my mama didn't raise a fool.

My attention returned to the present and the skirmish at hand.

"Ain't nothin' you got to say that I need to hear. Nothin' I ain't heard umpteen jillion times before," Fisheye grunted petulantly. "Near as I can tell, nothin' in this school ever helped me with anythin' that counts."

What had begun as a well-intentioned counseling session had quickly deteriorated into a standoff. Fisheye had drawn a line in the sand and dared me to cross it. Others in this seventh grade class had drawn this line—for the most part, silently. Less shy than others in expressing his disillusionment with a system he felt was without practical value to him, Fisheye also enjoyed the rapt attention his behavior brought him.

I wasn't supposed to call him by his nickname, despite the fact that few in the school would recognize Fisheye's real name. "Eugene," I began, "if you spent half as much time trying to get to the eighth grade as you do on extra-curricular activities—"

Dismissing me as irrelevant, he turned his head and looked out the window.

As I mulled over what I could say to Fisheye that would make any difference, my mind drifted back a few months—which already seemed like an eternity—to before I had ever heard of Abraham Lincoln Attendance Center. I recalled standing outside Connor Hall on the Ole Miss campus and yelling "Glory Hallelujah!" at the thought that I had taken my final exam and, after graduation, would embark on an exciting new life.

This was the new life, all right, but not the *Leave It To Beaver* one I'd left behind. The realities of Lincoln were a far cry from my WASP existence that, up to now, had been my only point of reference: two parents, a comfortable home in a middle-class, all-white neighborhood, a segregated high school. My security had been overseen by our cocker spaniel, my probity assured by attendance at our Methodist church each Sunday.

My mother was co-owner with my dad of J. G. Lusk & Company, which specialized in brokering cash commodities, primarily cotton seed and soybean products. The cash commodity business at that time was a male-dominated industry, and my mother enjoyed the status of being one of the first females in the trade.

My parents were both native Mississippians—my mother from Collins in south Mississippi, my father a Greenville native. Constancy is common in the Delta. My father was born in King's Daughters Hospital, the same hospital where my younger brother, Bill, and I were born. Some of my teachers had been my father's as well. His family had been old Greenville middle class. Though never wealthy, they had always been respectable. He had been raised by a prematurely widowed mom who was a well-established local seamstress. Nana, as we called her, lived in the old downtown section of Greenville, one block from the levee. The black section of town was less than a mile away. Blacks frequently walked past Nana's house on Central Avenue, more often than not to shop at the Chinese grocer down the block from her house. It certainly never occurred to me that they might have entertained even a passing thought of living there.

You qualified as being old Greenville if your forebears had lived there before the flood. All my life I had heard the stories of the infamous 1927 flood and how Nana had allowed a black preteen, Kitty, to evacuate with the family. Kitty, when she herself had grown old, returned to pay her respects and attend Nana's wake when Nana died at age ninety-six.

I reviewed the incident that had triggered the confrontation with Fisheye. At the back of my classroom, before class started, Fisheye had been dealing out ice cream sandwiches he'd bought at Jones Grocery. He wasn't doing this out of the goodness of his heart but was demanding the recipients' lunch money in exchange. The ice cream was beginning to melt, and it was imperative that he get rid of the stuff. His entrepreneurship also extended to dill pickles, which he had stuffed into his socks.

Is this how Cornelius Vanderbilt got started? I wondered. Is this what my four-year college degree has gotten me? Have I become Lincoln's Dick Tracy—my specialty being bringing to justice teenage culprits who sold ice cream sandwiches and pickles in school?

I enjoyed college, and getting an advanced degree had always appealed to me. I knew, however, that if I pursued further education, most of the financial burden would be mine, since my parents still had my younger brother to educate. So barring getting drafted for the Vietnam War, as many of my contemporaries had been, my only option was to get a job and save my money.

In an optimistic frame of mind, I had sent out twenty résumés with high hopes that several acceptances would show up in a short period of time. Instead, in reply I received twenty form letters which were brief and to the point: "Thank you for thinking of us. At the present time we have no openings, but please try us again in the future." What's the matter with these people? Don't they realize I'm a college graduate? Hadn't my father told me since I was a small child that if I got a college degree, doors would open for me that had been closed to him because he didn't have one?

It was now July 28, 1969. Bill and I were home: Mom and Dad had gone to the lodge for a Masonic–Eastern Star function. My brother, a budding artist, sat in the den with a sketch pad on his lap while listening to the evening news on TV. As usual, when he had a few moments free, he sketched whatever crossed his line of vision. This time it happened to be our grandfather's shotgun, which Daddy had hung on a wall of the den.

I sat at the dining room table typing up résumé number twenty-one on Mama's manual Smith-Corona. To this point, the résumés sent to Fortune 500 companies had met with a dismal reception. I considered this résumé, sent to the superintendent of schools in Leland, Mississippi, inquiring about a teaching position, my last resort. Leland was just down the road from my hometown of Greenville. I reasoned that since I planned, somehow, to go back to the university for an advanced degree, staying in the education field would be a good idea.

As I typed the address on the envelope, I could hear the evening news from the den. The Huntley-Brinkley nightly news was detailing the big events of the day. Neil Armstrong's spectacular walk on the moon had replaced Ted Kennedy and Mary Jo Kopechne's plunge off the Chappaquiddick Bridge. "I bet Senator Kennedy won't hesitate to vote for NASA's next appropriation," I called to Bill, "now that Neil Armstrong's adventure bumped his catastrophe off the news."

The Kennedys hadn't been popular with most white adult Mississippians after Jack and Bobby spearheaded the federal government's efforts in 1962 to integrate the University of Mississippi, and a large portion delighted in Teddy's shame when that plunge off the bridge resulted in Mary Jo's tragic drowning.

The next news item outlined President Nixon's "Vietnamization" program, in which the emphasis had been changed to training and equipping the South Vietnamese to fight their own war so that we could begin to extricate ourselves from that seemingly endless conflict. The last bit of news was short: the Nixon Department of Justice and HEW (Health, Education, and Welfare) had filed a motion with the U.S. Supreme Court to delay integration once again throughout the country. Little did I know at the time that this item would have far more relevance for me than any of the other stories.

I folded my résumé, inserted it in the envelope, and applied the stamp. "Wish me luck," I called to Bill as I headed for the mailbox that hung by the front door.

That twenty-first job application did the trick. Three days later I received a letter asking me to come to the office of the Leland superintendent of schools for an interview.

I was elated.

∽

It was an ordinary hot and sticky Mississippi Delta summer day. The temperature was in the upper nineties, and the humidity was even worse that August 8 when I dressed in my only khaki poplin summer suit and set out on Highway 82 in my bright yellow 1962 Rambler American. The car had a push-button transmission on the dash to the left of the steering wheel, and air-conditioning, which I used sparingly since the engine overheated if I drove faster than fifty-five. My father had paid half the $500 cost of the vehicle because he thought it was heavy enough to keep me safe in case of a wreck.

The route was familiar—past the Joy Drive-In theater where, as a teenager, I'd enjoyed watching a movie in the car and necking with my date; then Thompson-Hayward Chemical Company, my employer during five summer vacations; and Valley Chemical, where my best friend, Dick, had worked. Dick was now an army officer on his way to Vietnam.

I knew I was getting near Leland when I passed the juke joint called Tillie's. This establishment was a blue-collar hangout frequented by towboat workers and their spouses or girlfriends. Often, the spouses or girlfriends wouldn't wait for the towboat workers to return from their labors before indulging themselves at Tillie's with a few beers or some short-term companionship. Age limits for alcohol consumption weren't strictly enforced, fights were a regular occurrence, and rumor had it that a killing was not unusual on the weekend. It was a rite of passage for teenage boys in the Delta to go there.

It was surprising that although Leland and Greenville were a mere ten miles apart, I knew very little about the inner workings of the town. I'd been to an occasional Methodist Youth Fellowship meeting here. I had heard of the Stoneville Agricultural Experiment Station, where research on growing hardier, disease-resistant cotton was done. I'd also come with my family at Christmas to drive the street beside Deer Creek, which bisected the community, to admire the decorated floats anchored midstream.

Outside Leland, a town of about ten thousand residents, was some of the richest farmland in the world. Every spring for millions of years, the Mississippi River had overflowed its banks into the surrounding delta. When the water receded, it left behind vast deposits of silt. This annual ritual was interrupted when man took control, building levees to hold back the water so that crops could be planted on the fertile soil.

The Delta was the wild new frontier of Mississippi in the early 1800s. Despite the hardships of living in this vast fertile wilderness, the slavocracy (the term coined by David G. Sansing in his book *The University of Mississippi: A Sesquicentennial History*) fostered a feudal aristocracy supported by the massive number of slaves demanded by the labor-intensive cotton industry. This left the planters very poorly equipped to deal with a labor force that suddenly developed negotiating power after the Civil War. This impotence by both sides carried forward to modern times. Descendants of the slaves composed about 70 percent of Leland's population. However, most of the work that in former eras had been performed by slaves was now done by machines. Thus a large displaced group of blacks had been created, many of whom lived in ignorance and poverty, existing on welfare.

The closer I got to my destination, the more nervous I became. How would I come across on this, my first-ever job interview with a stranger? The start of the school year is approaching. Why does Leland still have an opening? Will the superintendent find out that I'm not really qualified? What will I do if I don't get this job? Then came self-admonition. Don't keep asking stupid questions to which you don't know the answers. Just be grateful to have applied for the job before someone else did.

With these and similar thoughts churning in my mind, I parked in front of the red brick, one-story building with the sign in the front yard announcing that this was the Leland's school administration headquarters.

Adopting a purposeful gait, I made my way the short distance to the front door and opened it. Halfway down the hall next to a doorway was a sign: Superintendent's Office. There were no other visitors in chairs lining the walls of the reception room when I entered. The receptionist looked up as I crossed to her desk. Mrs. Letha Phillips, her nameplate announced. Thin and middle-aged, she wore a blue cotton dress with a jacket. Her hair was in the bouffant style popular with middle-aged women.

I introduced myself. She nodded, waved to one of the chairs. "Have a seat, and Mr. Bigham will see you shortly," she said.

I didn't have long to wait. I'd barely had time to peruse the headlines of the newspaper I'd picked up from a nearby table when I heard a buzzer at her desk. A moment later she looked at me over the top of her glasses and announced, "Mr. Bigham will see you now."

She ushered me into the superintendent's office and introduced me to the man sitting behind the large desk covered with papers. Displayed on the wall behind his desk were his college degree, a past president's Rotary plaque, and a picture of his wife and children. He stood up, shook my hand, and indicated a chair on the other side of his desk. Mr. Bigham looked to be in his mid-fifties. He was balding, perhaps shorter than me by three or four inches, and wore horn-rimmed glasses. He was clean shaven.

"Have a seat, Mr. Beckwith. Welcome to Leland. I hope you're the man we're looking for."

Elated at his warm welcome, so different from the brusqueness of the replies to my other job applications, I murmured something appropriate.

As we sat down, he continued, "You know, there are a lot of people who would like to work for the Leland Public Schools. We're mighty proud of what we've accomplished here." Not waiting for a reply, he looked down at my résumé. "I see you have a degree from Ole Miss in Business Administration. Do you have a teaching certificate?"

"No, sir, I don't," I answered. "My majors were marketing and finance."

"No education classes?" he asked.

I shook my head. "With my other workload, I didn't have time."

"Well," he frowned, "perhaps we can work around that. Are you married?"

"No, sir," I smiled. "Haven't had time."

He smiled back. "That may be an advantage at this point in your life. I see from your résumé that you've had six hours of English and made a B in history—'Western Civilization.' That's good." He looked up. "Are you considering any other positions presently?"

"This is the only interview I've set up so far," I answered, hoping it sounded as if others were just over the horizon.

"We have openings at the junior high level in both English and history," he went on. "Do you have preference?"

"English," I answered quickly.

"You are decisive," Mr. Bigham nodded. "I like that in my teachers. If you're available to teach when school begins, I think I can make you an offer."

Before I could reply, he continued. "By the way," his voice had taken on a schoolmasterish tone, "we are a God-fearing, Christian community, and we expect our teachers to live up to our standards. Unfortunately, many people your age go to juke joints, and we certainly have more in this town than we should. I know what kind of cars our teachers drive. I often ride around on Saturday nights to check out the parking lots of juke joints. I will not tolerate my teachers presenting the wrong image to the community by being seen patronizing those places, nor do I want to hear any reports from townspeople that they saw one of my teachers in a juke joint. That is grounds for dismissal."

"And," he added, "it does look nice for our teachers to be seen at church on Sundays. I'm a Baptist myself."

I nodded gravely.

"Well," Mr. Bigham continued. "What do you say? Are you interested? I can offer you $5,300 a year. Starting salary is usually $4,800, but I like you. I think you have the potential to be an excellent teacher."

I tried to hide my elation. It sounded like a princely sum. After three months of sending out résumés and getting rejection letters, I couldn't believe this job had been so easy to wrap up. "You won't be sorry," I said. "I'll do a good job for you."

"Fine!" Mr. Bigham said. "I'll get the contract worked up, and we'll let you know when to come in and sign it." He stood up. "It's been good to talk to you."

I floated out of the office on a cloud. I had a job! I couldn't wait to get to a phone to call my folks. It wasn't until I was in the car heading back to Greenville that I realized I hadn't asked the name of the school where I'd be teaching.

"Mom!" I exclaimed when she answered the phone at the office. "I did it! I got a job!"

"Doing what? Where?" she asked.

"I'm going to teach at a junior high school in Leland! The superintendent offered me the job on the spot. It pays $5,300. I must have really impressed him! I didn't have to mention any of your contacts in Leland. He wanted me just for my qualifications."

"But David," she said, sounding puzzled, "you don't even have a teaching certificate."

"It wasn't a problem. He said they could work around that."

"What are you going to teach?"

"He gave me a choice of English or history," I answered. "I told him I'd rather teach English, and he said that was fine."

"Well, you always were good at English," she said. "What's the name of the school?"

I laughed. "I was so excited at getting the job, I didn't ask him. I'll find out soon enough. I'd think all the schools in Leland are about the same. I guess I oughta look for an apartment in Leland. I'm sure gonna miss y'all, but if I'll be working in Leland I should live there and be part of the community. I think things are startin' to roll!"

So, with a less-than-crystal-clear understanding of all the details of the new position, I'd become a teacher.

2

For the next three days I stewed and fretted by the phone. I stewed about my youth and inexperience. I fretted about my lack of a teaching certificate and about the possibility that Mr. Bigham was regretting his offer of a contract. In short, I never had a thought about how I could or would teach a class, and it didn't seem important what subject I would teach. My only thoughts were about possibly losing the opportunity to try.

Feeding my paranoia was the media's preoccupation with reporting about the flood of baby boomers fresh out of college scrambling for a trickle of job openings, the weakening economy, the stock market's decline, riots against the war in Vietnam, and turmoil in Richard Nixon's presidency.

The barrage of bad news not only magnified my concerns but also convinced me that there couldn't possibly have been a worse year to graduate from college than 1969. Only a few years before, the media was reporting that new grads were writing their own tickets; now we were begging for any job we could get.

Early on the morning of the fourth day, the phone finally rang. It was Mrs. Phillips saying that my contract had been prepared.

"When would it be convenient for you to come to Mr. Bigham's office so he can go over it with you?" she asked. She sounded very official.

Relief washed over me, and I wanted to shout "Right this minute!" Instead, in my most detached manner, I responded, "It's great to hear from you so promptly. I have to be in Leland for some other commitments later today. My schedule does allow some time about 9:00 to come by your office and talk with Mr. Bigham."

"That would be fine," she answered, matching me cool for cool. "He'll be expecting you."

Man oh man, I hope I didn't lay the BS on so thick she had to lift her feet off the floor, I thought as we hung up.

As I hurried through my morning shower and dressing routine, I sang my spur-of-the-moment improvisation of the popular song "Bobby's Girl": "I'm not a kid anymore; I'm not a kid anymore. I want to be Bigham's boy. I want to be Bigham's boy. That means everything to me."

In one hour, barring a disaster, I would officially be Bigham's boy and simultaneously would become a member in good standing of the adult working world. I would finally have made it to the threshold of the other side, that grown-up side where my folks and all their friends were.

I dressed conservatively in the middle-class male uniform: navy blue pants, white shirt, striped tie. A jacket in this kind of weather was intolerable as well as unnecessary considering that the job was all but mine.

I was too excited to notice any of the familiar landmarks along the way as I tried to keep the Rambler below the speed limit. I was also glad that I didn't have to worry about what to say when I got there. It was a done deal. All I had to do was sign my name, and soon I'd be collecting a paycheck. I wondered, for the first time, what was included in the seventh grade English curriculum.

"It's good to see you again," Mrs. Phillips welcomed me with unexpected warmth as I walked into the reception room. "We're glad to have you on board. I'm sure you are going to enjoy your first year as a teacher. I won't see you often, but do call if this office can ever be of assistance. And now," she went on, "Mr. Bigham is expecting you. You can go on in."

The friendliness of her welcome made me feel that I was already a member of the team. What a contrast it was to my initial visit!

When I entered the office, Mr. Bigham was seated at his desk working on a stack of papers. He looked up, smiled, and repeated Mrs. Phillips's cordial greeting.

"I'm glad you've had time to think over our offer and decided to join our little family," he began as soon as I'd sat down.

Before I had an opportunity to even give a cursory response, he continued: "I've tentatively decided that you will teach four seventh grade English classes and one seventh grade world history class. I'm assigning you to the Abraham Lincoln Attendance Center over on Roadway. I've already mentioned that your salary will be $5,300 a year. If that's agreeable, we'll get the contract signed."

He reached in the top drawer of his desk, took out the legal-size document, and slid it over to me. "It's a standard contract that all county teachers sign, but if there's anything you don't understand, I'll be glad to explain."

I scanned the contract, pretending that I was absorbing it. In reality, it might as well have been written in Chinese. What I was really looking for was the line with my name typed underneath where I was to sign.

He noticed my hesitation and offered to explain any wording that wasn't clear. I shook my head, and on the last page found my name. I signed it and handed it back to Mr. Bigham. It wasn't until after he'd added his signature alongside mine that I felt a sense of pure relief. I was hired!

"Let me tell you a little more about the challenges we face here in the Leland Public Schools. As you know, we have traditionally had a 'separate but equal' school system in which I am convinced we have delivered a good education to the diverse segments of our population. Local option, however, is in danger of becoming extinct."

He leaned back in his chair and waved at the stack of papers he'd pushed aside in order to sign the contract. "These are the new regulations and requirements the federal courts have laid on us. We can't afford to ignore them, or we would be deprived of our federal funding." He shook his head. "I guess I don't have to tell you that we couldn't even come close to balancing our budget without it. We are under federal court order to begin the integration process in our local schools or be declared in contempt of court."

Again he shook his head and sighed.

"I'm also convinced that we can't do this all of a sudden. The system as we know it—the system that educated you—was developed over almost a hundred-year period. It's not in the best interest of this community to dismantle it overnight. I can hold the federal courts at bay for a while if I integrate my staff."

"Lord willing and the creek don't rise, this will buy enough time to bring a measure of acceptance so that when we face total integration, I can do so without disrupting the entire community."

By now I was totally focused on what he was saying rather than on whether

I would be hired or not. "The Abraham Lincoln Attendance Center is one of our black schools. It goes from kindergarten through twelfth grade. Enrollment is approximately twenty-four hundred students. You're the first white teacher I've been able to hire to work in a black school." He paused, his hands nervously twirling his ink pen. "I'm sure you can understand that I had to give my existing staff the choice of what school they wanted to work in, and none of them chose to be pioneers in the black system."

His eyes hadn't left my face during this lengthy discourse as if to gauge what my reaction would be to this revelation. Bemused would describe it, but a light had gone on. No wonder my dearth of education courses had seemed unimportant. My chief attribute from his standpoint was that I was white!

"I'm asking you to trust me," he urged. "Things are going to work out fine. I am trying to hire more white teachers to work at Lincoln, and I'm sure I'll find some before school starts."

He leaned forward and laced his hands together on the desk. "I hope you'll take this assignment with an open mind. You're going to find that these are good-hearted, generous people who will not resent your being there, but will welcome the contributions you can bring to their school.

"Let me add that you'll be working for a progressive school district. In 1950 Leland was one of the first school districts in Mississippi to organize a 'Colored' consolidated school district. The school you'll be teaching in was built for $100,000, $75,000 of which was generously financed with a local bond issue. The creation of this taxing district gave us a mechanism we needed to target taxes for ongoing maintenance. I hope you appreciate that this created one of the finest Negro schools in the entire state—a school that was then and still is fully accredited.

"I haven't known you long, but my gut tells me you'll make a contribution to their school. I can tell from your face that I've blindsided you with this conversation. If you want me to, I'll hold your contract and give you time to digest all this, or I can just tear it up right now. Whatever happens, I won't hold it against you."

I've always heard that there are no free lunches. If something sounds too good to be true, it probably is. But the fact remained that I needed a job, and I sure didn't have anything else working. It was more money than I'd expected to earn, and this sure as hell beat being shipped out to Vietnam—I hoped!

Despite feeling some uncertainty, I nodded. "I'll take the job."

"You won't be sorry. You're doing the right thing," Mr. Bigham said. "I'll let you know when I find the other teachers."

Among the myriad thoughts crowding my mind as I stood up to bid him good-bye was one that had piqued my curiosity as soon as he'd mentioned it. "Why is the school called the Abraham Lincoln Attendance Center?" I asked. "That's not a term we use in the Greenville school system."

"If you're not in a hurry, Mr. History Teacher, I can give you a short history lesson," he said with a smile.

I glanced at my watch, recalling that I had told Mrs. Phillips that I had other appointments while in Leland.

"Time enough for that," I hedged. "Hey, 'Mr. History Teacher' has a pretty good ring to it," I added.

He smiled, leaned back in his chair. "We both know what a rural state Mississippi is. Before your time as well as mine, hundreds of one- and two-room makeshift schoolhouses served rural communities around the state. They offered little more than a dry roof, four walls, a few desks, and a blackboard. They were manned by whatever talent happened to be in the community. In the early 1900s the state power structure decided to gather together these little country schools into larger ones that would serve an entire county. This consolidation was spurred on by the advent of school buses which could transport children to a center located much further away than walking distance from their homes."

He raised his eyebrows: "Are we on the same page up to now?"

"We are," I answered.

"This made it possible to have science labs, gyms, libraries, sports teams, and bands—facilities that we take for granted today—under one roof, so to speak," he went on. "These schools often served from first grade through high school. Students were bused to attend these amalgamated institutions. Someone came up with the idea of calling them attendance centers. This was supposed to be a temporary name, but it stuck—kind of like that fast-growing vine and ground cover we Mississippians call kudzu. So, that's why your school is called Lincoln Attendance Center. By the way," he added, "did you know that our white school is called Dean Attendance Center?"

"I do now. Thanks for the history lesson." I smiled as I stood up.

"From time to time, us old codgers come up with some interesting all-but-forgotten tidbits of information."

We bade each other good-bye and I made my way down the hall, through the reception room, and out to my car. Interesting as his account had been, worry reared its persistent head. What if he's unable to get any other white teachers? I will be the only white person in the all-black school. What will it feel like to be a member of the minority?

As I contemplated all these new issues, I turned on WDDT-AM, where Sam and Dave were singing: "I'm a soul man. I'm a soul man . . ."

I answered them and tapped the rhythm on the steering wheel, "I'm a soul man . . ."

I laughed out loud. Maybe I wasn't a soul man yet, but I soon would be. I recalled the night while I was at Ole Miss that I had been one of a select group of whites who had attended a Sam and Dave concert at the Mid-South Coliseum in front of a packed house of ten thousand screaming black fans.

As I attempted to harmonize with Sam and Dave, I tried to analyze the black/white relationship that had been so ingrained in me since birth, I'd never questioned whether it was right or wrong. It was just the way things were.

Blacks had been assigned "their place" by the whites, and that's where they stayed. This seemingly brought order and stability to the two groups, who otherwise would have had trouble dealing with each other.

Whites interpreted this willingness of blacks to stay within the confines of "their place" as confirmation of the fact that this was the way things were supposed to be. What was not openly admitted was that blacks stayed in "their place" not only because of economic dependence on whites but also for fear of what might happen if they didn't. The White Citizens Council and the Ku Klux Klan primarily kept watch to ensure that blacks didn't overstep the bounds of "their place."

The White Citizens Council was formed in Indianola, Mississippi, in 1954 after the U.S. Supreme Court decision commonly called *Brown v. Board of Education* barred segregation in public schools. Indianola is a town about the same size as Leland and about ten miles east on Highway 82. This local group spread, and within three months a state association of White Citizens Councils was formed in Winona.

By 1956 the organization extended beyond the borders of Mississippi, and a national group calling itself the Citizens' Council of America was formed in Jackson, Mississippi. This new organization reportedly received funding from the state of Mississippi.

The Citizens' Council of America wasn't simply a local or southern phenomenon. Chapters were formed as far away as Los Angeles. In their battle to fight *Brown v. Board of Education* and other measures that followed, many whites perceived it as a respectable alternative to the Klan. Subsequent events contributed to this smoldering of white resentment. High-profile incidents such as President Eisenhower's sending U.S. Army troops into Little Rock in 1957 to enforce school desegregation, and the 1961 Freedom Rides, which focused on the issues of integration on public buses, served to galvanize the already hardcore members of the Citizens' Council and added to its membership rolls.

Membership in the local group, known as the White Citizens Council, was made up mostly of right-wing businessmen and professionals who had a vested interest in the status quo. The Klan, which often functioned as its enforcement arm, was largely made up of lower-class, uneducated whites whose jobs and place in society would be threatened if blacks rose on the economic and social ladder. Therefore, it was vital to members of both organizations that this status quo be maintained, no matter by what means. Those means were unrelenting and sometimes vicious, and more often than not they went unpunished by authorities.

Change had always come slowly and grudgingly. In a court case in 1948, Gladys Noel Bates successfully challenged the unequal pay scales for black and white teachers in the public schools in Jackson, Mississippi (though Bates won the court case, she and her husband both lost their jobs, their home was firebombed, and they were forced to leave the state). In 1954 the law making it a felony for blacks and whites to attend the same school was struck down as unconstitutional by the U.S. Supreme Court. And in 1962 James Meredith led a bitter but successful fight to gain admission to the University of Mississippi.

Meredith's admittance was the climax to a struggle that had begun eight years prior when Mississippi civil rights leader Medgar Evers first tried to enroll in the Ole Miss School of Law. Mississippi's leaders during that time believed strongly that states ultimately held the right to control education and educational matters. In 1962, federal troops called in during the Meredith crisis forced the state to recognize the sovereign power of the national government. In the melee that followed Meredith's forced registration at the University of Mississippi, two people were killed and more than two hundred National Guardsmen were wounded. Soldiers were bombarded with brickbats and Molotov cocktails by a mob of white citizens who chanted,

"Two, four, six, eight, we will never integrate." The campus became a war zone. Before the crisis ended, more than thirty thousand National Guardsmen, federal marshals, and troops—including units from the 82nd and 101st Airborne—would be mobilized and sent to the University of Mississippi in Oxford to restore peace.

James Meredith's daytime world at the University of Mississippi was turned into a nightmare odyssey as federal marshals escorted him to class past name-calling students. Through all hours of the night, students in his dorm, Baxter Hall, bounced basketballs on the floor just above his room. When Meredith was escorted into the cafeteria for meals, the students eating would all turn their backs. If he sat at a table with other students, all would immediately get up and go to another table. The final troops deployed for this incident would not be removed until the spring of 1963, and even then a small group of marshals remained with him through the remainder of his stay at the university.

Meredith would later write a revealing account of these events in *Three Years in Mississippi*. He would be honored decades later by having this same university dedicate a life-size bronze statue to him in a ceremony with dignitaries like actor Morgan Freeman assisting. Meredith's statue was inscribed with terms such as "courage," "perseverance," "opportunity," and "knowledge."

When I entered Ole Miss in the fall of 1965, the university was still trying to accustom itself to the concept of integration. If the board of trustees had had its way, Ole Miss would have remained an all-white school. In 1964, Cleveland Donald, an honor student from Tougaloo, had applied for admission. He was issued a certificate of enrollment for the summer session but was later denied admission for the fall term because of board concerns over "exploding tensions" and fears of a possible "long hot summer." He was admitted that fall under court order, received a bachelor's degree in history, and earned a doctorate at Cornell University. In 1978 he was named the first director of the University of Mississippi's Black Studies program.

In the fall of 1964 Ole Miss admitted its first black student, Irwin Walker, who did not have a court order. By 1966 there were fourteen black students, and the following year the number had risen to thirty. Among these black students was Reuben Anderson, who later became the first black justice of the Mississippi Supreme Court.

The black students didn't go unnoticed, but I never had the opportunity to get to know one. I never had a black student living in my dormitory,

Hill A. I never had one in any of my classes. I simply saw them occasionally on campus or from a distance in the cafeteria. They usually kept a low profile, causing as little disruption as possible on their path to earning a degree. They chose to avoid functions like football games and pep rallies, which could elevate their vulnerability and lead to trouble.

One memorable event that I attended occurred in March 1966. The law school speaker's bureau invited Bobby Kennedy to speak at the university. Mississippi's governor, Ross Barnett, had used the Kennedys as the scapegoat for the James Meredith "trainwreck" in 1962. The majority of Mississippians and southerners couldn't believe that Kennedy and his wife had the nerve to make an appearance at the university. His appearance created so much interest that his speech had to be moved from the small law school auditorium to the coliseum. Senator Kennedy and his wife were greeted with a standing ovation. The press screamed that Ole Miss had become a "hotbed of liberalism." Kennedy told his side of the Meredith crisis and dispelled a lot of the myth that Barnett's actions were based on idealism and that his sole motivation had been the good of the university. Using the words of James Silver, Kennedy pronounced that the days of Ole Miss being a "closed society" were over (Dr. Silver, a tenured professor since 1936, had been forced out in the aftermath of Meredith's admission).

With rare exception, however, interaction between blacks and whites remained limited to dealing with each other through their stereotypical roles. As is the case with many people we meet in the routine of life, the relationship was too often one-dimensional. For example, while living at home with my parents, I spent very little time dwelling on the personal life of my parents' maid, Hattie Brown. By 1950s southern standards, she was treated very well. Hattie was given used clothing and household goods that we no longer needed, took home excess food we didn't eat, was driven to the doctor when she was ill, and was transported to and from work. Once when Hattie was injured due to a hazard caused by city negligence, my mother pleaded her case before the city council and convinced them to be fair with their settlement. Hattie's health eventually deteriorated from her injury, and when she could no longer work she introduced us to her cousin, Celie. Even after Hattie no longer worked for our family, we stayed in touch with her, providing her with food and other assistance.

Large numbers of black males were hired as farm laborers or yardmen or to perform other menial jobs. They fed the cotton into the cotton gin, then baled it when it came out, just as their forebears had been hired to chop cotton. It was hard, dirty work. They represented the bottom of the black labor ladder.

There were few black businessmen. The clergy, trained in "separate but equal" seminaries, as well as teachers and principals trained in "separate but equal" colleges, were considered by both the black and white communities to be the cream of the crop. They held the ultimate positions for which to strive and were often extremely influential in the black community.

My main contact with a black man was with Willie Smith, who worked at the Greenville Yacht Club. Willie was steadfastly servile and helpful when I wanted to take our boat out on Lake Ferguson or fish off the side of the club's dock. He was quick to remind me how long he had known my father. "Yessir, Mr. David, looks like a good day to catch bream. You remind me of Mr. Bobby when he was growing up. That boy loved this lake."

We were grateful to those blacks who helped make our lives more pleasant, and while they were viewed as part of our family, our view of them was usually limited to their actual presence in our lives. In essence, we usually didn't dwell on the multifaceted roles of their lives. We viewed them as being different from ourselves, with different values and different aspirations.

Outsiders were critical of this "caste" system, but natives of the Deep South took it for granted. This had been the social fabric for as long as anyone could remember, and most white people saw no reason to upset the applecart now.

Now, things were beginning to change. I would be teaching at an all-black school. I would be on their turf. I would be the minority. We would become more familiar with each other than in any other situation that I had encountered in my life. It would be a situation where they made the rules. As if this weren't enough for me to be concerned about, I had no idea what kind of teacher I would be, or what level of competency seventh grade black students had attained.

3

Of more immediate concern was finding a place to live in Leland. I got copies of the *Leland Progress* and the *Delta Democrat Times* and visited places listed in the classifieds. I also got rental listings from the Leland Chamber of Commerce and the Board of Realtors office. Every place I looked at had two things in common: it wasn't furnished and I couldn't afford it. Three hundred and thirty dollars a month in after-tax income does not get you into the Taj Mahal. Now I could appreciate what my parents had meant when I ran deficits at school. "You must think money grows on trees and falls to the ground like pecans that you just go out and pick up," my father would admonish me. "Wait'll you start having to support yourself. I guarantee you'll look at things differently." As usual, Daddy was right.

I was amazed that no matter where I inquired, people knew about my being the new teacher. One day I stopped for lunch at a local café, and while I was trying to decide what to order, the waitress volunteered, "Mr. David, the fried chicken looks awful good today, and I've been shelling butter beans all morning to go with it."

"Do we know each other?" I asked.

"I heard about you through my uncle Leon. He's got this friend named Ray who does the yard for Mr. Bigham's next-door neighbor," she answered, as if that were the logical road anyone took who was desirous of information about a newcomer.

At the dry cleaner where I left some shirts, the clerk filled out the inventory slip, having already written my name at the top. "I hope you're gonna like it here in Leland," she said as I bid her good-bye.

One afternoon I drove along Deer Creek Drive, the shady, two-lane road that paralleled Deer Creek. Deer Creek wasn't just one of Leland's most attractive residential areas; it was also known for its history. General Ulysses S. Grant used the waterway to transport his Union soldiers to the attack on Vicksburg which culminated in the surrender of the Confederate forces there. In a lighter vein, Muppet creator Jim Henson is believed to have gotten his inspiration for Kermit the Frog on Deer Creek. Kermit's name was taken from that of Kermit Scott, one of Henson's childhood playmates. Henson's father had worked at the Stoneville Agricultural Experiment Station outside Leland.

Behind one of the attractive white wooden homes facing the creek was a one-story, one-bedroom garage apartment. The newspaper ad listed it at seventy-five dollars a month. A pleasant-looking middle-aged lady in gray slacks and a faded blue shirt was raking leaves in the front yard. She looked up as I pulled into the graveled driveway.

"Are you the owner of the apartment for rent?" I asked.

She pushed a lock of graying blond hair back from her face. "I sure am," she answered. "My name is Mildred Young. Would you like to look at it?"

"I'd appreciate that very much," I answered.

She watched me get out of the car and walk toward her. "You're the nice young man that's been hired to teach at Lincoln School."

I nodded. "Everybody in town seems to know."

She smiled. "We're just a small town—don't get excitement every day."

The apartment was perfect—living room, bedroom, kitchen, bath, a covered front stoop, and a carport for one car. The furniture was old but clean. After the tour, Mrs. Young invited me into her kitchen for a glass of sweet iced tea and some brownies. She told me she was a widow who lived a tranquil life; she'd been looking for a tenant who was quiet and well behaved. Evidently she thought a schoolteacher would fill that role, and she had me sign the lease.

"Would it be possible for me to move in tomorrow?" I asked.

"Certainly! I should be able to have your phone connected by then," she said.

I thanked her and told her how pleased I was to find such a nice place to live.

"Things have a way of working out, don't they?" was her parting comment.

Now that I had a job and a roof over my head, I could concentrate on the real reason I was here—to teach school.

At the end of the week, Mr. Bigham telephoned me. "Good news," he said. "You're not going to be the only white face at Lincoln. I've hired two additional white teachers. I told you I wouldn't leave you hanging out to dry."

You didn't know that at the time you hired me, I thought to myself. "That's great," I said. "What subjects are they going to teach?"

"One is a fourth grade art teacher; the other is going to teach English at the junior high," he answered.

I waited. "So now you have two white English teachers in the junior high?"

"The one I've just hired is a licensed teacher with over twenty years' experience in Alabama school systems," Mr. Bigham answered. "I'm sure you won't mind teaching world history instead of English."

Having that sprung on me just before school was scheduled to start jarred the hell out of me. The only history I'd taken in college was a required course in "Western Civilization" when I was a freshman! "I'm more confident in my knowledge of English," I answered, "but with her teaching certificate and twenty years' experience, I can see she would do a better job."

"I'm sure you'll make a real good history teacher," Mr. Bigham said heartily. "After all, these are just seventh graders. Surely you can stay one step ahead of them."

That remark did little to bolster my ego, but since it was already a done deal, further objection seemed pointless. "Yes, I'll teach history," I agreed.

"You'll do just fine," he said enthusiastically. "I know you're gonna have a great year. You can pick up your textbook and syllabus at the first faculty meeting at Lincoln."

Hanging up, I felt anything but confident about that "great year"!

⁓

Through business contacts in Leland, my parents had learned more particulars about my hiring. Not only was Leland under federal court order to desegregate, but the courts were using it to initiate what would be the desegregation of all public schools in Mississippi. Mr. Bigham's willingness to cooperate by hiring white teachers for black schools would delay desegregation of the student bodies for a short while, and it would also ensure that Washington County public schools would still get federal funds. I now knew that my being white was far more important than I had imagined. If

I hadn't come along when I did, he would have been forced to transfer one of his white teachers to a black school—an action that had the potential to produce an explosive situation. If he picked the wrong "sacrificial lamb" for the transfer, all his teachers might have gone on strike. He was thus caught between two equally undesirable alternatives when a hungry, young, white out-of-towner showed up on his doorstep. Thinking back on it, I decided I'd really missed the boat. If I'd known during my interview how important I was, I could have asked for a lot more than $5,300 a year!

No southerner is unfamiliar with the expression "the dog days of summer." They start in July and continue through Labor Day. During these days the temperature readings in Mississippi often approach or exceed one hundred degrees, and humidity readings are equally elevated.

I felt the heat and humidity even more than usual on August 28; I was nervous at being en route to my first faculty meeting of the teaching staffs of every public school in Leland. The meeting was held in the auditorium of Leland's all-white high school, called Dean. I'd been warned to be on time. Mr. Bigham always started his meetings on time, and it was said that he remembered who was late. I stood at the door a moment to look around. It was a large room with a red carpeted floor and rows of blue plush fold-down seats facing a stage. On the stage, which was large enough to accommodate school plays and band concerts, sat a stern Mr. Bigham and a man I didn't recognize. In front of them was a lectern with a microphone.

As the new kid on the block as well as the first white person who had agreed to teach at Lincoln, I'd expected to be welcomed by some of the other teachers and wished good luck in the coming year. Instead, when I walked alone down the aisle and took a seat midway from the front, no heads turned, no one smiled a greeting. This was certainly different from the reaction I'd gotten elsewhere in town. I noticed that whites and blacks didn't mingle; each group seemed to have staked out a section of the auditorium as its own territory. There was no exuberance—no feeling of expectancy in the air. Instead, it was as if the audience had heaved a resigned sigh: the peace and quiet of the summer was over, and the turmoil and disquiet of the school year lay ahead.

A few moments after I sat down, the man occupying the stage with Mr. Bigham walked to the mike and thumped it a few times to be sure it worked. He didn't introduce himself—I suppose he assumed he was so well known that an introduction would be superfluous—and announced without ceremony: "The meeting will come to order. We'll now have the invocation, which will be followed by the Pledge of Allegiance. Please rise."

Those preliminaries done, the audience sat down and Mr. Bigham took over the microphone.

"Welcome back for another school year. I'm sure it's going to be both interesting and challenging." Mr. Bigham went on to say how much Mr. Hammond, a math teacher who had recently retired, would be missed.

"And now," Mr. Bigham continued, "I want to make a few comments about setting examples for your students. If y'all are here every day, it sends them a silent message that attendance is important. If you cut school when you don't feel like working, and someone sees you downtown, the message that gets back to your students is that whether they show up in class or not doesn't really matter. I don't mean you should work when you're sick—that's why we have substitutes—but if I hear that you were not at school and you really weren't sick, you can expect to get a call from Mrs. Phillips or me. Don't make it necessary that we take that unpleasant step."

He braced a hand on each side of the lectern and leaned over it. "The next topic I want to emphasize concerns the image I'd like my teachers to present to the community. You are a reflection, whether you want to be or not, of the school system as a whole. Don't make the fine folks and taxpayers in this community think we hire lowlifes to teach school. My teachers are here to set an example for the young people to follow. You all know that juke joints are out of bounds and that church attendance is encouraged. I want you not only to do as I say, but to do as I do."

He straightened, folded his hands on the lectern. "Unless anyone has any questions, you will now report to your respective schools for the first faculty meeting. It will start promptly at 10:30. We have some unusual challenges facing us this year, but nothing we won't be able to handle. Good-bye for now, and good luck."

I sat a moment wondering if I'd missed something. Not a word had been said about the pending desegregation; no introduction of me and the two other white instructors who would be teaching in the all-black school. It was as if, by ignoring the subject, the magnitude of the problem would diminish.

As the audience filed out, no one spoke to me or acknowledged my presence. Were they trying to tell me not to expect any encouragement from them? I wondered who among the white teachers had refused to act as pioneers.

As I made my way across the teachers' parking lot, I observed a young woman standing at the driver's window of the car next to mine. She was clutching a sheaf of papers under one arm and, with her other hand, was fumbling in her purse—for her car keys, I assumed. Not bad, I thought, as I inventoried her attributes: early twenties, shoulder-length, light brown hair, must weigh in at 120, give or take a pound, and look at those legs! Sure beats the old-maid teachers I had in school. Nearing the driver's side of my Rambler, I heard a muffled "Damn!" and the metallic clunk of a bunch of keys hitting the asphalt.

"I'll get those for you," I offered. "You seem to be having a problem."

I picked up the keys and held them out to her.

She smiled her thanks. Her eyes were light blue and fringed with long, black lashes. Looks good up close, I mused. As she took the keys with her left hand, I noticed that she wasn't wearing a wedding ring.

"I don't know why I never remember to get my car keys out of my purse *before* I pick up a pile of stuff," she said as she juggled the sheaf of papers under her arm. "I must be a slow learner."

"It doesn't show, so I won't tell anybody," I promised. "By the way, my name is David Beckwith."

"Glad to know you," she answered. "I'm Michelle Lynn. I'm new here. Isn't it exciting—the school year beginning! I've wanted to be a teacher since I was a sixth grader. Are you elementary, junior high, or senior high? What room are you in?"

"Junior high," I answered. "And I haven't been assigned a room yet."

"I hope we have the same lunch hour. It sure would be nice to eat lunch with someone I've met," she suggested.

"I'd like that," I answered. "Too bad we won't be able to. I'm over at Lincoln."

"What's Lincoln?" she asked.

"It's the black school on the other side of town," I answered.

"Oh, really?" I watched her smile ebb away. "Well," she said, "maybe we'll meet again anyway."

"Hope so," I said cheerfully.

She was still sitting in her car when I left the parking lot. I can kiss off the possibility of getting to know *her* better, I decided. Too bad, I grimaced.

On my drive over to Lincoln, I reviewed what I knew about the school complex where I was to teach. It included kindergarten, elementary, junior high, and senior high schools. Each school had its own principal, and each principal reported to a Mr. A. B. Levison, the administrator for the whole compound. Not counting administrative personnel, there would be twenty-one teachers with whom I would be interacting.

The faculty meeting was held in one of the classrooms in the junior high. It was a typical classroom: rows of desks, blackboard, teacher's desk—a classroom that could have been in Greenville, Mississippi, or Miami, Florida. It had an almost sterile look, as if it hadn't yet been outfitted with equipment or supplies. As I hesitated at the door and looked around at those already assembled, I decided that at six foot two, blond, blue-eyed, and fair complexioned, I couldn't have stood out more if I'd been a giraffe. The atmosphere here was the opposite of that I'd experienced at Dean. People were smiling, joking with each other. As I entered the room, a tall, thin, middle-aged black man came up to speak to me. He had graying hair, wore a coat and tie, and had an air of assurance. "Welcome to Lincoln," he said, as if he really meant it. "You must be Mr. Beckwith." He held out his hand. "My name is A. B. Levison. I'm the principal of the Lincoln complex."

As I put my hand in his, I realized what a seismic change this was for me—my first handshake with a black man. In this situation, Mr. Levison was not in a position of subservience. He was the big boss, and I was the neophyte—the one who had to earn his respect. His handshake was firm and certain. I had noted also that except for an occasional word, his speech pattern lacked the idiosyncrasies that I associated with black speech. He didn't appear to be preoccupied with the fact that I was white, and he didn't mention that I was a new white teacher or say that we were pioneering integration. I was merely a new teacher and this was the beginning of a new school year, which, as far as he was concerned, was to be like any other school year.

As we chatted, a middle-aged lady joined us. Mr. Levison put his hand on her arm as he proudly introduced her. "This is my wife, Cora. She's the school counselor. Cora, this is Mr. Beckwith, the new history teacher."

She was pleasantly plump, dressed in a simple, blue-flowered cotton dress. She was one of those people who wore clothes well. I couldn't imagine her in blue jeans, or shorts with a shirttail flapping in the breeze.

"Welcome, Mr. Beckwith." Her warm, genuine smile and quiet self-confidence had a calming effect. She wasn't trying to impress me, and I had the feeling that she was a person in whom one could safely confide. "We're glad you've become a member of our faculty. If I can help you in any way, please let me know."

"I'm new at teaching," I answered. "I'm sure I will be calling on you."

Just then, a young man carrying papers strode with a purposeful gait through the door and up to the front of the classroom. He had a streetwise look, a little cocky; his eyebrows arched as he sized up the room. He wore a short-sleeve white shirt and multicolored tie, was of medium height, and was nice looking except for a pronounced scar stretching from behind his ear up into his hair.

"That's Theodore Rollins," Mr. Levison said, nodding toward the newcomer. "He was a math teacher in Greenville last year; this year he's the principal of the junior high school. You'll have lots of dealings with him, and I'm sure you'll find him very helpful. He's a good man."

As Mr. Rollins asked everyone to be seated, I felt a kinship with him, though he seemed unapproachable. Both of us were venturing into uncharted waters—he as an administrator, I as a teacher. Maybe the cocky, somewhat officious air was a put-on to mask uncertainty about his new job.

The desks in which Mr. Rollins had asked us to sit were designed for twelve-year-olds. One end of the armrest was attached to the back of the chair and curved around to form a broad, flat writing surface at the front. Trying to shoehorn myself into such a seat took some maneuvering. I hoped the meeting would be short!

"Welcome," Mr. Rollins said when the bustle of getting settled had ended. "We all look forward to a productive year, and I hope our aspirations will be fulfilled." He had a strong, deliberate voice. His penetrating eyes made eye contact with everyone in the room. "And now," he continued, "before I introduce everybody, the principal of our Lincoln complex, Mr. Levison, would like to share a thought with us."

He stepped aside as Mr. Levison came up to the front of the room. From the breast pocket of his jacket, the senior principal took a pair of glasses which he settled on his nose. From a side pocket he drew out a piece of paper. "I'd like to read a poem which expresses, better than I could, what we should strive for during the coming year. Its title is 'Be Strong.'"

Be strong!
We are not here to play, to dream, to drift;

We have hard work to do and loads to lift.
Shun not the struggle, face it, 'tis God's gift.
Be strong, be strong, be strong!

Be strong!
Say not, "The days are evil—who's to blame?"
And fold the hands and acquiesce—O shame!
Stand up, speak out, and bravely, in God's name
Be strong, be strong, be strong!

Be strong!
It matters not how deep entrenched the wrong,
How hard the battle goes, the day, how long;
Faint not—fight on! Tomorrow comes the song.
Be strong, be strong, be strong!

When he finished, Mr. Levison didn't attempt to editorialize the poem. He let it speak for itself, aware that anything he added would likely reduce its impact. People nodded, murmured words of approval as he took his seat.

"Thank you, Mr. Levison, for those inspiring words. I hope we will all take them to heart," Mr. Rollins said. "Now I'm sure most of you remember when Stokely Carmichael made national news over in Lowndes County a couple of years ago by coining a phrase that subsequently became a household expression, 'Black Power.' I think he must have made a trip over to Leland," Mr. Rollins went on with a twinkle in his eye, "because we have Mr. Brown Power working for us in this very school. Just ask any student at Lincoln to define 'black power' and you'll get only one answer," he said, gesturing with his palm up to a man sitting two rows in front of me, "Mr. Caldwell M. Bibbs."

Smiles on the faces of the veteran teachers made it clear that they knew what Mr. Rollins meant: Mr. Levison made policy, and Mr. Bibbs enforced it. We newcomers couldn't yet appreciate Mr. Bibbs's importance. I guessed, however, that we would soon come to understand that Lincoln now had an additional "black power"—Theodore Rollins.

Mr. Bibbs was dressed in dark pants, a white short-sleeve shirt, and tie. He was an extremely light complexioned, balding, black man. Appearing to be in his early forties, he was tall, slim, and well muscled as if he had done his share of hard physical labor. He stood seemingly relaxed with his arms at his sides, a benign expression on his face, yet even we rookies could sense that, should the occasion arise, this was a man who could move swiftly and decisively.

After Mr. Bibbs's presentation came the self-introductions of the junior high faculty. Trying to fix in my mind the name of the teacher and subject taught quickly became too cumbersome, and I decided that would have to wait until my contacts with them became more personal. They, of course, would have no problem remembering me—the sole white face in the room. Mrs. Juanita Hadley, the white English teacher, had not yet arrived from Alabama.

The introductions over, Mr. Rollins walked over to the desk where he'd placed a stack of papers. "I'll hand out your teaching syllabuses, your class schedules, your schedules for monitoring the morning and afternoon school buses, and the schedules for monitoring the lunchroom. If for some reason you have to miss one of your scheduled sessions, it is imperative that you get someone to replace you. Are there any questions?"

No one spoke up, and he handed out the various papers that would control our lives during the coming school year. After that task was accomplished, the women in the group left for lunch while the men remained to gossip and discuss duties for the Friday night football game between the high school teams of Lincoln and Cleveland.

The male teachers were assigned to patrol the bleachers, keeping order as well as overseeing the arrival and departure of the buses. Since I wasn't included in that group, I was wondering what my duties would be when Mr. Rollins asked if I would take tickets at the gate. After I agreed, the meeting was over and we dispersed to have lunch. I wasn't invited to join the others, as eating in a restaurant would be awkward for them if I tagged along. I understood this and was amused again at the shoe being on the other foot. They would never have been allowed in a white restaurant with or without me.

When I returned to the classroom that afternoon, Mr. Rollins drew me aside.

"I've changed my mind about you taking up tickets Friday night," he said. He looked me in the eye. "I'm going to be frank. You would be the only white in the stadium. None of the students would know you. As you can imagine, there are always some who'll try to sneak in without paying, and there might be some belligerence on their part if you try to prevent them. Some students, too, will be climbing over the fence, which also would present a problem. Perhaps later when they've become accustomed to you, it will be different. Do you understand where I'm coming from?"

"Of course, and I appreciate your telling me like it is," I answered. "I know I'm a minority of one, but I hope you know that I'm here to pitch in and do whatever it takes to get the job done."

He nodded. "That's good to hear. Incidentally," he added, "will you be at the PTA meeting tonight? It's held in the gym."

"In the gym?" I asked.

"The gym doubles as an auditorium. Bleachers that are hinged to the wall pull out and provide seats."

"OK," I nodded. "See you then."

As I watched him hurry away, I thought: how odd that the teachers and administrators that I'd met here were so much more appealing to me than those I'd encountered at the faculty meeting at Dean. Perhaps teaching and school administrative positions in this community attracted superior blacks because so few career options were open to them. In the white community, with many opportunities available, teaching—with some notable exceptions—wasn't a calling but just a job until something better came along.

While my experience at the faculty meeting at Lincoln had been positive, the PTA meeting that evening in the gym deflated my euphoria. In chairs facing the bleachers sat Mr. Levison, Mr. Rollins, and two members of the Washington County Board of Education. Seated in the bleachers were about twenty women.

The speakers took turns explaining the desegregation steps that the schools had been ordered to take, the academic goals they hoped to achieve, and the Title I program involving federal aid.

Following their explanations, the meeting was opened for questions. A large woman sitting on the first row spoke up. "My son in the seventh grade got a stomach problem. Where do I sign up for the medical care?"

"My girl in the fifth grade is down in her back," the woman behind her said before any of the speakers had a chance to respond. "She need somebody tell her what to do 'bout it."

"Where do we get tickets for the free-lunch program?" a third broke in.

Listening to the questions, my first reaction was disappointment. What's wrong with these people? Don't they understand why we are here or what is important? I thought they'd want to know more about desegregation, and talk about academic goals. Instead, their total focus is on the Title I program (the Elementary and Secondary Education Act of 1965), which provided funds for helping disadvantaged students meet higher standards. As I mulled over why their inquiries were so limited, I recalled a discussion led by my sociology professor at Ole Miss on Abraham Maslow's theory of the hierarchy of needs.

According to Maslow, all human beings have five levels of needs: physiological, safety, social, self-esteem, and lastly, self-actualization. Only when more basic needs are satisfied can a person's concerns move to the next level. As a teacher, I was eager to impart to my students the knowledge needed to achieve self-actualization. These parents' concerns, however, had not advanced beyond their physiological or safety needs—not one level away, but several levels removed from what I considered most important.

Though I wondered how the speakers could leave the meeting with any feeling but despair, these questions didn't seem to faze them in the least. I decided that I was the one who needed some self-examination.

4

On Friday, August 29, at 9:00 a.m., the faculty of Lincoln Junior High met in the school library. Among those present was Mrs. Hadley, the white lady who had replaced me as an English teacher. She was of average height, matronly, with a dignified air. She wore glasses, and her brown hair was worn in a style that was popular in the 1950s. She also looked very ill at ease. I went up to her and introduced myself.

"You're from Alabama, I hear," I said as an opener.

"Florence," she answered.

"How did you come to Leland, Mississippi?" I asked.

"It's a long story," she answered wryly, "and not very interesting."

"I'd like to hear," I countered.

"My husband had a job transfer to Indianola. I tried the white high school there, as well as Dean High School here." She sighed. "No luck. There were no openings.

"So . . ."—she looked around the room—"I ended up here as a last resort. I've never taught under these conditions before. I don't know if I'm cut out for this or not."

"Don't feel alone," I said. "At least you've had years of teaching experience. I've never taught anywhere before."

"But they're"—she made a face—"black. Can they read? Will they even know what I'm talking about?"

Mr. Rollins's entrance interrupted our conversation. He crossed the room to a table and put down a stack of papers. "All right," he said, facing us, "let's get started. First, please make a circle of friendship."

With much shuffling and rearranging of positions, we configured ourselves into a circle. "Will you bow your heads, and let's say the Lord's Prayer in unison."

"Our father, who art in heaven," he started us off in his strong voice; by ones and twos, the rest of us joined him.

As the "Amen" brought the prayer to a close, I mused that Madalyn Murray O'Hair would have taken a dim view of this religious warmup in a secular school setting. However, if starting my classes with a prayer would hone my teaching skills, I was all for it. Hoping to locate a more comfortable chair than the one I'd occupied during the combined faculty meeting, I was about to survey the room when Mr. Rollins went on to say, "And now, please take the hand of the person on either side of you." He held out a hand to each of his neighbors. They responded by placing their hand in his, then turning to the person beside them to repeat the maneuver.

Mrs. Hadley stood beside me, but on her other side was a black English teacher with an Afro hairdo, Pearlie Brantley, who was a couple of years older than me. When I glanced at Mrs. Hadley's face to see her reaction, I saw that her expression was rigid. She stared straight ahead as she held her hand out to Pearlie. The man next to me was a history teacher, Bill Hayes, whom I had just met. I must admit that I felt a little odd as we joined hands. I had never encountered this level of intimacy with blacks before.

There was no opportunity to ponder this new experience, as Mr. Rollins had begun talking about friendship—the bonds we could form with each other, the help we must offer our fellow teachers when it was needed. His speech—well thought out and to the point—lasted only a few minutes, but I wondered if Mrs. Hadley had heard a word.

Then it was time to get down to business—the scheduling of classes. There were six periods in the day: four for academic subjects (English, history, math, and science), one for athletics, and the last for music and art. When the dust had settled, I'd been assigned a homeroom class and six classes of seventh grade history.

At noon we broke for lunch. I ate in the school cafeteria with Mr. Rollins, history teacher Bill Hayes, and Mr. Bibbs, the assistant principal. All were older than me by a few years, and all had had teaching experience. I felt quite the novice, and I didn't get some of the inside jokes, but on the whole they were good company. I felt sure that, among themselves, they'd had discussions about me, the new guy.

After lunch, I happened to pass Mrs. Hadley's classroom. She was sitting at her desk, staring at the empty room. I stopped in to speak to her.

"How was lunch?" I asked.

"I ate here at my desk—alone. None of them included me in their lunch plans. I didn't shut them out—they shut me out. I don't know how I'm going to stand this place."

"This is the first day!" I reminded her. "You're new to them, just like they're new to you. It's going to take a while for them to accept you. That goes for me, too. I'm sure they weren't eager to have either one of us show up."

"But you're young; you're flexible. You know what they say about teaching an old dog new tricks."

I smiled encouragingly. "I don't mean to preach, but that doesn't mean you can't change."

Back in the classroom, the afternoon session of the faculty meeting got under way. Mr. Rollins was again in charge.

"Those of you who have just joined the faculty probably don't realize the extent of Mrs. Levison's duties as school counselor," he said. "She provides a shoulder for students to cry on and acts as a semi-policeman when they misbehave. She also supervises standardized testing and instructs graduating students on how and where to apply to a college or to look for a job. She can be an invaluable asset to you, so don't hesitate to call on her when you need help."

He followed that information with instructions on how to register students and fill out book cards, and then he explained the lunch policy. Each class was paired with another class. One teacher took to the cafeteria those students whose lunch was subsidized by the federal government as well as those who could afford to buy lunch, which cost twenty-five cents. That teacher stayed with them while they ate. Those students who did not qualify for the free-lunch program because their family income was above the poverty level stayed in the classroom. The classroom teacher supervising those students was brought lunch, which he or she ate at the teacher's desk in front of the students who were not eating.

Later I protested this policy to Mr. Rollins. He gave me a patient smile. "I know it sounds heartless, but you have to face reality," he said. "Many of these kids don't have lunch money because their parents don't give it to them, thinking that if they look hungry the school is going to feed them, or because the kids get the money and spend it on something else. Call it what you will. We just don't have the resources to be more liberal in matters like these."

"It still doesn't make me feel any better about the situation," I answered.

"If you've got a better solution, I'll be glad to listen to it," he said.

"I guess I don't," I admitted.

The afternoon session lasted until a little after 4:00 p.m. "Since Monday is Labor Day, I'll see all of you here on Tuesday, September 2," Mr. Rollins said. "There will be a meeting of all students and faculty in the gym where members of the faculty will be introduced. After the meeting, you'll report to your homerooms to fill out registration cards for your students. When the registration is complete, all students will be dismissed to go home. So, if there are no questions, we'll see you Tuesday. Have a good weekend."

Labor Day was the official end of summer. After Labor Day, it was fall; it was football season; it was time for the school year to start. Labor Day was not to be wasted. My folks, Bill, and I took the boat out on a crowded Lake Ferguson and swam, lazed in the sun, and grilled steaks. As evening approached, our little sunburned group returned to shore confident that we had celebrated Labor Day to the fullest. That night I finished off the festivities at the Paramount Theater with my occasional girlfriend, Sally Stein. *Alice's Restaurant,* the Arlo Guthrie spoof of the sixties establishment, was playing. Sally was leaving in a few days to return to Indiana University for the fall semester, and I wouldn't see her again until Christmas holidays.

Sally was excited about returning to her college sorority with all her well-dressed, well-spoken, well-to-do sorority sisters. I would be returning to Lincoln School on the other side of the tracks to my students, who would probably never even get a high school diploma and who had a high likelihood of never darkening the doorway of any college. The evening was fun, but our worlds were as far apart as they had ever been. After I took her home, I thought to myself, this is certainly a cultural case study: David Beckwith, southern WASP, spending the evening with a Jewish princess, telling her about his ghetto junior high school.

On Tuesday, school opened with the meeting of students and faculty in the gym. Mr. Rollins and Mr. Bibbs sat in chairs facing the students and faculty, who were seated on the metal bleachers. Of course. Most of the faculty was known to the students, and when they were introduced they were greeted with friendly ovations. When Mrs. Hadley was presented, however, there were hoots and catcalls. Her face turned beet red, and I thought for a moment she might leave. Instead, she dropped into her seat and stared at her clasped hands. When I was introduced, there was not a sound. I was the white male figure which, for them, represented repression. Any self-confidence that either of us had was tested. Mrs. Hadley squirmed in her chair when she caught me glancing at her. I just tried to smile like nothing was wrong.

After the meeting, we adjourned to the homerooms that had been assigned to us the week before. There I registered seventh grade students. They were well behaved. In fact, no one made a sound—trying to figure me out, I surmised. They were timid when I tried to get information to fill out their registration cards. I had a difficult time understanding many of them, especially when I asked for parents' names. Often the father and mother did not have the same last name—or live in the same house. Only one in four students lived in a home where the family had a telephone, eight were on welfare, and more than half of them had failed one or more grades. I registered twenty-seven students. Most lived out in the country and rode buses to school. At 10:30, after registration was complete, we dismissed them to go home.

5

On Wednesday morning my alarm failed to go off, and I didn't wake up until 7:35. Teachers were supposed to be in their homeroom at 7:50. How I made it exactly on the dot, I'll never know! I registered two more students that morning, a boy and a girl. The girl, who was a little old to be in the seventh grade—having failed a couple of grades along the way—lingered at my desk, made a point of touching my hand, regarded me with a wide-eyed expression in a not-very-subtle effort at flirting. These two brought to twenty-nine the number of students in my homeroom. Since all junior high students were now registered, they were dismissed for the day.

In my homeroom that afternoon I was trying to decide how to make the bare-bones space look more attractive to the students when Anita Yarbrough, the new white art teacher at the Lincoln elementary school, stopped by and introduced herself. Since we had been attending separate faculty meetings, we'd never met. She was twenty-three, a graduate of Mississippi State College for Women, and was stunning, with large hazel eyes and a flip-up hairdo. She had married a guy from Mississippi State. She had that sorority look in her pleated skirt, pink blouse, and penny loafers, and certainly didn't look like she belonged at Lincoln.

"So what brings you to Lincoln?" I asked.

"My husband got a job at the experiment station. We moved here from Corinth. I applied at every white school in the county, but I was too late." She grimaced. "This is the last place in the world I wanted to end up. My folks had a hissy fit when I took this job. Maybe I should have listened to them. I don't think I belong here, and I'm not at all sure I'll make it a whole year. But I wanted so badly to show Mama and Daddy that Jimmy and I could make it on our own."

"Have you been around black people much?" I asked.

"I was born and raised in Carrollton. We had a few black people, but nothing like here in the Delta," she answered. "Mama and Daddy had a maid and a yardman. We always got along fine. Mama told Lelia, the maid, what to do; Daddy dealt with Roy, our yardman. But we always knew they weren't our equals. They were hired help. This is different," she sighed. Then she smiled. "Now I'm the hired help."

"Aren't we all," I nodded. "You know, I bet if our new black colleagues were honest with us, they'd say they weren't all that happy to have white teachers like us thrust on them. But I'll tell you this: so far everybody around here has treated me better than the white faculty did at that meeting we all went to at Dean." I smiled. "Wouldn't it be funny if a few months from now, you and I confessed to each other how much we like it here?"

"Want to bet on that?" she asked. Her mouth turned down.

"Yep. Twenty-five cents."

"You're on," she answered.

"In the meantime, do you have any ideas about how to improve the looks of this room?" I asked.

She looked around at the drab assemblage of the required equipment, and her glance settled on the bulletin board. "Fixing that up would help." Her eyes brightened. "I love doing things like that. Would you like for me to—"

"I sure would!" I interrupted. "I'm all thumbs when it comes to decorating."

She headed for the door. "I'll be back in a jiff. I'll bring some things with me that we can work on."

While she was gone, I searched in the teacher's desk for a ruler, magic marker, paste, or anything that would be helpful in decorating a bulletin board, but came up empty handed. Back then—and probably today—it was understood that teachers would supply their rooms with the extras beyond the bare essentials of books, and chalk for the blackboard. By the time I had finished hunting in vain for those extras, Anita was back, her arms loaded with supplies which she piled on a student's desk.

She handed me a piece of red construction paper and a pair of small children's scissors and pointed to the teacher's desk. "Sit there and draw big, block letters spelling 'Welcome,' then cut the letters out," she instructed me.

"Yes, ma'am," I said meekly.

She laughed. "I'm sorry. I'm so used to talking to kids when I'm teaching, I get carried away."

"You can talk to me any way you want to as long as we get the job done," I said with a smile.

An hour later she had transformed a dull bulletin board into a bright, inviting display of pictures cut from magazines, a little red schoolhouse she'd made from construction paper, figures of children playing ball and reading books, and a caricature of an absent-minded professor drawn with magic markers.

She stood back to view her handiwork and nodded. Then she turned to me and asked, "Is that OK?"

"Perfect! It brightens up the whole room," I enthused. "I'd have been here until this time tomorrow trying to figure out where to start."

"This was fun." Her smile faded as she gathered up her supplies. "Made me forget for a little while what I'm going to be facing the rest of the year." She headed for the door.

"Remember, they're just kids," I said. "Anything you can teach them will be new."

She gave me a patient "I've heard that before" look, then nodded. "See you around," she said.

As she disappeared down the hall, I reflected on what an odd threesome Anita, Mrs. Hadley, and I made. Yet how similar we were! We had arrived here as a last resort, having exhausted all other avenues of employment. We were steeped in a lifetime of prejudice. And we were white, thus providing Mr. Bigham the opportunity he needed to stave off total desegregation.

After Anita left, I was doing odds and ends—counting textbooks to be sure I had twenty-nine, making a list of equipment I'd need to get for my classes, such as wall map, thumbtacks—when I sensed that I was being watched. I looked toward the door and was somewhat disconcerted to see a black boy standing there, eyeing me. He was of average height, gangling, and ill at ease.

"Hi," I said, hoping my greeting disguised my surprise. "Can I help you?"

He shuffled toward my desk. "You the new teacher I been hearin' about?" he mumbled.

"I guess I am," I answered. "Are you in one of my classes?"

"Yessir. My name is Eddie Watts. I'm supposed to be a eighth grader." He shifted his weight from one foot to the other. "You got time to talk a minute?"

"Sure." I nodded toward one of the student chairs. "Have a seat."

He lowered himself into one of the chairs facing me. I waited for him to speak, but he seemed reluctant to begin. To break the silence, I nodded toward the bulletin board. "What do you think of that? The new art teacher just finished helping me decorate it."

He examined it and nodded. "You and her did a good job."

"She did most of the work," I said. "I'm not all that good at decorating."

He took a deep breath and looked back at me. "I been in the seventh grade before, but when the teacher wrote on my report card that I should repeat seventh grade, I dropped out. Just couldn't see no point to the whole thing— all that history, science, and stuff—it wasn't gonna help me make any money. And," he examined his hands on the desk top, "I wasn't good at readin'. I just quit."

I waited, not wanting to interrupt.

"My momma tried to make me go back, but I didn't listen to her. Made no sense to me to sit here all day just to get a free lunch. I reckoned with a job, I could buy lots of lunches and have plenty of money to spend on girls."

He shifted in his seat; slumped a little lower. "But when I left school, nobody gave me a chance at a job. They kept axin' me if I'd graduated from high school, an' when I said I hadn't, they didn't want me around. I ended up bussing tables over at the café on Highway 82, but that don't pay nothin', and I had to work nights and weekends. I didn't know it was gonna be like that—not getting anywhere, not seeing my friends anymore. They were over here at Lincoln. I thought I'd be the big shot. Instead, here I am—don't belong nowhere no more."

He sighed. "So I decide to go back and finish school. Then I can go to college and wear a tie like you and Mr. Bibbs. You went to college, didn't you?"

"I sure did," I answered. "They wouldn't have given me this job if I hadn't been a college graduate. What do you want to be when you get out of school?"

"I don' know, but I know I don't want to bus no more tables and wash no more dishes. I wants to have it easy, like you. And to have some respect. Yeah," he nodded, "that's what I want. Respect. I wanna be somebody. Maybe go to Chicago. I hear everybody in Chicago makes money. I got a cousin who went there and you oughta see the postcards he sends my momma."

I leaned back in my chair. "What makes you think that being a history teacher is easy?"

"'Cause you get paid lots of money to stand up in front of the class and tell the students about things that happen long time ago," he answered.

"And how did I learn those things?"

"'Cause you got to go to college."

"You don't think I had to study hard to pass tests and make good grades in high school so I could get accepted in college?"

He shrugged. "I guess so."

"What makes you think you wouldn't have to do the same?"

He shifted uncomfortably in his seat.

"Eddie, if you'll really try, I'll do what I can to help you," I went on. "If you don't, then I'm not interested in you. First, we need to get you in a remedial reading class. I'll see what I can find out about that." I looked at him fixedly. "It's up to you."

"I'll try," Eddie nodded earnestly. "I promise."

"I'm going to hold you to that. It's up to you," I repeated.

As I watched him shuffle to the door, I couldn't imagine a less likely success story than his. What if he's borderline intelligent and really can't learn to read beyond a third grade level? I sighed. I've stuck my neck out. I've got to see it through.

A few minutes after Eddie left, I hurried down the hall to the school counselor's office, hoping I could catch Mrs. Levison with a few moments to spare. She welcomed me, indicating the chair beside her desk.

"I didn't mean to use your services even before the first day of school," I apologized as I sat down, "but something's come up that requires more experience than I've got."

"That's what I'm here for," she smiled warmly, "to help wherever I can. What's the problem?"

I related my encounter with Eddie, and also my promise to help him if he cooperated. "He says he's serious about wanting to succeed. Since he's already experienced being rejected in the business world because he's not a high school graduate, I believe him. Could he be tested to find out if he is capable of doing seventh grade work?"

"Yes, we can do that," she nodded, "and we'll also find out if he has a physical problem." She thought for a moment. "Sometimes we like to team up a slow student with one who's doing well, and both of them benefit. Next Friday, when school starts, let me know if there's someone in one of your classes who you think might make a good mentor. If that student and Eddie aren't in the same history class, we can shift their schedules around."

I sighed, relieved. "You make it sound so easy. I know it isn't, and I appreciate your help. Thanks." I pushed myself to my feet. "I hope I won't be bothering you again for quite a while."

"David, get that notion out of your head. Asking for my help is not a problem. That's what I'm here for. If you don't 'bother' me again, I will be very put out with you."

We parted with mutual hopes that the coming year would be a good one.

6

7:30, Friday morning, September 5: D-DAY.

As I drove toward Lincoln Attendance Center on this first day of school and contemplated the task of teaching seven classes of twenty-nine restless students, I thought of many places in this world I would rather be. To pass the time during the twenty-minute drive, I conjured up words that began with D which would describe my feelings of inadequacy, hoping that the calming effect of acknowledging my shortcomings would carry over into instructing my classes: deficient, desperate, despairing, despondent, discomfited, disaffected. It didn't help. The bald fact remained that I had no idea how much these seventh graders knew or whether I could convey to them in a class setting what I knew and they didn't. First of all I had to get them beyond the fact that I was white and they were black.

At 7:55, I looked around my homeroom and savored the blessed silence before the storm. The student desks were lined up neatly in rows, the new bulletin board which Anita had decorated showed off to good effect, the table next to my desk held the twenty-nine textbooks, chalk was ready in the blackboard tray, and the seating chart upon which I had spent time was at hand. I was pleased with myself that I hadn't forgotten anything.

I now knew that Eddie Watts, the boy who had talked to me about coming back to school, was in my homeroom and first-period history class. I hoped he would justify my giving him a second chance by working hard and being attentive. I didn't have time for further reflection, because the silence was broken by loud voices calling to each other in the hall, the scrape of shoes, the rhythmic thump of someone hitting the wall, a yell, "Stop that! I'm gonna tell teacher on you!"

Some days are embedded in one's memory for life. For me, my first day teaching at Lincoln is one of those days.

As they came into the room, the students were silent, eyeing me suspiciously I greeted them with a cheerful "Good morning!"

Only Eddie Watts responded. He gave me a half-wave and tentative lift of his eyebrows as if questioning whether I remembered him. I smiled at him and nodded.

"Sit down anywhere for now," I said.

As they decided where their temporary seats were to be, there was much shoving and jabbing.

"Stop pickin' on me, Fisheye."

"You call me Fisheye again and you gonna get a black eye to go with your black behind," came the retort.

"That's the seat I want!"

"Well, that's too bad, 'cause I got it."

"Willie poked me!"

Finally, everyone had taken a seat.

"I have a seating chart which will seat you alphabetically," I said, taking the chart off my desk. "As I call your name, raise your hand, then take the seat I assign you."

"Ruby Anderson."

A light-skinned girl with pigtails sticking straight out from her head raised her hand. I indicated the first seat in the row nearest the door. As she moved to it, the girl already sitting there stood up and looked at me. I pointed to the seat left vacant by Ruby.

We're on our way, I thought gratefully.

"Leroy Baker." Another hand shot up. I indicated the seat behind Ruby.

"I can't sit by him," Ruby objected. "He picks on me all the time."

"That's 'cause you ain't no good," Leroy answered.

"Louise Beasley," I went on, ignoring Ruby's comment. "Sit behind Leroy."

"Our teacher didn't do this last year," Louise objected. "She let us sit anywhere we want."

"Doris Brown," I continued determinedly. "Where are you, Doris?"

A tall girl who looked like she was too old for the class raised her hand.

"Take the seat behind Louise," I instructed.

Instead, she came up to my desk and handed me a piece of paper. "This is a note from my momma to ax you if I can sign up my cousin for school." She pointed out a smaller girl. "She didn't have no chance to sign up before."

"I can't do that now," I answered. "You'll have to take your cousin to the office and get it straightened out."

The two of them left.

That was only the beginning. Almost every student had an objection to where he or she had been assigned to sit. Either they wanted to be by a window, or they did not; they couldn't stand the person sitting in front, behind or beside them, and became graphic in reasons why—from "he stink" to "my momma don't want me to have nothin' to do with her."

The wrangling continued even after everyone had a seat. I felt like I'd been working on the project for a week. I decided to try out something I'd heard a public speaker say: "Stand up in front of a group of jabbering people and be silent, and they will become silent also." I stood there and didn't say a word. Gradually, the room grew quiet.

"My name is Mr. David Beckwith," I said, "and I will be your homeroom teacher as well as your history teacher. I am new at Lincoln and look forward to getting to know you. If we try, if we work together, we can make this a memorable and productive year."

This speech was greeted with blank stares.

At that point, the bell rang. Frowning, I glanced at my watch as the students stood up and began milling around.

"Sit down," I said firmly. "There must be something wrong with the bells. It's not yet time to leave."

There were groans, and muffled "We be's late for our next class."

"Mr. Beckry, Leroy hit me!"

"You hit me first."

"No, I didn't."

"I don't like this seat!"

"Well, sit in it anyway," I finally yelled.

Surprised, they remained mute for a few seconds.

I handed out their classroom schedules, which identified the rooms they were assigned to for their classes during the day. "As I said before, this room will be your homeroom as well as your first classroom. When you arrive in the morning, you will come here for me to take the roll and make announcements," I continued, "and then you will have your first-period history class. It's important that you take care of your schedules so you'll know which classroom you need to be in at what time. Any questions?"

There were groans, mutters, objections.

I pointed to the blackboard and told the students to copy into their notebooks the page numbers of the lesson for the next school day, and also the grade scale.

"I cain't copy nothin' on account of my pencil is broke," Anthony said.

"Mine ain't got no point either," Louise added.

As a babble of voices chimed in with reasons why their pencils wouldn't write, I realized that, despite all my efforts at preparation, I'd forgotten a vital piece of equipment—a pencil sharpener. I racked my brain. Where would I go to get a pencil sharpener? The custodian was my only hope. Yet how could I leave a class of twenty-nine unruly youngsters to go look him up? In desperation I decided to risk it.

"I blew it," I admitted. "We don't have a pencil sharpener. I'll try to get one from the custodian."

They were delighted to have the teacher be the one who'd struck out, and there were shouts of pleasure. "Teacher done messed up," a boy in the back crowed.

"Please behave while I'm gone," I said in a voice that was just short of desperate. "Let's see how grown-up you can be."

They were silent until the door closed behind me. As I raced down the hall, I could hear the shouts that erupted when they thought I was out of earshot. I didn't know what else to do. There was nothing to keep them busy unless I could sharpen their pencils. Their behavior appalled me. I couldn't imagine a classroom that I had been in as a student which would have allowed this kind of conduct.

My attempt to locate a pencil sharpener proved frustrating and time-consuming. An ancient black custodian, dressed in bib overalls, shuffled around in the maintenance room and finally dug out of a drawer a pencil sharpener that looked as ancient as he did. He couldn't, however, supply either screws or a screwdriver to attach it to a wooden surface. I took it anyway and raced back to the class. Halfway down the hall, I could hear them, and was glad that the other classrooms had their doors shut.

They quieted as I walked into the room. "We've got a problem," I said. I held up the sharpener and explained about the lack of screws and screwdriver. "I need some help with this—a couple of boys to hold this steady while we sharpen the pencils."

Everyone wanted to help. I picked out two of the worst troublemakers to do the job, thinking that if they were occupied, they'd keep their mouths shut.

Leroy and Anthony swaggered up to the front of the room, proud of their role in rescuing the teacher. They were dressed in blue jeans and cotton shirts and looked bigger than twelve- or thirteen-year-olds. I let them figure out how to hold the pencil sharpener steady on the windowsill so everyone could come and sharpen his or her pencil. I called the students up row by row. Oddly enough, they behaved better during this activity—no denigrating remarks, no jabs with elbows—than they had since the bell rang.

"Thanks, you did a great job," I congratulated Anthony and Leroy. "I couldn't have managed without you."

They shrugged, pretending it was nothing, but I could see in their eyes their pleasure at having been useful as well as the center of attention for a little while.

Once the fun was over, however, it was back to normal. I pointed to the blackboard nearest the window and asked everyone to copy what I had written there: the pages in their textbooks that I wanted them to read for the next day. I ignored the groans. "On the blackboard next to it is a chart that shows which grades on a test are equivalent to an A, B, C, D, or failure. I hope I'm going to have a good number of A's in this class. We'll learn a lot of interesting things and have fun doing it."

"I ain't never wrote down that much at one time," a complainer in the back offered. "We gon be here all day doin' that."

"I betcha I ain't going to get even a 70. This is really going be a hard class," offered another faultfinder. "I wish I had Bill Hayes. He looks good."

"Son, don't pull the hair of that girl in front of you," I interjected, "and Ruby, stop waving at whoever that is out in the hall, and pay attention," I snapped.

I was about to tell them how exasperated I was with them when I noticed a girl in the second row diligently at work. I glanced down at the seating chart on my desk: Shirley Foster, age thirteen. She was small, and her dress was too big and looked old and faded, yet it was clean and ironed. Her hair was neatly braided, and someone had cared enough to put a pretty blue barrette in it. She hadn't taken part in the raucous catcalls hurled from one row to another, nor the jabbing or poking of nearby classmates. Is one student soaking up knowledge out of a class of twenty-nine enough to keep a teacher in the classroom? Then I had another thought: Eddie's mentor!

"My momma said I need to be excuse from taking PE," piped up a girl in the back of the room.

"I don't know anything about that," I answered. "You'll have to go talk to Mr. Rollins."

"Can I go now?" she asked.

"No, just stay put. You'll have time to talk to him—"

Rrriiiinnnnnng! The bell again.

"Don't pay any attention to it," I said, ignoring the jubilation the raucous sound had brought. "Finish copying the information on the blackboard so I can give out the textbooks."

I couldn't figure out why it would take so long to copy the pages in the textbook to read for the next school day, and a simple chart that showed A being 90–100, and on down the list, to below 70 being an F. I waited a few more minutes. All told, I'd given them enough time to write their life history!

"All right," I broke in, "it's time to give out the textbooks. I'll start on this side of the room," I said, pointing to the row opposite the door. "Y'all come up one at a time. Bring your book card with you and I'll give you your book."

I sat at my desk and motioned for the boy in the first seat in the row to come up to the table.

"I din't bring my book card," he said. "My momma didn't have the time to sign it."

I decided not to argue that he'd had the card for two days, and went on to the girl behind him. She came to the desk and handed me the card that had been signed by her mother. I wrote her name on the inside cover of the book, then wrote on the book card today's date and the serial number of the book. Though this task didn't call for extraordinary skill, it did require concentration so that the information was recorded accurately.

The distribution of the books went well for the first row. I was heartened by the lack of disruption. But as the tedious task wore on, the students lost interest and went back to the bickering and poking that seemed to be a necessary part of their behavior.

"Those of you who have gotten your book, read the first chapter," I said in a firm voice, hoping they would surprise me by doing what I asked.

A halfhearted flipping of pages consumed at least thirty seconds, then it was back to:

"The whole first chapter! That's a lot."

"That's too much work for the first day of school."

"I got to go to the bathroom."

"Willie poked me again."

"JoAnn steal my pencil and broke the lead."

"I rilly got to go!"

By the time the twenty-nine books had been distributed, I felt I had done a hundred push-ups. Would the entire school year be like this? Could I last the course? As a novice, I had nothing to compare this class to except my own experience of being a student. That didn't appear to be an apples-to-apples comparison. Had I misbehaved in school, I would have been punished not only by a school official but also my parents when I got home. My parents' initial reaction to my being punished at school was inevitably, "What did you do to deserve it?" Only after I mounted a lengthy defense might they consider the possibility that the punishment was unjust.

I was heartened by the fact that, on his way out, Eddie Watts stopped at my desk and said that he would bring a screwdriver and some screws the next day and attach the pencil sharpener permanently to the windowsill.

"Thanks, Eddie, I appreciate that." I went on to tell him that I'd spoken to the school counselor about him and that she would be getting in touch with him soon.

He nodded agreement. We had no more time for conversation, as students from the next class had begun drifting into the room.

The first day continued its chaotic course. The bells continued to ring erratically, and I didn't know—nor did anyone else, it seemed—which of the two shifts for the lunch period was ours. Too many classes crowded into the lunchroom for the first period, and not enough for the second. My classroom was adjacent to the lunchroom. When I'd first learned this fact I had thought that it would be a convenience, but I soon found out that the seasoned teachers had chosen classrooms as far away from the lunchroom as they could get, and that I, the newcomer, had been assigned what was left. For both lunch shifts there was noise of running feet, yells, thumping on my classroom wall, loud conversations just outside the door. The tenuous hold I had on my students' attention at the best of times disappeared entirely during lunch hours.

That first period of the first day was a portent of what was to follow. My history class 7C was replaced by 7B. I had hoped that, with my first class, I had hit bottom. Such was not the case. 7B pretty much followed the course set by 7C. The letters after the number 7 indicated the perceived abilities of the students. 7B and 7C had been average in intelligence, 7E and 7G were markedly less so. A good number had failed classes in the elementary school, and many were well into puberty. Several of the boys were almost as tall as me. It was as if I was trying to teach individuals with adult bodies who had had children's brains implanted in them. Every instruction had to be repeated; no information was grasped the first time. With some of my lower groups I was glad I didn't have to grapple with the pencil sharpener problem, for we might never have gotten that solved.

I recalled that when, during my high school career, my parents had expressed disappointment with a deficiency in one of my grades or a shortcoming in my motivation and lack of direction, I had always joked: "Don't worry about me. I can always teach school." One must be careful what one jokes about, I now decided.

7

Monday, September 8

Oh what a beautiful morning,
Oh what a beautiful day . . .
("Oh, What a Beautiful Mornin'," Richard Rodgers and Oscar
Hammerstein III)

The words and music from *Oklahoma!* followed me around my apartment as I was getting dressed. I had put the record on my stereo hoping its
upbeat message would inspire me to think positively about facing my classes
of seventh graders. I'd gotten up early and, after consuming a hearty breakfast of bacon, eggs, grits, and toast, had walked over to Deer Creek to listen
to the tranquil murmur of water flowing and the sound of birds singing in
the overhanging hardwoods. A touch of fall was in the air. The sun was shining. I told myself that since I had already made every mistake in the book, I
would have the weekend to reflect and prepare. Friday had belonged to them;
the week coming up was going to be mine!

Since I hadn't yet been assigned to an early morning detail—such as meeting the school buses—I stopped by Mr. Rollins's trailer-office to say hello. He
was already hard at work.

"Good morning, Mr. Rollins," I chirped.

"You seem to be in a good mood this morning," he answered. "And I see you're an early bird like I am. I like to get a running start on the day. Did you have a good first session Friday?"

"Yes, sir," I nodded. "I think I set the stage so we can accomplish something this week. I can't wait to get started teaching!"

If you're going to lie, you might as well tell a big one.

"Go get 'em, Tiger," he smiled.

As I turned to leave, he said, "Oh, by the way, David—"

I paused. "Mrs. Levison mentioned to me that you had a visit from Eddie Watts," he went on. "She said she was surprised when he re-enrolled in school this year. When he dropped out, she was afraid he was gone for good. For some reason, he didn't have his school physical when he was here before. A nurse from the health department is coming Wednesday about 9:00 to check some of the kids so we can get our records on them up to snuff. How about sending Eddie down while the nurse is here and she can check him out too?"

"Sure thing," I answered. "I'll see that he gets here."

With mutual wishes for a successful day, we parted.

The brief interlude of blissful quiet in my room was banished by the shrill clang of the bell, followed by the shuffling of feet and jabber of voices in the hall. I plastered a smile on my face.

"Good morning," I greeted my students, as they more or less filed into the room.

There was no response as they were occupied with poking the student ahead of them or dragging their feet to delay the student behind. A rather large girl wore a skirt so short that one wondered why she bothered to wear it at all. I made a mental note to detain her after class to send her to the office—by regulation, skirts could be no higher than the top of the knee. One of the bigger boys had his shirttail out, which was also an infraction. When all were seated, arguments began that some students were in the wrong places. I didn't interfere, and finally they took their assigned seats.

"Let's have a little drill," I suggested pleasantly.

They eyed me warily.

"When I greet you with 'Good morning,' it would make my day start off real nice if you could respond, 'Good morning, Mr. Beckwith.' Let's try it."

I looked around the class. "Are you ready? Good morning," I said cheerily.

A few of the older boys rolled their eyes and shook their heads, but the rest came up with some form of greeting. Almost everyone mispronounced my name: Beckry, Bucky, Beckwey, Buckwort, and so forth.

"Very good," I said.

I had noted that three students were absent, and glanced at my seating chart to pinpoint who they were. "Does anyone know why Rosa, Leroy, and Robert aren't here?"

No one answered. I marked them absent on my roll.

I looked up and scanned the room, still unsure about the lunch situation—whose parents were on welfare and thus had free lunches, who didn't qualify for free lunches and would thus stay in a study hall, and which students would be paying their quarter. I decided to ask.

"Do those of you who are paying for lunch have your lunch money?"

Amid the babble of responses, a boy who was seated toward the back made his way up to my desk. He was thin and not as tall as an average pre-teen. His clothes were too big for him and not very clean. I'd also noted that when others around him had moaned and groaned over every chore I'd assigned, he had remained quiet. In his hand he held a piece of paper.

"This is from my momma," he said. He didn't look at me but waited with downcast eyes, swaying from one foot to the other, while I read:

Dear mr Dave will ya
Let Samuel have 25 cents
For his lunch I will
Pay you for it
his mother Marie P

I had a gut feeling that Samuel's mother was not numbered among Mr. Rollins's freeloading parents, nor did I believe that Samuel had spent his quarter on something else. Unfortunately, I knew that if I gave him a quarter, I'd be opening the door for twenty-eight other students to badger me daily for money.

I handed the note back to him. "I don't have any control over this, Samuel," I said. "Show the note to the lady taking up the money in the lunchroom. She's the one in charge."

As he scuffed his way back to his seat, I tried to imagine how he must feel to be so needy that a quarter would make a difference between eating and going hungry. Bitterness, anger, humiliation, and a feeling of helplessness would cover it. I made a mental note to find out something about Samuel's family background so that, if there was real need, he could be included in the free-lunch program.

The ringing of the bell for first period to begin interrupted my musing; now it was time to get to the job I was hired to do—teaching history.

"OK, class, settle down," I said firmly. "Let's get to work. Open your books to the first chapter."

Instead of the groans, moans, and catcalls that I thought this suggestion would elicit, there was total compliance. I was amazed. I decided not to push my luck and ask how many of them had actually read the chapter. I was right, I told myself. This week is going to belong to me!

Speaking in public was a relatively new experience for me. I'd been a member of the high school debating team and had given oral book reports, but those were short speeches during which one had the polite, undivided attention of one's audience. Here, I was expected to speak for an hour in an unstructured situation, to a juvenile audience who was free to interrupt and ask questions about topics sometimes totally unrelated to my script. It was a daunting prospect.

"In studying world history, we are going to start at the beginning. And that means we will talk about prehistoric times," I began. I wrote the word *prehistoric* on the blackboard and asked them to copy it into their notebook.

I waited a few minutes to allow time for the mutters of "this sure is a hard class" and "this teacher going work us to death" which accompanied any request I made.

"The 'pre' in the word means 'before.' And the 'history' part of the word means a written record. So, can anybody tell me what the words 'prehistoric times' mean?"

I waited, looking hopefully around the room for a response. Finally, Shirley Foster raised her hand.

"Yes, Shirley?" I said encouragingly.

"That means the time before writin' was invented," she replied timidly.

"Very good," I answered. "So, we have no written record of what life was like in prehistoric times." I walked toward the windows. "Did prehistoric people live in houses like we do?"

"No," came a chorus of replies.

"Where did they live?" I asked.

"They lived in caves" came from different parts of the room.

"That's right, and so we called those people cavemen," I answered.

"Where did the cavewomen live?" Brenda McGary asked.

"The Bible don't say nothing about no cavemen," challenged Dorothy Myers before I could answer Brenda.

"I know, Dorothy," I said, realizing I was treading on dangerous ground, "but the people who wrote the Bible didn't know about the cavemen because their caves hadn't been discovered then."

"Next thing we know, you going tell us we descended from monkeys," an incensed Dorothy shot back. "Reverend Ike say that God made us in his image. He say that we all come from Adam an' Eve who live in the Garden of Eden. He say that's in the Bible." She was almost in tears.

"Everybody doesn't have to believe the same way," I tried to reason. "That's one of the things that's great about our country. Some people believe that the stories in the Bible were written to make a point or to teach a lesson."

"You must be one of them atheists!" Dorothy retorted. "I'm going tell my momma on you. You don't believe in God. We don't come from monkeys!"

I noted heads nodding around the room and wondered when I'd be hearing from some irate parent, which would lead to hearing from Mr. Rollins. Pursuing the topic of evolution at this time wouldn't be in anyone's interest, I decided, conceding defeat. I was about to change the subject when a hand shot up in the back of the room.

"Yes, Ruby?" I asked.

"Mr. Beck," she blurted. "When did the vampires live? Did they live in the caves with the cavemen?"

Now, where did *that* idea come from, I wondered. "Vampires are just imaginary creatures," I answered. "Somebody just made them up and told stories about them. You don't need to worry about vampires."

The mind of a seventh grader is a wonderful thing—open, uninhibited, imaginative—so out of touch with reality!

"Mr. Beckry, why was them cavemen so ugly? Didn't they ever brush their hair or their teeth?" Willie Mae Jackson asked.

Before I could answer, I had an authoritarian statement from an expert in the second row: "I think the cavemen came before Adam and Eve."

"Mr. Beckry, were Jesus' parents cavemen?" Glenn Oakley wanted to know.

As I was about to say that Jesus came many centuries after cavemen, Albert Lewis asked me what kind of guns cavemen had.

Ada Ware in the middle row stood up. "Mr. Teacher, I know something about history that I'd like to tell the class," she announced.

"What is that, Ada?" I asked.

"This is from my gramma. She say that when the world was young, the animals and the birds had a big war all over the world. The bats thought that the animals gonna win so they left their friends, the birds, and joined the animal army. But," she paused for dramatic effect, "the birds beat the animals and won the war. The birds chased the bats into the caves an' made them live there. They wouldn't let the bats have any friends. That's why the bats live in caves."

Several heads nodded in agreement. "Thank you, Ada, for sharing that interesting story with us," I said, wondering how, as a history teacher, I could compete with an authentic account like this from Ada's grandmother!

Now seemed to be a good time to try to insert at least a modicum of reality into our discussion. I went to the blackboard and drew a line that extended about four feet.

"This is called a time line," I said. "On this time line we're going to list important events that have happened in the world and put them in relation to each other. For instance, we'll put cavemen at the beginning, and at the end we'll put something that happened recently. In between let's list some important events in world history."

"Mr. Beckry, Mr. Beckry," a hand shot up in the back of the room. "Call on me, call on me."

"OK, Oscar," I agreed. "You first."

"Eight o'clock. That's when we got to be at school," he answered.

"Tuesday," yelled another. "That's when we going to have the next pep rally."

"January," a third participant offered.

I didn't know whether to laugh or cry. "I mean a famous date in history."

"The Fourth of July," proposed an eager contributor.

"No, no," I answered, my voice edging toward hysteria. "I mean a famous event. Like the discovery of America by Christopher Columbus."

"I know! I know!" Leroy almost fell out of his seat in his enthusiasm. "When Martin Luther King Jr. got killed."

"When President Kennedy got killed," chimed in another.

"When Abraham Lincoln got killed," a third contributed.

Once again, I had to retreat in defeat. "Thank you for those suggestions. It's about time for the bell to ring, so I want to assign some homework."

I waited for the moans and groans to diminish. "I want you to read over the first chapter again, because tomorrow we're going to have a little quiz on it. It's not going to be hard. I just want to find out what you've learned."

8

Let the sun shine,
Let the sun shine in
The sun shine in . . .
("Aquarius/Let the Sunshine In,"
Galt MacDermot, James Rado, and Gerome Ragni)

The radio alarm clock blared the Fifth Dimension's famous rendition of the song from *Hair,* the Broadway hit of the year. The rock musical had shocked the old guard and pioneered rock and roll's invasion of Broadway.

I turned over and hit the button, silencing the radio. Yesterday's failures, which I had evaded while I slept, now paraded before my eyes—the disaster of the time line, the Adam and Eve controversy, Ada Ware's grandmother's explanation of why bats live in caves! How can I reach them? Is my lack of teaching experience the reason why they don't understand?

The clothes closet was opposite my bed, and through the open door I spied a pennant from Ole Miss that I'd tossed on the shelf. It had been there since I'd unpacked and moved into the garage apartment. If only I was back there, I yearned, where life was simple and straightforward and progressed one day at a time toward a goal.

I threw back the covers and headed for the shower. I didn't have time for self-pity. Mr. Rollins had called for the faculty to meet before school started, which meant getting there earlier than usual. I dressed quickly, gulped down breakfast, and hurried out the door.

"This will only take a couple of minutes. I just need to reemphasize a few things," Mr. Rollins said after we had assembled in the gym.

"One: you are to use no profanity in the classroom. I don't care how badly they frustrate you, and believe me, they frustrate me, too. Remember also to use appropriate language. Some parents told me that teachers last year had used words that were inappropriate. I will not tolerate unsuitable language—even though that language may be used in their homes and their neighborhoods.

"Two: I do not want to hear that any of my teachers are having an intimate involvement with a student. Let there be no doubt that should this happen, it is grounds for dismissal.

"Three: I don't want to see any of you coming to work with a hangover. I like a good drink as much as anybody in this room, but if I see you showing up here with a hangover, I will deal with you severely." He smiled. "I don't need to tell you what Mr. Bigham thinks about drinking.

"Now, to other things: let's see who's going to do what at the football game. For the first game, we should have a full house. If you want a specific duty, speak up. If you don't have a preference, I'll just assign you a job."

As he looked around the room, I held up my hand and volunteered to man the fence to keep people from getting in without paying. Others spoke up and were assigned other positions. The bell rang, and we disbanded to get to our respective homerooms.

As I followed a couple of other teachers toward the door, I heard Mr. Rollins call my name. When I turned around, he beckoned me. "Can I speak to you a minute?"

"Sure," I answered, and as the others left I hurried to the front of the gym where he was waiting.

"I've got some good news on Eddie Watts," Mr. Rollins said. "The nurse that examined Eddie discovered that he's very nearsighted. That could be the reason he hasn't done well up to now. Everything written on the blackboard is a blur, and he has trouble focusing on the printed page. Also, Mrs. Levison found out that the Fosters live down the street from Eddie Watts and his mother. They've known each other for years. Shirley's mother said Shirley would be happy to help Eddie. 'It would make me feel like a teacher,' her mother quoted Shirley. I'll find out if their church has some kind of fund that would buy the glasses that Eddie needs. Most do."

"That's really good news," I exclaimed. "I like Eddie. He's not a troublemaker; he seems to really want to learn. I appreciate your following through on the case."

"Sometimes problems have happy endings," Mr. Rollins said with a smile.

"I think this one will." Then he grimaced. "I wish problems that some of the other kids have were this easy to solve."

Since that interlude had taken a few minutes, and I still had a way to go from the gym to my classroom, I dreaded what mayhem I would find that my class was causing with no one there to take charge. I jogged the last few yards and sure enough, through the open door, the decibel level was impressive.

"OK, calm down," I called as I closed the door behind me. "I'm sorry I'm late."

"You going to be marked tardy on your report card," one of the older boys in the back row gloated.

I nodded. "Fair enough, but I wasn't just goofing around. I was at a meeting." Before someone else thought of something smart to say, I added, "Shall we go through our little drill?"

"Good morning, class," I said, beaming.

"Good morning, Mr. Beckry," replied most of the class. I smiled as I heard them once again butcher my name. I had long ago given up on correcting them on this subject. As long as whatever they called me was preceded by "Mr.," I responded. Some of the older boys still held out on this childish behavior, but the response was becoming more and more widespread.

Then it was on to taking roll and checking the money for lunches. After the fifteen-minute homeroom chores were over, it was time to teach history.

"I hope everybody has read the chapter I assigned yesterday. And now, we are going to have a little quiz. All the questions are covered by the chapter in your book. And, since this is our first quiz, I'm going to be lenient and let you keep your books open."

"That's not fair givin' a test on the furst day of school," complained Fisheye.

"This isn't the first day, and I told you yesterday what to study," I replied as I put a stack of tests on the first desk in each row.

"What I supposed to do with these?" Ruby Anderson asked.

"Try to figure it out, Ruby," I suggested. "You're in the first desk and have all the tests. Nobody behind you has one, so what are you supposed to do?"

She grimaced as if I'd asked her to move a mountain, took one of the sheets, and passed the others to the seat behind. Eureka! I wanted to shout. We're making progress.

"Does everyone have a test?" I asked when the pages had all been passed.

"Sure are a lot of questions on this test," grumbled someone from the back of the room. "Going to take a long time to finish."

"We'll be here all day long," agreed another contributor.

"Start working and you won't be," I suggested.

I let them have the whole period to work on the test. There were ten simple, unambiguous questions on material in the first chapter. I had great hopes that this would start us off on a road of accomplishments. Except for various grunts and groans, foot shuffling, and an occasional poking, they seemed to be hard at work. The peace and quiet was heavenly. Maybe I had judged them—and myself—too harshly.

A couple of minutes before the bell rang, I asked them to sign their papers and pass them up to the front. This brought on more complaints about the difficulty and length of the test.

"I'll grade your papers and give them back to you tomorrow so y'all can talk about them. In the meantime, read the next chapter for tomorrow."

The usual complaints continued as they made their way out the door. Several wished aloud that they had some other teacher.

I gave the same test to my next history class, 7B, and while they were busy on it I graded the papers of the previous class, 7C. The first paper—Fisheye's—got a grade of 20! I couldn't believe it. This must be a fluke. I'd really better spend some one-on-one time with him.

The second paper, turned in by Stanley Gildart, scored a 10. He missed nine out of ten questions. The score on the third paper was 30. What's the matter? This was supposed to be an easy test to bolster their self-esteem and begin the year with a good grade. My spirits dropped lower with each paper I graded. When I finished, Shirley Foster was the sole student to make a passing grade. Only three out of the twenty-nine had scored 30 or higher. The words used to fill in the blanks made no sense: Charles Robinson stated that man's history could only be traced back ten years; a classmate opined that man's history only went back to 1890. Why 1890, I wondered. Where did Robert get the idea that the Pharaohs were cavemen, and Frank the belief that an educated Egyptian child was a Christ?

And so it went through the four classes that I taught that morning. All the grades were in the twenties and thirties. The millennia of civilization had been reduced to a few short years. I had the feeling that this history had been written by the editors of *MAD* magazine.

Just when I'd concluded things couldn't get any worse, an announcement was sent around that the water had gone off in the whole building and the cafeteria had to be closed. This meant that the lunch schedules were thrown out of sync. It also meant that the students were confined to their classroom, and I had nothing planned for them to do in an emergency such as this.

"I'm hungry. When we gonna get lunch?"

"I needs to go to de bafroom."

"Fulton hit me!"

"We gon' be here all day long."

"Give me your attention, everybody," I said in what I hoped sounded like an authoritarian voice. "I was very disappointed with your quiz results. Eugene, if you don't sit there and shut up, I'm going to send you to Mr. Bibbs."

He shut up momentarily.

"Didn't I do good on the test?" called out someone in the back.

"It was too hard," another voice chimed in. "I don't like that history anyway. We ought to be talkin' about Martin Luther King Jr. 'stead of the king o' Egypt."

"If I did bad, don't sen' me home. My momma'll beat me."

"I wisht I had Bill Hayes. My sister had him last year and he don't give no test the first week o' school."

"I was very disappointed with your test results," I interrupted. "Kenneth! Don't try me. You're this close to getting sent to the office," I said, holding up my fingers an inch apart. "As I was trying to say, you didn't live up to your potential on the test this morning."

"I don't want t' know nothing about no cavemen. I ain't got no business with them."

"I need to go to de bathroom."

"You must be de hardest teacher in the seventh grade."

I'd finally had it. "Stop! Right now. Just sit there and shut up! You all flunked the test. Every one of you failed. Maybe one reason you failed is that you don't keep your mouths shut long enough to pay attention so you can learn something. Larry, one more time—and Randolph, don't egg him on or you're both out of here! This was an easy test. My opinion of this class is down around here!" I leaned over and held my hand level with my knees.

Deafening silence greeted my outburst. Suddenly, Brenda McGary started to cry. No one picked at her or poked her. They sat there staring at their desks. At that moment, the bell sounded, and without a word they gathered their belongings and filed out.

I had never been so glad to see the backs of a group of people leaving a room. "God help them!" I mumbled to myself. "And don't forget me!"

On the way back to my apartment that afternoon, I clicked on the car radio. Elvis Presley was singing:

We're caught in a trap,
I can't get out . . .
("Suspicious Minds," Mark James)

9

It's Friday! It's Friday! Thank God it's Friday! Only one more day of facing six classes of undisciplined seventh graders before the weekend.

A good night's sleep had diminished the impact of the humiliation of the day before. As I lathered my face and began to shave, my mind replayed some of those events. What should I have done differently? I had used the same methods that my teachers had used on me when I was a student, but then they had worked! Was I the problem?

As I mulled over that conundrum, I recalled Leroy's complaint following the test: "I don't wanna know nuthin' about no cavemen. I ain't got no business with them."

In truth, so much history had no relevance to the lives of Leroy and his classmates. What difference did it make to them that the Roman Empire rose and fell, that Napoleon terrorized Europe, or that the Spanish Armada was sunk by the English? Leroy's locale was Lincoln Attendance Center, his state was Washington County, his country was the state of Mississippi. To him the chief executive officer was Theodore Rollins, not Richard Nixon. Caldwell M. Bibbs was his vice president. A world traveler to Leroy was someone who had been to Chicago or Detroit; he had probably never been farther than twenty miles away from home in his life.

The more I thought about the relevance of what I was attempting to teach these children, the more I decided they weren't dumb, but rather uninterested. Unfortunately, getting a passing grade in history was required for graduation. I'll give the test again, I decided. I'll jumble the answers and write them on the blackboard. This "pick a winner" test might restore their self-respect by giving them a chance to succeed.

Armed with this well-thought-out rescue plan, I welcomed my 8:00 homeroom class with an upbeat "Good morning" when they shuffled tentatively through the door. All were wary, having heard about my explosion, I was sure, from the other students.

Then came a subdued "Good morning, Mr. Bockwort," or "Brekwit," or "Bref-wurf," and so forth.

I scanned the room to determine who was absent. "Does anybody know why Reginald isn't here? Or Louise? Or Ed Allen?" I asked.

No one commented, and I filled out the absentee list to be sent to the office.

Fisheye waved his hand in the air. "I needs to take a note to Mista Rollins from my mama," he said.

"You can take it between classes," I answered.

"But my next class after this one is at the other end of the hall," he objected. "By the time I get to the office and back to my class I be late."

Not knowing Fisheye then as well as I would later, I innocently agreed. "All right. Ruby is going to take the absentee list to the office now. You can go with her."

Just then, Louise sauntered into the room. "You're ten minutes late, Louise," I said. "I'll have to mark you tardy unless you have an excuse."

She shrugged.

Ruby and Fisheye left. That was the last I saw of Fisheye that day.

The bell rang for the first period. I told the class that I would give them a second chance to take the test they had failed.

Instead of the smiles and upbeat comments I had expected at this chance to redeem themselves, I was greeted by:

"Again!" in an aggrieved tone.

"That hard test? I got to do it agin'?"

"This class sure ain't no fun!" and other, similar comments.

Gratitude for second chances? Forget it. I wondered how I would react if, just once, someone would say "Gee! that's great!" or just a simple "Thank you."

"I'm going to write on the blackboard the answers to the test," I went on.

"The answers will be jumbled, so you'll have to figure out which answers to put in the right blanks."

Again, I placed the test papers on the first desk in each row, to be passed from front to back, and the class settled down to choosing their answers. On three occasions I reprimanded a student for copying from a neighbor's paper. Being caught in the act of cheating never seemed to embarrass them. The result of cheating, an automatic zero, posed no threat.

Again, a project that should have taken twenty-five minutes lasted forty-five. After the test was over and I'd taken up the papers, I launched into the next topic in the book: the history of man around 4500 B.C. Living in the fertile valleys of the Nile, these people had furnished us with the first indications of man's historical existence. I went through the motions of assigning them the chapter on the subject, not very hopeful that they would read it. The bell rang, 7C made their exit, and 7B took their places.

While the second class took the test, I graded the papers just handed in by the first. I all but groaned aloud. More than 50 percent of the first class flunked, and the rest, again with the exception of Shirley Foster, did poorly. The pattern repeated itself in the other two morning classes. The morale of the kids seemed unaffected by their performance, though mine was all but destroyed. Are my communication skills that bad? What can I do to inspire them to at least try?

The big event of the afternoon had nothing to do with academics. As I explained how the small Egyptian communities along the Nile River gradually joined to form a unified nation, develop the calendar, and introduce agriculture, I noticed that some of the students sitting next to the window began pointing at Sam Trotter and giggling. Wondering "what now," I saw that the front of the boy's shirt was stained with a large, blue splotch. Basking in the attention, Sam grinned. The whole inside of his mouth and his teeth were stained the same shade of blue. I thought he was suffering from some strange malady.

"Sam, what's wrong?" I yelled. "Are you hurt?"

"Nawsa," he said, his grin getting bigger now that the teacher was concerned. "I was jes' chewin' on ma pen an' it broke off in my mouth. That's all."

The headline "Student Poisoned by Ink Cartridge" flashed through my mind. I hurried to his seat and took him by the arm. On the way out the door I appointed Dorothy Myers to take down the names of troublemakers while I was gone, then dashed for the principal's office.

I explained to Mr. Rollins what Sam had done; he didn't seem perturbed at Sam's appearance. He just smiled and shook his head. "Leave Sam with me," he said. "I'll take care of the problem. You better get back to your class."

When I returned to my room, things were out of control and, oddly enough, there were no names on Dorothy's list of troublemakers. I groaned when I saw that during my brief absence the ink on the floor had been smeared up and down the aisle.

"Wouldn't it be as much fun to do something constructive as to do something you know you shouldn't?" I shouted. "You work so hard to make trouble, I swear it would be easier to behave yourselves!"

The only reply I got from my outburst came from an unidentifiable source at the back of the room. "Mr. Beckry, you not s'posed to swear in school!"

The rest of Thursday passed in a blur of just trying to maintain control. Even the first chore of taking the roll was a toss-up as to who was in charge—them or me. "Anthony, don't shoot spitballs at Eddie. Louise?"

No one answered, and I looked up to see Louise at her desk busily painting her fingernails. "Louise!" I all but yelled.

"I'm here," she answered, annoyed that I had interrupted her concentration.

As she spoke, another spitball whizzed by her head.

"Anthony! One more time and you're in trouble. Velma? Where are you, Velma? Stop talking to Louise and pay attention. Oliver? Answer when I call your name. Anthony," I yelled. "Are you deaf! Spitballs are dangerous. You're out of luck now. Go to the office with JoAnn when she takes the absentee list."

The day that had begun on a negative note continued on a chaotic course. Each class seemed to repeat the pattern set by the one before: continual complaints about too much homework, comparison of my teaching with that of the year before, persistent punching and poking of fellow students. The fact that several students were repeating seventh grade made no difference in their knowledge of the material. It was as if I was giving them a new set of facts.

I tried to think of some bright spots, and there were some. I'd spoken to Mr. Rollins about Samuel Ross, whose mother had sent the note asking if I could loan him a quarter for lunch. Arrangements had been made so that Samuel could get a good hot meal at noon. Here was a bright child who read the lessons, contributed to discussions, and took no part in the misbehavior of the others. I must look out for him to see that Samuel was not bullied by the older boys. And then there was my poster-child student, Shirley Foster. One afternoon when the final bell had rung, the students were barreling from the room in their usual disorganized way. My morale had hit a new low. I watched them leave, wishing I was anywhere but in this classroom. Shirley lingered behind the others and came up to my desk.

"Mr. Beckry," she said, shyly, "did you notice that Eddie did better on that last test? I been going over to his house in the afternoon after school and helping him with his homework."

I smiled. "Is *that* why he's so improved! That's very good of you, Shirley."

"I enjoys pretendin' like I'm a teacher," she replied.

"I think you'd be a good one! I know Eddie and his mother really appreciate what you're doing for him. And so do I," I added.

Watching Shirley leave, I tried to imagine the joy of teaching a roomful of students like her.

~

Friday arrived: the day of the big game—the first football game of the season. All summer, baseball had reigned. The voice of Harry Caray on the radio—the primary means of broadcasting sports at that time in the Delta—announcing the St. Louis Cardinals games had dominated the athletic picture. Now football, the foremost sport in Mississippi every year, would begin a new season.

The periods throughout the day were abbreviated to allow time in the afternoon for the pep rally. During fourth period, Mr. Levison came to my classroom and "borrowed" all the boys to help him set up the bleachers in the gym for the pep rally. I wondered if I was the only one in school concerned that this extracurricular activity took precedence over academic subjects. But—what the hell! It was such a relief to have the boys gone! The girls were very subdued. I didn't have to yell at a single one of them, and we actually covered the day's material in an organized manner. When the bell rang I felt satisfied that I had actually accomplished something.

The tension mounted as the hour for the pep rally approached. Finally, any semblance of holding classes ended, and the student body en masse streamed toward the gym. Even at some distance, one could hear foot stomping, hand clapping, and boisterous yells. When everyone was assembled, Mr. Rollins and Mr. Bibbs walked into the gym. All eyes were focused on the two men as they raised their hands for the crowd to be quiet.

"Are we going to beat Rolling Fork tonight?" Mr. Rollins roared.

"Yes! Yes! Yes!" the crowd thundered.

"Let me hear all you Braves! I can't hear you! Braves '69! Braves '69!" Mr. Rollins orated like an itinerant preacher warming up the crowd for a revival. "I've watched Coach McCall and his staff all through August, and I can tell you: this is gonna be the most exciting football season Lincoln has ever had. Does anyone agree?"

"We do! We do! We do!" shouted the audience—teachers as well as students.

"I can't hear you!" Mr. Rollins egged on the crowd. "Who's going to be best?"

"LINCOLN! LINCOLN! LINCOLN!"

At this point, the cheerleaders ran into the gym with the football players thundering behind. Now the gym vibrated with foot stomping and hand clapping. Studying history can't hold a candle to participating in a pep rally like this, I decided.

The senior class president stepped in front of the cheerleaders and the players and held up his hands for silence.

"Let's all rise and sing our school song," he said.

As the band played the opening bars, the audience stood up and joined the president in singing:

Oh, Lincoln dear
Oh, Lincoln dear
You are the pearl of my heart.
And true to you we'll ever be
No matter what the future holds.
Though time may take us from thy halls
And cares may our spirits enthrall
Yet deep within our hearts still lie
The noble thoughts thou has instilled.
Oh, Lincoln dear, oh blue and gold
To you we ever will be true.
Oh, Lincoln, Lincoln, we love thee,
For you our prayers will always be.

There was a spirit of unity in the gymnasium that I certainly had not seen in the classroom. Even my flagging spirits were raised. As the last notes of the song became silent, the head cheerleader yelled: "Extra! Extra!"

The crowd responded in perfect unison: "Extra! Extra!"

Read all about it (clap)
We got a team (clap)
We got a team (clap)
We gonna shout about it! (clap)
Here we come! (clap)
Yeah, man! (clap)
Have we got rhythm? (clap)
We gonna shout about it! (clap)

Feet stomped, voices were raised to a higher pitch, bodies swayed back and forth. The students were totally involved. No one poked anyone else; punching was absent. The coach stepped to the microphone and added to the din with incantations of "Here we come!" "We got the rhythm!" and "We gonna win!"

If I'd been a stranger walking into the gym, this atmosphere would have seemed eerie, like something from a different world. Somehow, it didn't seem quite as unnatural to me as it might have even a week ago. I glanced at Mrs. Hadley, who was sitting to one side of me, two rows ahead. She remained silent, observing the commotion engulfing her with a combination of fear and disdain. She had taught for many years and was used to pep rallies, but nothing that would compare with the intensity, the total concentration of the participants from Lincoln. The kids seemed to have reached a trancelike state, exhibiting an almost zombielike involvement. I imagined her visualizing naked native children, spears in hand, body and face paint gleaming, running through the jungle, screaming "Kill the pig, cut her throat, spill her blood!" as William Golding famously wrote in *Lord of the Flies*. Eye contact confirmed my supposition.

I didn't have much time to weigh her reaction, for we were off and running again, launched into the next part of this frenzied script.

There's a little ole school on the shady road
On the west side Choo Choo
It's run by the braves
Come be our guest
On the west side Choo Choo

Lots of girls, you bet
Even more than you can get
On the west side Choo Choo.

This was shouted over and over, each class trying to drown out the one preceding it.

"Now all the freshmen," shouted the head cheerleader.

"Now the sophomores.

"Let's hear it from the juniors.

"Show your spirit, seniors."

Then came introduction of the players, with each one getting a boisterous acclaim with yells, whistles, foot stomping, and hand clapping. One would have thought they were national heroes. In a sense, for this audience, they were more than national heroes. These were their superstars—not those imposed upon them by a white establishment or the black adults of their world. I had played football in high school, but my teammates and I would have been bowled over at the acclaim these players got.

Once again the contrapuntal exchange began between the audience and the person at the microphone. Every exchange was upped a notch in the decibel level, and all exchanges were repetitive. I glanced again at Mrs. Hadley. Her eyes were closed. Seeming to have shrunk down in her seat, she was conspicuous by being the only person in the gym who was silent.

Mr. Rollins finally took over the microphone, and after repeating some inflammatory remarks about what we were going to do to Rolling Fork that night, he dismissed us.

I made a quick exit, went home to change clothes and to grab a bite to eat. Even more, I wanted a few moments to unwind before I had to return to school to do my duty as captain of the fence. I had never realized that teaching school was a sixteen-hour-a-day job.

10

Kickoff was at 7:30 p.m., and Mr. Rollins had instructed us to be on the job at 6:30. The days were getting shorter, but there'd been no letup in the heat. The empty stadium at dusk gave one a feeling of tranquillity. I savored it, knowing the peace would be short lived.

I was both excited and apprehensive. Mr. Rollins had decided that the Lincoln community by and large knew who I was. That being the case, he should treat me no differently than any of the other men on his staff. Tonight was to be my debut.

My duty was to patrol inside the chain-link fence surrounding the stadium. At first glance this would seem to be a pretty cushy job. When I'd gone to Greenville High School, fans getting into the stadium by any means other than through the gate with a ticket was never an issue. Tickets were cheap and easy to purchase. I assumed the same would apply here, and that I would have a carefree evening enjoying the game from an excellent vantage point.

Soon after I'd taken up my post, the crowd began arriving. They converged on the ticket taker at the stadium entrance. The stands filled quickly, and there was the usual hallooing and waving to friends and classmates. I was basking in the pleasure that came from seeing people having a good time when, out of the corner of my eye, I saw a body slither up the outside of the fence and drop to the ground on the inside. I ran to him and took his arm.

"You can't come in this way," I said firmly. "You'll have to go around and come through the gate."

"I won't be here but jest a few minutes," the boy answered, not missing a beat. "My brother's in the stand, and my momma told me to bring him something."

"Let me see your ticket," I said.

"That's why I had to come in this way. My brother got my ticket," he answered, looking me straight in the eye.

"You aren't allowed inside the stadium without a ticket," I answered in what I hoped was an authoritarian tone.

"But my brother got my ticket. Please lemme go, Mister. You'll see. I bring it right back to you. Won't take me more'n three minutes."

"I'll be right here waiting," I said.

"Yessir, I be right back. You'll see. Thank you, suh. You're a pal."

Before I could respond, he was off and swallowed by the crowd.

As the evening wore on, my position at the fence became the most demanding job at the stadium. Unlike some chores that were taxing during certain times of the game, my assignment absorbed my attention through almost the entire evening. Almost as many of Lincoln's fans used the fence for a port of entry as they did the gate.

I developed a new respect for the U.S. Border Patrol's effort to keep out illegal aliens. In Texas there was too much border and too few officers to patrol; here, I had too much fence and no other "officers" to help me. If I maintained watch at one location, the incoming traffic merely moved to another. Agile youths would shoot up the chain-link fence, and as I futilely yelled for them to stop, they would vanish into the crowd. When I did occasionally apprehend a transgressor, he would take defeat graciously and leave, only to make a more successful attempt from another launch site. I imagined that in after-game gatherings there would be mutual congratulation at how they'd outfoxed whitey.

Needless to say, I saw little of the football game, which, it turned out, we lost 19–6. The frustrating evening seemed a fitting end to my disastrous first week. My lack of control in the classroom had been mirrored at the game.

I didn't see the first boy who had slithered up the fence until the end of the game. He was talking with his buddies at the exit gate oblivious of my presence. Then he glanced my way, noticed me looking at him, and grinned. He'd won; I'd lost. I had trusted him; he'd used that trust to accomplish his goal. He seemed surprised that I remembered his face, and surmised that by next week's game I would probably have forgotten it.

Discouraged, beset with doubts about my ability to connect with the students much less teach them anything, I drove home and fell into bed, probably more tired and defeated than the athletes who'd lost the game that night.

~

As September progressed, the idealism I'd had when the term began—that I could make a difference in these children's lives—was replaced by the reality that success meant surviving the daily mayhem. Each day brought a different challenge. Once, I sent Dorothy Myers to the office because she felt compelled to circumnavigate the room during the class period, punching the other students as she passed by their desks. Fisheye was a never-ending irritant to those beside, in front of, and behind him. I learned that he had repeated the fourth grade three times, finally outgrowing the grammar school desks. He was catapulted into the seventh grade, not because of his academic prowess, but because he would at least fit in the seats!

~

Before the month was out, I had to resort to corporal punishment. From bull sessions in the teachers' lounge, I'd learned that most of the spankings occurred in the classroom rather than in the principal's office because it was too disruptive to bring the class to a standstill every time a misbehaving student was punished. Mr. Rollins's office discipline was saved for repeat offenders or for the worst breaches of the rules. The embarrassment of being punished in front of one's classmates also served as a deterrent, the teachers agreed.

"If you feel squeamish about striking a child in punishment," said Leroy Cain, a math teacher, "just remember that the punishment meted out at school is no comparison to what they're used to getting at home."

"When I was in school," I said, "being punished by having to do extra homework or being required to stay after school was a great embarrassment in front of your classmates, not to mention what you faced from your parents when you got home."

"That won't help much here," he answered. "Since so many of the kids don't do any homework, assigning extra work would be a joke. If you keep them after school, they'd miss their bus ride, and guess who has to take them home? You! What you need is a gin strap," he went on. "That's the most commonly used weapon in school for administering punishment." A canvaslike belt, twelve to fifteen inches long, six inches wide, and a quarter inch thick, a gin strap was an essential component in the operation of a cotton gin.

"Weapon?" I asked. "These are children! We're teachers, not soldiers."

"Yeah, weapon," Leroy replied without hesitation. "To wage war you need a weapon. It's you or them. He who hath the biggest weapon winneth the war."

"If I'd wanted war I would have gone to Vietnam," I grunted.

"At least in this kind of war, they can't hit you back," Leroy got the last word.

"Where can I get one?" I asked.

"Any of your students can get you one—from their male relatives who work in the cotton gin," he answered. "Gin operators don't mind if employees take home worn-out belts." He smiled. "It'll cost you a quarter, though. Think you can handle that?"

"It'll be worth every cent," I answered. "Thanks for the tip."

As I mulled over who among my students would be the one to obtain my weapon, Eddie Watts sprang instantly to mind. He had been fitted with the glasses he needed—thanks to Mr. Rollins's effort with the church fund—and they had transformed his life. Seeing the blackboard and the printed words on a page was still a miracle to him. Eddie had told me to let him know if there was anything he could do for me. Getting me a gin strap would fit the bill. When I approached him with my request, his face lit up.

"No problem!" he said. "I got an uncle workin' at the gin. He can get me a gin strap. I'll bring it to school soon's he give it to me."

Two days later, he appeared in class with a paper-wrapped package and placed it on my desk. Rather than open it in front of the other students, I waited until the period was over. When the bell rang, Eddie stayed behind and approached my desk. "I got a good one," he said proudly as I unwrapped his bundle. "My uncle picked it out special."

I held it up, admiring it on all sides. If there was a Rolls-Royce of gin straps, this was it.

"My goodness, Eddie. This is a beaut!" I tested it for heft, slapped it against my leg with a crisp snap. "It must be worth a lot more than a quarter," I said, reaching into my pants pocket for some change.

"I don't want no quarter," Eddie said, "This is just a little return on everything you done for me."

We looked at each other, and I saw that behind the glasses his eyes glistened. Feeling close to tears myself, I put my hand on his shoulder. "We're all proud of you, Eddie. Keep up the good work."

He nodded, ducked his head, and hurried from the room. As the door closed behind him, I decided that if I didn't accomplish anything else during this year, Eddie's redemption would have made all my efforts worthwhile.

Shortly after the gin strap discussion in the lounge, Mr. Rollins sent a notice to our classrooms about a faculty meeting in the library the next morning before school. Another early rising! The time and effort demanded of teachers in just the teaching process, not to mention the extracurricular activities, had given me a new respect for the teachers I'd encountered through my school years. I vowed to go back to my high school the next time I was in Greenville and tell some of my favorite teachers how much I appreciated them now—even if I hadn't then.

The next morning, after the faculty had assembled in the library, Mr. Rollins walked in with a determined look on his face and opened the meeting with no preamble.

"I was under the impression that I'd made it clear what the school district's policy is concerning proper haircuts, how we expect all students to keep their shirttails tucked in while on the campus, and the proper length of girls' skirts. We will not tolerate the miniskirts that are becoming popular. Personally, I agree with these standards, and even if I didn't, I would feel it is my duty to enforce the district's rules."

He had been pacing back and forth across the room in front of us. At this point, he stopped and looked at the gathering directly. "It has gotten back to me that there are certain members of my staff who have chosen to not only disagree publicly with these policies but to instigate a movement to organize the parents of our students to encourage the violation of these policies. I would like to remind those members that the district office has methods to deal with staff members who are being a disruptive influence on our system. Contracts are reviewed and renewed on an annual basis."

Again he began his pacing. "I would be a hypocrite if I said that I agree with every policy in this school district, but as long as I accept a paycheck from them, it's my duty to either keep my differences to myself or discuss them privately with my superior. My door is always open if anyone would like to discuss these matters with me. Are there any questions?" He paused, looking over the group. No one spoke.

"Then I guess it's time you get to your homerooms," he said.

As the days passed, I noticed that a tentative bond had begun to form between the black teachers and me. This probably resulted from my being willing to work side by side with them at the Friday football games, participate in discussions in the teachers' lounge, and eat with them in the cafeteria. Mrs. Hadley still avoided these situations. Demonstrating that I could take kidding from them in a good-natured manner also helped build our rapport. The black teachers must have sensed my increasing ambivalence to skin color, and this lowered the barriers still further.

Mrs. Hadley, on the other hand, not only refused to eat in the cafeteria but was also reluctant to use the teachers' lounge. She confined herself to her room most of the day.

One day I was having lunch in the cafeteria with a math teacher, Leroy Cain, and a science teacher, Gwen Stewart, when a female student suddenly came over to our table and whispered something in Gwen's ear. After the student had left, Gwen shared the whispered message with us:

"That Mr. Cain sho' is a gorgeous hunk o' man!"

My joining in the heckling of Mr. Cain which followed that revelation further cemented the fact that even if I was a whitey, I wasn't such a bad one.

Gwen's reply made me turn beet red. "Honey, for a honky, you got real possibilities yourself."

～

I continued to be confronted with sometimes challenging, sometimes amusing events. One day Mrs. Hadley stopped me in the hall. She had a shocked look on her face; her mouth was set in a grim line.

"David," she whispered, as if she could be overheard in the din that always accompanied class changes, "I passed your room just now while you were at lunch, and saw one of your boys lying on his back on the floor. One of the girls was standing over him, and he was looking up her dress!"

Was that better or worse than shooting spitballs across the room, I wondered, as I tried to give her a measure of relief by saying I would handle it. What I would do to "handle" it? I had no idea.

Another day, Anita Yarbrough stopped me as we passed in the hall. "This morning I was sitting behind my podium reconciling my grade book," she said, "when one of my little first grade boys stooped down in front of me and looked up my dress. Then he blurted out to the class that 'Ms. Yarbrough is only white from here up,'" and drew a line at his waist. "I was so embarrassed, but thank goodness, I kept my cool. You'd have been proud of me. I told them that I was white all over just like they were brown all over, but that I was wearing a pair of pantyhose which were darker than my skin."

I tried to keep a straight face, but failed. I started sniggering as I told her about Mrs. Hadley's experience earlier in the day. That set her off, too. Before we could regain our composure, tears were rolling down our faces.

11

September passed in a blur of trying to maintain a semblance of order in the classroom and even, as a sideline, teach history. Some days I succeeded with one goal or the other, but rarely with both. Early in the month I caught Fisheye trying to steal an encyclopedia from the classroom. If I'd thought there was a ghost of a chance he'd read the book I would have been glad to let him keep it, but, of course, it was just something he would sell to make a little money. He'd already been accused of stealing another student's radio for that purpose.

At the end of the first week of school, I had experimented in all my classes with having students take turns reading aloud from the text. Fisheye and his fellow troublemakers read at what seemed to me to be about a third grade level; many of them needed help with even one-syllable words. It came as a shock, but it explained why school held no interest for them. Why hadn't the school given them remedial reading lessons before the seventh grade?

My patience was pushed to the point of resorting to corporal punishment at the end of the third week. This involved spanking the hands of the miscreants with a ruler. For one student, it was outright disobedience: "I ain't gon' do dat stupid lesson, and you cain't make me do it!" For another, it was picking on the students around him so that the class was continually interrupted by complaints. The third incident involved a girl who was sent to the office for punishment. She had been an irritant since the moment she walked in the room—interrupting my explanations, talking to other students, and defiantly chewing gum (which was forbidden). The fourth incident was in a lighter vein. Mary Bishop went tripping in front of my desk across the room to the pencil sharpener. For whatever reason, before she got there she untied the shoulder straps holding up her dress. It fell to the floor at her feet. I was speechless; the class went into hysterics. She finally got her dress adjusted, sharpened her pencil, and returned to her desk.

Soon after that incident, she raised her hand.

"Yes, Mary," I bit, assuming she wanted to apologize for her earlier behavior.

"Mr. Bekwort," she said sweetly, "please tell Charles to stop callin' me a nigger."

As a fitting end to this perfect day, during sixth period Johnny Hampton passed wind that permeated the entire room. Half the class ran to open the windows and stuck out their heads to breathe while I stood with my mouth open trying to think of an appropriate response. I didn't know whether to laugh or cry.

～

Monday, September 22, was the first day of fall. I woke up with a bad cold and felt really rotten. In class, I showed filmstrips so I wouldn't have to summon the energy to teach. Asking the classes to behave because I felt so bad did little to improve their conduct. Larry Harold picked this day to do whatever he could to aggravate me. First he dropped his textbook from shoulder height to the floor, where it landed with a bang as loud as a gunshot. He apologized, saying it had slipped out of his hands. Next he gave a jab in the back to Leroy sitting in front of him. Leroy cried out in pain and whirled around ready to strike back. I interceded and warned Larry that any more misbehavior would be punished with a spanking. Undeterred, he took a crayon from his pocket, turned to the girl behind him, and scribbled on the page of notes she was taking.

"OK, Larry, that's all I'm going to take," I said, hoarsely. "You have a choice of a spanking here or being sent to Mr. Bibbs."

"I ain't gonna have no spankin' nowhere," he said defiantly. "Eveythang I dun was a accident."

"You know that isn't true," I replied. I looked at Louella sitting in the first seat of the first row. "Go ask Mr. Bibbs to come to my room, please."

She darted out the door, eager to be the one to summon punishment.

Mr. Bibbs showed up a few minutes later, and I explained the problem. Larry was a big boy, but Mr. Bibbs was bigger.

"OK, Larry, you've got a choice," Mr. Bibbs informed him. "You can come to the office and take your punishment now, or we can send you home for two weeks, and when you return you'll get double punishment. It's up to you."

"I'm goin' home—for good," he declared flippantly. "I ain't goin' come back to dis stinkin' school."

"You're fourteen," Mr. Bibbs answered in a reasonable voice. "The law says you're required to stay in school until you're sixteen. I tell you what," he added, as if it were an afterthought, "let's go see Mrs. Levison and get her advice about dropping out."

The two of them left, and in about thirty minutes a chastened Larry returned and took his accustomed seat. I found out later that Mrs. Levison persuaded Larry to accept the punishment meted out by Mr. Bibbs and then return to class. She was a marvel as a counselor, with unlimited patience and wisdom in dealing with students like Larry whose lives were fraught with problems.

When I got home I drank lots of water, took aspirin and cough medicine, went right to bed, and slept twelve hours. The next morning, I felt like a new person. I gave a pop quiz to all my classes on the material we'd covered, and was delighted that as a group they scored higher on this test than any other. Perhaps the Egyptian civilization appealed to them more than the cavemen of Europe. In fifth period Charles Robinson asked me what poor Egyptians had to pay in taxes to the white men. He then got very embarrassed and corrected himself.

"I means how much taxes did they pay to de rich men?"

If it could have, Charles's face would have been a glowing beet red. The other members of the class were not as embarrassed as he was. This was a golden opportunity for them to humiliate Charles, absolutely too good to pass up. For all intents and purposes the history lesson was finished for the day.

∼

That same day, Mr. Rollins initiated a new lunch program. It involved the homeroom teachers taking the twenty-five cents from students who bought their lunch and giving them a plastic token in exchange. The tokens would be collected by the lunchroom attendant. This method was aimed at eliminating the problem of students losing their quarters before lunch period as well as the extortion of lunch money from the younger children by the older ones. The down side was that it added another chore to the homeroom teachers' already frantic fifteen minutes of taking roll, reporting absentees, and maintaining order.

~

Keeping control in the sixth period was becoming increasingly difficult. Some of the boys were as tall as I was, and trying to paddle them myself would be absurd. They had failed grades in the grammar school and had had to repeat them, which meant they were now fourteen and fifteen years old instead of twelve. Some were just marking time until they turned sixteen and could drop out.

The last school day in September, I filled out the required end-of-the-month report on my classes that was due in Mr. Rollins's office when school let out. As I signed the report, I reflected on the composition of my homeroom. I had an average daily attendance of twenty-seven out of twenty-nine registered students. The typical student had attended school for 7.7 years and was fourteen years old. Five students had parents who were unemployed. Only six students had never failed a grade. Obviously, they weren't Rhodes Scholars, but it wasn't for lack of attendance. Now if I could figure out a way that they could accomplish more than just sitting in school, perhaps there would be some hope for this year. And maybe—just maybe—some hope for their futures.

12

October is a marvelous time of year in the Mississippi Delta. The enervating, sticky summer heat has departed, replaced by temperatures in the comfortable seventies during the day and the fifties at night. An irritation that had seemed major during the September doldrums could now be viewed in proper perspective.

October brings a marked change in the landscape. Oak, ginkgo, and maple trees shed their leaves, and the ground is covered by a red, gold, and orange carpet. Pecan trees drop nuts which children gather and sell to earn money for Christmas presents. The cotton is ready to be picked, and farmers can realize revenues for the backbreaking work and the risks they have taken during the spring and summer. Prior to the 1950s, the cotton would have been picked by hand, a process that would have lasted through Thanksgiving. Since children participated in the process, education took a backseat in importance. Now, most cotton is picked mechanically, making fall less disruptive to the education system.

I was in a good mood as I drove to school that morning. I couldn't wait to tell Pearlie about Lily Tomlin's antics on *Laugh-In* the night before. In her latest skit she'd snorted to a customer that "We're the phone company! We don't have to care." The car window was down and the crisp air ruffled my hair. I tuned the radio to WDDT. A folk-rock song made popular by The Byrds was playing and took me back to my Ole Miss days.

To everything there is a season . . .
A time to laugh, a time to weep . . .
A time to build up, a time to break down . . .
A time to gain, a time to lose . . .
A time to love, a time to hate . . .
("Turn! Turn! Turn!" Pete Seeger and Jim McGuinn)

While I was at Ole Miss I had thought of the song as an anti-Vietnam anthem. I guess my life has become more multidimensional since then. I had added a few more "times" of my own: a time to teach, a time to punish; a time to be angry, a time to try and understand; a time to ask for help, a time to work things out on my own.

As I made my way along the now-familiar streets, I realized that I wasn't driving with my shoulders hunched, and I didn't feel the vague anxiety that had always accompanied me on the way to school. If I wasn't serene, at least I wasn't dreading the day ahead. I had settled into a routine—I was feeling less like an oddity and more accepted for what I was, rather than what I represented—the white, male boss. Or maybe I'd reached my highest level of incompetence, I thought wryly, thinking of the current best-seller, *The Peter Principle*.

Part of my more relaxed attitude could be attributed to the evolutionary changes in the way we teachers treated each other. Our initial mutual forced courtesy was daily being replaced by the more relaxed attitude that familiarity brings. Last week, when a group of us were grading papers in the teachers' lounge, Gwen Stewart called math teacher Tommy Seaton a nigger. Instead of being embarrassed because I'd heard the epithet, Tommy draped an arm around my shoulders. "We got to keep this guy another year at Lincoln. It's going to take more than one year to make a 'nigger' out of him."

Another day, Coach McCall embarrassed me in the teachers' lounge by presenting me with a miniature plastic Lincoln High School football. He made a big to-do of the ceremony, bowing at the waist and holding it out in both hands as if it were a valued trophy, all the time accompanied by the hoots and jeers of everyone present. I had taken it home that afternoon and placed it on a stand on top of the refrigerator as a memento of my acceptance. Even Anita and Mrs. Hadley had begun to thaw as the color line began to fade. Anita mentioned to me how cute some of her pupils were and noted that two or three had real talent. "I think they're beginning to regard me as their teacher, not their 'white' teacher," she told me.

Another opportunity to strengthen my standing as "one of them" came when I joined the faculty men's basketball team. It was a school tradition for male faculty members to play a game of basketball with senior members of the varsity team, and for the female members of the faculty to play the women's senior basketball team. Coach McCall was in charge of our team; our newest black faculty member, Miss Feltus, coached the women.

Faculty participation was voluntary. Anita and I both chose to take part; Mrs. Hadley, citing age, declined. "I don't know that I'd be much of an asset to the team," she smiled. "I'll help by monitoring the children in the stands."

Faculty practice sessions were few and involved more bragging than actually getting the ball through the hoop. The students wore their basketball uniforms; we wore T-shirts and shorts. On the day of the game, classes were dismissed after lunch. All the kids could talk about was how the seniors were going to cream the faculty. No admission was charged, and the stands were packed. When the seniors were introduced one by one, there were whistles, clapping, and encouraging cries of "Go get 'em!"

Then Mr. Rollins boomed through the loudspeaker: "And now the starting lineup for the faculty! First we have Meadowlark Lemon Cain." Whoops of laughter resounded.

"The incomparable Wilt 'The Stilt' Chamberlain McCall," he bellowed. Raucous jeers exploded.

"Third, Marques Haynes Seaton." Catcalls reverberated.

"The Magnificent Clarence Wilson Hayes." Jeers, raucous taunts and boos.

"And last, the mainstay of the team, Goose Tatum Beckwith!"

Even louder scoffs and boos rose to the ceiling. "He's a goose all right," one of my fans yelled from the stands.

The students were convinced that the varsity teams would crucify us. We didn't exactly feel like the Harlem Globetrotters—more like a circus act.

The ball was tossed, the varsity team got it, and the game was on. We substituted players frequently, claiming it gave the students a chance to see all the faculty members play. In reality, we got winded quickly—about three trips up and down the court would do it—and needed relief. No one was more surprised than the faculty members when we ended up beating the varsity team 42–41. We strutted back and forth in front of the stands, hands clasped above our heads in the victory salute. The women's teams tied their game 9–9. More and more barriers were breaking down.

The goodwill produced by my participation in the faculty-student game led to my first opportunity to socialize with one of my black associates off campus and after work hours. This icebreaker was a chance to attend the Ike and Tina Turner show at the black Veterans of Foreign Wars (VFW) club. Some performers have such a strong identity with the public that they need use only one name; Madonna and Elvis come to mind. In the black community, Ike and Tina achieved that status on the rhythm and blues circuit (often referred to as the chitlin' circuit). Ike is credited with having recorded the first rock and roll song, "Rocket 88." Ike and Tina with their backup singers, the Ikettes, were considered one of the greatest live touring shows of the period.

As a child, I'd always been interested in black music. We had only limited exposure to it through crossover hits that were played on white radio. Occasionally, we were able to listen to black radio via WDIA in Memphis, which broadcast throughout the Delta. When I was old enough to buy records without my parents' supervision, I sometimes patronized record shops in the black district on Nelson Street in Greenville to buy music not available through my normal outlets.

I was excited when I overheard Tommy Seaton tell some of the black teachers that the Ike and Tina Turner Revue was going to play at his VFW club. I would certainly not feel welcome to attend, since I was neither black nor a VFW member.

I approached Tommy one day at lunch. "Did I hear you say that Ike and Tina are playing at your VFW club Friday night?"

"You know Ike and Tina?" he asked, surprised.

"Do I ever," I nodded. "Everybody listens to 'A Fool in Love.'"

"Maybe there's some hope for you tightass white boys after all. I'd take you as my guest, but I'm sure you wouldn't want to be seen in that part of town on a Friday night. It's not the country club."

"Try me," I suggested. "I'd owe you one."

"If you're willing, I am," he said. "Keep your eyes open. Before the night is out, you just might learn what it's like to be a brother. Meet me at the VFW at 7:30. You'll be my guest."

Since blacks could not participate in established white institutions, they established those institutions in the black community. They had their own

Masonic lodge, Elks club, VFW club, and their own version of debutante society.

At 7:30 I was waiting in my car in front of the VFW (I'm sure Mr. Bigham would have considered this a juke joint, but that didn't bother me). Tommy showed up shortly thereafter, and I hardly recognized him: tight pants, zipper boots with an inch-and-a-half heel, a striped vest over an open, partially unbuttoned shirt, body jewelry, and very strong cologne. I got out of the car as he approached. "Wow!" I exclaimed. "If your students could see you now they wouldn't recognize you."

He laughed. "Those are my nine-to-five clothes, but we're here to party." He looked me over. "I need to take you shopping so you can get some real threads. You white boys look so dull most of the time. We got to get you some soul."

I followed him into the club, and he introduced me around to his friends. From their reaction, I could tell they'd heard of the white teacher at Lincoln and were glad for the opportunity to size me up. More than one of them offered to buy me a beer. I felt like the center of attention as Tommy introduced me to more people than I could remember. They didn't make me feel that I was invading their turf; in fact, I sensed that they were glad for the opportunity to show off one of their institutions. It wasn't lost on me that I was being warmly welcomed in their club. Unfortunately, these same blacks would not be so welcomed at a white establishment.

The din in the club was deafening as everyone talked at once catching up on jobs, families, children, new possessions, and general gossip. I noticed that the banter and small talk at a black function was very similar to what I was accustomed to hearing at an all-white event. The atmosphere was more boisterous, and people were less inhibited.

When showtime arrived at 8:00, I was so busy being introduced to people that I didn't notice that the band was on the bandstand until I heard a familiar funky guitar rift followed by the high-decibel voice of Tina Turner.

Hey! Hey! Hey! Hey!
Beat is getting stronger
Beat is getting longer too—oo—oo
The music's soundin' good to me
I wanna . . . said I wanna . . .
I wanna take you higher

Yeah, let me take you higher
Baby, baby let me light your fire
Ooh Yeah! little bit higher
Boom-shaka-laka-laka
Boom-shaka-la—boonka-boo
("I Want to Take You Higher," Sylvester Stewart)

I didn't just hear the bass guitar notes; I felt them pulse in my chest. The floor filled with bodies like God had emptied a giant container of liquid dancers that had run all over the dance floor and sprung to life. Ike was menacingly sultry, and communicated primarily with the slashing guitar strokes. He was a master. Tina wore the long wig that was her trademark. The walls resounded with the loud, gospel-like vocals her fans expected.

The moment the opening number was completed, and before the crowd had a chance to catch a breath, Tina boomed:

If you want some loving
That I can give to you
If you want some hugging, said I can hug some too
All I want, baby now is some parts of you
And just a little of your affection
You know will see me through
'Cause you know that you're my man
And I want you forever to be mine
I idolize you (Yes, I idolize you)
("I Idolize You," Ike Turner)

By now, Tina was drenched in sweat, as were the dancers who were determined to keep up with her. The Ikettes seemed to have boundless energy. The already loud room got even louder. Song after song continued unabated. All the crowd favorites took turns receiving the Ike and Tina treatment: "A Fool in Love," "It's Gonna Work Out Fine," "Twist and Shout," "Shake."

This wasn't a crowd of spectators, but a crowd of willing participants who were here to release the tension of the week and have a good time. Folks yelled to each other across the room and sang along with the band. Beer flowed, we ate salty snacks, which led to more beer. There were no fights; no one got out of hand. The "high" I felt was less from the beer I had drunk than from the energy of being in a room full of people having a good time. This wasn't a country club scene or a fraternity blowout, but a party in a mundane, all-but-ramshackle building for ordinary people who were making the most of what they had. On Monday, many of these revelers would return to menial jobs, working for employers who probably regarded them as second-class citizens, but tonight that world didn't exist. Is this what was meant by "If you were ever black for a Saturday night, you'd never want to be white again"?

At midnight, the party was over. Ike and Tina disappeared, band members began rolling up amplifier cords and packing up instruments, and tired, smiling people said good-bye to each other. What a party it had been! As Tommy and I parted outside the club, I thanked him and told him I'd had a fantastic time. He knew it wasn't just the beer talking. As I rode home, I was glad I'd approached him about inviting me. Gradually, I was acquiring a better understanding of black people. They had always been a part of my life. Their subservient role had made my life comfortable from the time I was born. What a shame I hadn't had an opportunity to really get to know them until now.

13

The atmosphere in my classroom was subtly changing. The lousy conduct that had plagued me the first month had improved somewhat. Perhaps the progression of our history lessons had become more interesting to the students. The fact that slaves had played an important role in civilizations down through the centuries was a revelation, and students found it fascinating that white people had even enslaved other white people. They had always assumed that slavery had started when their forebears were brought from Africa to this country.

One day Shirley Foster raised her hand. Although she always listened intently and did well on her tests, she had never volunteered an opinion or asked a question. "Yes, Shirley," I said. "What is it?"

"Were the Jews Negro or white?" she asked.

"They can be either one," I answered. "Judaism is a religion, not a racial group. It's just like Baptists and Methodists can be of different races, You could become a Jew if you wanted to. Sammy Davis Jr. did."

"But aren't they all dark skinned?" she persisted.

"No," I answered. "Some white people have light complexions, some have darker skin. This doesn't make them better or worse than other people. It simply indicates the area of the world in which they originated. Some Jewish people have dark skin because they originated in the Middle East, which is a hot part of the world just like Africa."

I didn't realize until I'd finished the explanation that the room had grown silent. No one was shuffling feet, flipping pages in the book, or shooting spit-balls! It was a reminder to me that preoccupation with skin color is every bit as deeply rooted in the black community as it is in the white.

Another hand went up. "Yes, Brenda. What is it?"

"Is you or Miz Yarbrough the oldest?"

I mulled over her question, wondering what Anita's or my age had to do with black and white. "I guess we're about the same age," I answered. "Twenty-two."

"You can't be the same age. One of you got to be older," she maintained.

"Why?" I asked, puzzled.

"Since she's your sister, one of you got to be older."

I frowned. "Why do you think she's my sister."

"'Cause you look alike. Y'all got the same color hair and eyes; you both white."

I restrained a laugh. My God, the shoe is on the other foot. They think all white people look alike, just like we claim all blacks do! Wait'll I tell Anita that we're brother and sister!

"Just because we have white skin and light-colored hair and eyes doesn't mean we're related to each other. My father has brown hair and gray eyes and isn't as tall as I am, but he's still my father."

I wasn't sure this explanation satisfied them, but I had a lot of material to cover, and it didn't include whether or not Anita and I were siblings! So we left Egypt and in the following days made brief references to the Babylonians, Hittites, Phoenicians, Assyrians, and finally the Greeks, all of whom produced works and ideas important for the Western world. I tried to make the topics interesting with maps, pictures of how the people might have dressed, the tools they used, their money. Even so, it was far removed from the everyday problems these children faced. So many of the boys, particularly, were just marking time before dropping out of school at sixteen. I often felt I was talking past or around them instead of to them.

An incident occurred about halfway through October that put a damper on any relief I felt that disciplining the students no longer usurped the major part of each day. As I was clearing my desk after school on a Friday afternoon, I heard hurried footsteps in the hall and looked up to see a very agitated Mrs. Hadley rush into my room.

"David!" she exclaimed, even before I could greet her, "I'm on my way down to Mr. Rollins's office to resign!"

"Whoa," I said. "Take it easy." I put my books back on the desk. "Sit down and let's talk."

She slumped into one of the student's desks. "I can't take any more of these animals. That's what they are. Crude, lewd, jungle animals!" She took two deep breaths and closed her eyes a moment as if to block out an awful scene.

Horrible images flitted through my mind of two older boys knifing each other in front of her desk. "What happened? You've seen just about every stunt they can pull."

She took a deep breath. "Two days ago, I found them passing dirty pictures around class. These were disgusting, pornographic pictures. I didn't say anything at *that* time. But it's happened again. Today when I walked into my room, they were all huddled on the floor looking at a sex manual. They're disgusting little creeps! I'd rather quit than go through this the rest of the year."

"I know you've been around the block a lot more times than I have, but don't fly off the handle and do anything while you're upset," I cautioned. "Even in my short life, every time I've done that I've regretted it once I'd had a chance to cool down. It's been a long week, and you're tired. Although a sex manual isn't something that ought to be brought to school, remember that children this age are naturally curious about sex. We were. I never looked at a sex manual when I was a teenager, but it was probably because I never had one. Well, I did look at a few girlie magazines. . . . I'm not condoning it, but it's not a capital crime. Give the pictures to Mr. Rollins or Mr. Bibbs; they'll know what to do with them."

"I couldn't do that!" she retorted. "I'd die of embarrassment to show something like that to a Negro. I'm having a hard enough time telling you about it. That's why I didn't say anything about it the first time it happened." She shook her head. "This school isn't a place for somebody like me."

"Don't say that. You're such a good teacher. Talk to your husband about it when you get home. You'll have the weekend to get some perspective on it, and by Monday things will look different. You, Anita, and I started this thing together—we've got to stick together. Besides, I'd miss you."

Her shoulders relaxed; she sighed, and even managed a smile. "I appreciate that. Maybe I am overreacting, but it was just such a shock."

"Of course, it was. Understandably so," I agreed.

She pushed herself to her feet. "Thanks for listening."

"Have a good weekend," I said as she headed out the door.

She must have worked it out for herself over the weekend; she never mentioned the incident to me again.

～

The final week in October saw the blossoming of teenage crushes. I wasn't unfamiliar with the ailment, having had a full-blown crush on Miss Bush, my high school English teacher. I was fifteen, she was just out of college, and in my eyes she was gorgeous, sophisticated, the epitome of desirable womanhood. My crush manifested itself in my efforts to impress her with my interest in her English class. I would never have had the nerve to flirt or make any overt move to attract her attention, partly from awe, and partly from fear of reprisals by my parents if I'd ever engaged in disrespectful behavior. The crush lasted until spring, when I began noticing that girls my own age had some very attractive physical attributes.

The social boundaries that forbade my making advances toward Miss Bush didn't govern behavior here at Lincoln. The first episode happened while I was watching the exit gate at the stadium during the homecoming football game, which was played during the school day so that more students could attend. About halfway through the game, Mary Bishop, a student in my sixth-period history class, came up and started talking.

"You watching the gate?" she asked.

I nodded. "Yes, Mary. Mr. Rollins wants everyone to stay in the stadium during the game and not wander the campus unsupervised. You don't want to go out, do you? I can't let you, you know."

"Naw, sir! I'm not going nowhere. Football is boring. I just thought I'd come and keep you company. You don't mind, do you?"

"I'm always glad to see you, Mary. Do you like school so far this year? Is history interesting?" Having become eminently wiser, I glanced around in case she was being used as a decoy for others trying to leave the game.

"I like history, but only 'cause you're the teacher. You make history interesting." She glanced sideways at me, her eyes half shut. "You think I'm pretty?"

"I think you're a very attractive young lady," I answered. "If you really like history, why not try to make better grades?"

"I got lotsa boyfriends," she answered, ignoring the "better grades" suggestion. "They all say I'm pretty. You married?"

"No," I said. "I'm not ready to settle down yet." I was quickly becoming weary of this conversation and ready for her to shove off.

"You go out with women of different color?" she asked, raising her eyebrows as she looked up at me. "I bet you have a good time when you go out on the town."

"I pick my friends because I like them, and we have things in common," I said. "I'm sure you pick your friends that way, too."

Before she could answer, I said, "Hey listen to that noise. We must have made a good play. You better get back up in the stands so you can enjoy the rest of the game."

She looked disappointed. "Well, maybe I see you later. I sure hope you going to be my friend."

"Sure," I said, and smiled at her as she reluctantly walked away.

Just when I was congratulating myself on handling the situation so adroitly—avoiding making an enemy of her, but not leaving myself vulnerable to further encounters of this kind—three older girls whom I didn't know came up to make small talk. Their attempts to "accidentally" rub up against me and feel my hair convinced me that I hadn't handled it as well as I'd thought. The girls' brazenness floored me.

Several days later came the real shocker. One of my students, Stanley Gildart, who usually couldn't wait to leave the class, pushing and shoving the other students aside to get out, lingered after the others had gone. On guard at this marked switch in behavior, I asked if he needed help with something.

"Yeah, Mr. Beck. Mary told me you're not married. I've been thinking that maybe one afternoon you take Ms. Yarbrough and I get one of my girlfriends, and we all go ridin' together."

I wasn't quite prepared for this, but I managed not to gulp too noticeably. "I appreciate you thinking of me, Stanley, but Mrs. Yarbrough is a married woman."

"Is her husband around?" he asked, not missing a beat.

"Very much so," I said firmly.

"OK," he shrugged.

Ready to end the conversation, I began gathering my papers and books together on my desk.

"How many chirrens you got, Mr. Beck?"

"I don't have any, Stanley. As you know, I'm not married," I answered.

"None!" he blurted. "You must not be ripe yet. You know Johnny Hampton got two chirren. Both of 'em by the same girl. By the time I git to be your age, I'm going to have chirrens running all over the state o' Mississippi."

I looked at him and shook my head. "Is that anything to brag about? It doesn't take any brains to produce a child. Why don't you do something useful with your life?"

"It may not take no brains, but it sure is fun," he smirked.

"You're not dumb, Stanley. If you tried, you could do really well in my class. Have you ever considered reading the lesson and learning something?"

He frowned as if considering my question, then shook his head. "Histry ain't gonna get me on at the oil mill," he said. "You know, my uncle Ralph works over at Leland Oil Works and he don't know nuthin' 'bout history."

I bit my tongue. I was tempted to start a harangue about how he should have a level of aspirations higher than just being a manual laborer at the mill but decided that my comments would be construed as a slam on the role model that Stanley obviously idolized. Stanley lived for today. It was obvious but also very sad that education was only a dot on his roadmap of life, an experience not to be savored but a nuisance to be tolerated. Education had an intangible benefit in the far-off future; Stanley could only comprehend tangible present benefits.

The third incident occurred when I was grading some test papers. Bobby Ann Washington had added an extra page to her test.

TO MY GREAT TEACHER, MR. BECKWITH:
I'd like your eyes to look at this.

I wrote this poem especially for you.
Because you are my best teacher out of the few,
Mr. Beckwith you are a great teacher if you know it.
I knew, when you taught us history, you had a hit.
You're the greatest teacher I've ever known
To this great honor, you've shown
Out of this history book words you have blown
To this day, to that one,
I will always like you Mr. Beckwith for your teaching and your preaching
Without too much fuss,

by
Bobby Ann Washington

The "poem" didn't quite scan, but she had spelled almost all of the words correctly. What more could I ask?

I waited for a chance to see Bobby Ann alone. I didn't want to embarrass her in front of the others. We met in the hall a couple of days later, and I stopped to speak with her. "I want to thank you for your poem," I said. "It really touched me."

Embarrassed, she looked down at the floor while she swayed from one foot to the other.

"I feel that I have a lot to live up to, after all the nice things you said."

She looked more embarrassed than before. To put her at her ease, I took another tack. "I feel bad that I have to fuss at the class. Maybe you could help me by speaking to your friends. Everybody would enjoy it more if we all work together."

"I try," she promised, still not looking at me, "but they do what they want." And with her head still lowered, she hurried off.

As I watched her go, I remembered my three encounters with teenagers. Mary at the football game was a trollop in the making, Stanley a small-town Romeo hopeful, and Bobby Ann an idealistic, innocent preteen with a crush on an authority figure. During my school days we used to think that the black community was totally different from ours. We were wrong. I'd seen every one of these characters before, only their skin was as white as my own.

14

As a neophyte teacher, I had envisioned enriching the lives of my students by exposing them to stimulating outside influences. This vision inspired me to send a note home to their parents extolling the merits of the *Junior Scholastic Magazine* and requesting they send seventy-five cents to cover their child's subscription. In the teachers' lounge one day, I told the other teachers gathered there what I had done, explaining that the magazine would give students a broader vision of world events as well as act as a supplement to their textbook. I was somewhat annoyed when my recitation of these benefits as well as the method of paying for the periodical elicited shaking heads, raised eyebrows, and outright snickers of derision. I wasn't discouraged, however.

As a student, I was always excited when the teacher announced that the *Junior Scholastic Magazine* had arrived and was available for us to read. Articles in it stimulated me and my family to participate in dinner-table conversations that supplemented the news from TV and the local newspaper, the *Delta Democrat Times*. I hoped I would get the same reactions from my students and their parents and prove the scoffers wrong.

Anticipating that my students' parents would respond promptly to this request, as my own parents always had, I sent off the subscription. By the end of the first week, I had collected money from three students. The second week, I sent home a reminder. Two more payments showed up. For the first time, self-doubt began to creep into my mind. Two more payments showed up. By the end of the third week, I had garnered a grand total of nine payments. I fretted that the parents had sent the money and their children had spent it. I wondered if the parents could possibly be ignoring my note. I finally convinced myself that if they didn't respond, the school would find an alternate method of footing the bill, though I knew I would lose face.

One parent sent me a note asking why there was this assessment, since textbooks were supposed to be furnished by the state. And so it turned out that the "alternate" method of funding the project was—me. More determined than ever not to be proved wrong, I sent the company a check for the full amount, bringing my account down to the almost-overdrawn status that it had kept most of the time I was a college student.

The arrival of the magazine put me in a quandary. Should I allocate magazines only to those students who had paid for it? If I passed the magazine out to all students, would I ever collect from those who hadn't paid? If I punished those who hadn't paid by not giving them a copy, how could we have a meaningful discussion about events in the magazine, since two-thirds of the class wouldn't have been able to read it? Also, there was the problem of discussing current events while they were still current. Much as I disliked rewarding those who hadn't paid, the pluses outweighed the negatives, and I passed the magazine out to all the students, never admitting how I had gotten bagged.

~

When I began teaching at Lincoln, I had been critical of the inordinate amount of school time that was devoted to nonacademic pursuits. I had considered these pursuits as time wasted. As the weeks went by, I began to understand the burden imposed on the school by the poverty of the community. Most students were dependent on busing, having no other means of transportation. Therefore, the school schedule was dominated by the bus schedule. I began to see that if the school didn't take the lead in patronizing social events, these children would grow up more lacking than they already were in social skills.

The football homecoming was the most important social event of the fall season. Tradition dictated that funds had to be raised, floats built, homecoming royalty elected, a dance organized, and on and on. These events had to take place during school hours because bus schedules demanded it, and also because some students could not participate because they worked in the afternoon, and others had to take care of younger siblings while their mothers worked. An additional deterrent to after-school participation was that many parents had limited abilities not only to organize events but even to participate without the help of the more educated school faculty.

A guaranteed low-budget fund-raiser that never required much preparation was the sock hop. These dances usually lasted only about an hour, so school would be let out about 2:00, and the sock hop would end at the time the buses arrived. The sponsoring homeroom would reserve the gym, admission was ten cents, and the only props necessary were a record player and an extroverted disc jockey. The students brought their favorite records from home. All that remained was to put out advance publicity so the participants would be sure to have a dime to spend the day of the event.

Teachers were expected to be chaperones and participants. This gave students an opportunity to dance with members of the faculty and also gave faculty members a chance to dance with each other. In addition, it presented the faculty as being more than just one-dimensional figures behind a desk. A teacher's prowess on the dance floor was observed and critiqued by the students, often loudly. Like rooting for the home team at football games, students roared support or disapproval of their own teachers.

The week before homecoming, my homeroom was to sponsor a sock hop. All the students clamored to be included in the planning of the event. Portable stereos were volunteered, extension cords were offered, and countless records were donated—more than we could possibly play in an hour. It occurred to me how strange it was that records could be bought with such abandon, yet the seventy-five cents needed for a subscription to *Junior Scholastic Magazine* never materialized. I wished I could generate this amount of enthusiasm and participation in the history lessons!

Mrs. Hadley usually oversaw the study hall for those students who were not attending the sock hop. For my homeroom event, however, she was able to attend, though no amount of persuasion could get her on the dance floor. Although Anita's duties usually kept her in her classroom in the elementary school, she also managed to come to my sock hop. And she did participate! Our dancing together was a showstopper. As we whirled around the dance floor, there was much whooping and egging us on to wilder gyrations. Our willingness to participate in the sock hop and to take the good-natured verbal abuse further lowered barriers and made us more a part of the team.

Mr. Rollins and Mr. Bibbs gave us thumbs up and nods of approval from the sidelines. We counted the event a rousing success. It raised fifteen dollars for decorations for our seventh grade homecoming float.

~

Homecoming was set for October 17. The football team's opponent for the big game was Gentry High School in Indianola. Mr. Rollins asked me if I would serve on the committee to line up floats for the homecoming parade. Although I agreed, I had no idea what my duties would be. Three days later, I was informed that I was the chairman of the committee. I was promoted from being a member of a committee whose job I knew nothing about to being chairman of a committee whose job I knew nothing about.

Abbreviated school days became the rule as preparations for the big event swung into high gear. The day after my promotion, classes were suspended after lunch and the student body reported to the gymnasium for the important job of electing a homecoming queen. Five girls were running for the position. Each made a speech giving her reasons for deserving to be elected and followed this with a performance of some kind. The first candidate's performance was a dance so risqué and suggestive that it would have been in questionable taste in an all-adult locale and was certainly out of place in a school setting.

"Is that how Gypsy Rose Lee got started?" I murmured to Tommy Seaton.

"Can't you see her on homecoming night—boogeying while the band grooves to 'Please! Please!'?" he whispered in return.

"We could call her homecoming court the Go Go's or the Famous Flames," I responded.

We both glanced at Mrs. Hadley, who was sitting two rows down and to the right of our seats. Her face was a mask of disapproval. Tommy looked at me and mimicked her expression of disapproval so completely I had to look away or else laugh out loud.

The performances of the other candidates seemed pretty tame by comparison. One candidate treated us to a modern dance in which nothing moved but her hands. A third recited a poem, a fourth gave an imitation of a famous movie star, and the fifth read a story. After these performances, the girls tossed packages of gum and candy into the audience and released balloons. I wasn't sure how any of these performances would qualify a candidate to be a successful homecoming queen, but since I wasn't voting, mine was not to reason why. Classes returned to their homeroom to vote on their favorite candidate. As part of the drama, the name of the winner was kept secret until the week of homecoming.

~

Two days after the selection of the homecoming queen, serious planning began on the floats. The theme for the 1969 homecoming was "Blast Off." I had a meeting with my fellow seventh grade teachers, and we decided to mount a frame constructed of one-by-two-inch boards on each side of a cotton trailer. Chicken wire would be tacked to the boards. Threaded through the chicken wire would be crepe paper with a representation of a rocket ship in the shape of a football blasting off from earth streaming toward giant goalposts protruding from a crepe-paper moon. Now we had a concept, but as chairman of the float committee it was my task to determine how to implement it.

That night I made a list of necessary materials, and the next day, leaving my classes under the watchful eye of Mrs. Hadley, I went with fellow teacher Bill Hayes to buy lumber. During fourth period I took one of my students, Johnny Hampton, out to Stoneville where his father worked so we could borrow a tractor and a cotton trailer.

After school, my eager student volunteers and I began to build what we believed would be the prize-winning float. I was surprised to discover that these students who were disasters as far as history went were surprisingly adept as float builders. Finally finding something at school they could excel in as well as enjoy, they worked diligently.

The next day classes became an also-ran. Some of the kids reported to my homeroom, and as I could not supervise building the float *and* teach, they vanished for the day or roamed the halls until some teacher herded them into a study hall. That afternoon I went back to my old high school and picked up my brother, who was delighted to lend his artistic talents to an undertaking he'd never tried before.

If one word could describe our enterprise it was *underestimation:* of the time it would take to build the float, the supply of materials required, and the reserves of energy the task demanded. Early on we ran out of crepe paper. After exhausting the supply in stores in Leland, I drove to stores in Greenville and used up their inventory.

Mrs. Hadley traveled to Indianola after school and brought back more. It hadn't occurred to any of us to go to a store owner ahead of time and have him order extra inventory for our project, nor had we considered that we would be competing for available supplies against other classes trying to construct their float according to the same deadline.

On top of our other problems, we ran out of money, and my brother's ability to improvise was challenged severely. The gray moon became black, the brown football rocket ship became a mixture of brown and antique gold. The moon and earth took on a greenish tint that would have stopped Neil Armstrong in his tracks.

On Homecoming Day, bedlam reigned at the school. Students roamed from one room to another, rolls were not taken, the halls had more students than the classrooms, and people wandered the campus and the school who probably weren't students at all. Education took a holiday.

Bill Hayes, Anita, and I took her car downtown to view the results of our labors. The parade included six floats, four bands, eight cars, and a borrowed convertible for the homecoming queen and her court. Horns honked, bands played, everyone yelled at everyone. The seventh grade had the first float in the parade, and we were prepared to hear all around us shouts of approval and whistles of amazement at our handiwork. What resounded were Bronx cheers, for the decorations on our float were rapidly disintegrating.

"What the hell is the matter with our masterpiece?" I asked Bill.

Before he could answer, the reason became obvious. The chicken wire I'd bought to hold the crepe paper in place had large holes instead of small ones, and the paper was merrily sliding through the holes onto the street as the truck moved forward. I watched with dismay as the paper that we had made so many trips to buy and had spent so much time working on was being blown about the street like confetti. The children riding on the float were unaware that the decorations on their vehicle were disintegrating and waved gaily at the crowd.

Anita murmured sympathetically, but she couldn't keep a straight face. She began snickering. Bill and I joined her, and soon the three of us were roaring our heads off at the ridiculous sight.

"I hope a photographer from the *Leland Progress* isn't here taking pictures," I gasped.

"The newspaper called the school office this morning while I was there and wanted an interview," Anita said, straight-faced. "Mr. Rollins gave them your name as chairman of the Decorating Committee!"

That set us off again into gales of laughter. I don't remember the rest of the parade.

That afternoon, Lincoln pulled so far ahead in the football game against Gentry that it was a foregone conclusion that we would win. After the half-time homecoming ceremony, the crowd lost interest in the game and wanted to leave the stadium to seek more exciting entertainment. I'd been assigned to monitor the exit gate, and there was always a large group wanting to get out. On several occasions, students refused to go back to their seats and became so unruly that I had to call the police to come and herd them back into the stands.

By now, all I wanted to do was go home and collapse. After what seemed an eternity, the game was finally over and the buses came. There was still the float to dismantle and the tractor-trailer to return to Stoneville. All of my student helpers who had been so enthusiastic about building the float and had sworn they'd come back and help dismantle it mysteriously disappeared, and the chore was left to Bill and me. He went with me to Stoneville, where we returned the tractor-trailer and picked up my car.

After we had settled wearily into my car, Bill peered out of each of the side windows and then, over his shoulder, looked carefully out the back. "I don't see Mr. Bigham watching," he whispered. "What say we have an ice cold beer?"

"You took the words out of my mouth," I sighed. "Let's get the hell out of here!"

15

Even if I had taken education courses in college, I wouldn't have been prepared to deal with the realities of life below the poverty line. These had to be experienced in face-to-face encounters. My experience up to the present had been more or less with people in the same economic stratum as my family. In our world, deficiencies were hidden, and appearances were often more important than honesty in matters that threatened one's social status.

It was different, however, when the majority had few resources and little to gain by pretending. My peers in the white world would seldom confess to having limited resources or problems with members of one's family. It appeared that people in the black community, however, had little hesitation in making admissions of this sort, even to a stranger like their child's teacher. The following are letters I received from one child's parents.

Dear Mr Dave
We don't have no money for Samuel today. If ya would order his books for me I will send the money Monday.
his Father Joseph P

Dear Mr Beckwith
I will give Samuel his money for the candy Thursday to bring. I don't have it today.
His mother Marie P

Dear Mr Beckwih
I sprung a mucle in my back had to go the doctor I am down in my
back when get up I will send that money for the candy.
Samuel D mother
Marie P

~

Although homecoming dominated the latter part of October, some academic activity before that event had become the be-all and end-all of the
school calendar. Tests for the first six-week grading period took place the
week before homecoming. Since those tests would be a major determinant
in students' grade-point average, I gave 7B a practice test using questions
similar to those they would confront on the real test. On grading the practice tests, I found that Shirley Foster and Eddie Watts were the only ones who
passed.

I think I dreaded the approaching exams more than many of my students. Their attitude seemed to be: Ho hum. Another test. So what? Fifteen
minutes into the practice test, I had to give Mary Bishop a zero for blatant
and repeated cheating. Fisheye was next. His eyes seemed to be drawn by a
giant magnet to the paper of any student who sat near him. When I called
him down, he threw his test papers up in the air and watched them settle on
the floor. I let them stay there, not wanting to disturb the students around
him by fighting the battle to get him to pick them up. I now considered myself a war-weary veteran, but again my mettle was tested when, on glancing around the room to keep an eye out for other cheaters, I noticed Velma
Davis sitting at her desk staring straight ahead with a faraway look in her
eyes. Her cheeks were puffed out, and she looked like she was chewing a big
wad of gum.

"Velma, are you all right?" I asked.

"Yes, sir," she replied in a muffled voice.

"You sure there's nothing wrong?" I persisted.

"No, sir," she said, and then took a great gulp and swallowed.

I walked over to her desk to be sure she really was all right and discovered
that she had eaten the first page of her test.

"Why did you do that!" I demanded.

"I don't know. I jest felt like it," she answered nonchalantly.

I was too stunned to say anything. Then I noticed that Larry Harold, sitting in front of her, had just swallowed a page of his test. Jeez! Am I imag-

ining this? Is this real? "Here go some more zeros," I said through clenched teeth.

I continued to catch cheaters: Dorothy Myers and Sam Trotter. When I told them they would get zeros, they smiled and shrugged as if they didn't care. Having been around achievers and overachievers all my life, I couldn't fathom this mind-set.

Test grades confirmed my expectations: 7C had twenty-one failing grades, seven D's, two C's, and a lone A. The mean test score was 58.3. In 7B I had two A's—Shirley Foster and Eddie Watts; the rest were C's, D's, and F's. The other four classes repeated the pattern set by 7C. I felt I'd wasted six weeks.

As word got around to the classes that their grades were a disaster, I was bombarded not with inquiries on ways they could improve but with demands for an explanation. With all six classes, I went over the test, question by question, giving them the correct answer followed by an explanation as to why this answer was correct. Still, their demands persisted that they be awarded better grades. When I explained that they had to earn better grades, they grumbled that they deserved better than what I'd given them.

I'd finally had it—fed up with their persistent whining that I wasn't being fair. "The reason you don't make passing grades," I said through clenched teeth, "is because, first, you don't study, second, you don't try, and third, you act like a bunch of spoiled-rotten kids with no manners!"

Instead of head-hanging and looks of contrition, most of the class slumped down in their seats—except for the would-be Romeo, Stanley Gildart, who stuck his hand up in the air. Cover your ass, I told myself, since Stanley had never before adhered to such niceties as raising his hand before spouting off. I nodded at him.

"The reason you're giving us these low grades is 'cause you really don't like black kids," he said slyly. "If you liked us, you'd a give us passing grades."

The others nodded.

"You could be green, blue, or pink for all I care, Stanley." I forced my voice to be nonconfrontational, though it was by force of will that I kept my jaw unclenched. "Don't try to lay a guilt trip on me. It's not going to work. Your color has nothing to do with what grade I give you. Let me tell you something. You can't make a sirloin steak out of a cow patty. An F is an F; it doesn't magically turn into something better because you want it to. You're going to find out that's the way things work in life too. If you're going to use your race as a cop-out every time something doesn't turn out like you want it to, you've got a long, hard road ahead of you. That's the way life is."

He sulked through the rest of the class, but from that moment on the bitching from the rest of the students ceased.

At the time I thought their dismal academic record would cast a pall over homecoming events. As the week of homecoming activities progressed, however, it was evident that it had not. Another cold kept me in bed over the weekend following homecoming. This gave me time to think about my failure and what I could do to change the behavior patterns. I decided that, instead of lecturing, I would try to involve students in the teaching process. The following Monday, armed with my new method, I told my homeroom history class that we were going to take turns reading the chapters out loud, and then they would ask each other questions on what they had read.

I thought I had hit paydirt when they greeted this idea with interest. Their reading skills, with a few exceptions, were dismal, however, and I found myself having to all but read along with them to have any continuity. The questions they asked each other sometimes had no relation to what we had read, and if they did, the answer would have no relation to the question. Another tactic I tried was to ask them to write a report on the chapter I assigned, and then let them read it aloud in class so the listeners could ask questions. This, too, did not succeed, as often the person making the report didn't just tell the highlights of the chapter but read, word for word, what the chapter had said, often with no comprehension of what was read. The students quickly lost interest and looked for other diversions, which usually meant interrupting the speaker and poking or jabbing their neighbors.

As the end of October approached, disciplinary problems escalated. They sometimes became confrontational. Fisheye—embarrassingly enough, I had begun to think of Eugene Watson by his nickname—was an ongoing problem, and not just my problem. He caused trouble wherever he went. One day after lunch, as I was heading down the hall toward my room, one of the science teachers, Mrs. Little, came streaking past me in the opposite direction, seeming to look through me as if I wasn't there. This was so unusual for her, as she was always so pleasant and had time to chat, that I followed her, calling her name.

She slowed, then, looking over her shoulder and seeing me, she waited for me to catch up.

"What's wrong?" I asked.

"Honey child, God better grab a hold of me and hold on tight. If he doesn't, I'm going to commit a mortal sin before this day is out."

"Anything I can do?" I asked.

"That boy! That boy!" she cried, as if she hadn't heard a word I said. "Eugene Watson is the worst child I've ever seen in my life! You know I can usually find some good in everybody, but he's making it hard. He's rotten to the core. I told him to get his black behind out of my room and never come back." She looked me in the eye. "Mark my word—you'll read about that boy someday in the newspaper!"

With that she hurried on her way. I decided to pay Mr. Rollins a visit and headed for his office. I told him of meeting Mrs. Little and how upset she was.

"He's been giving you trouble, too, hasn't he?" Mr. Rollins asked.

I rolled my eyes. "Has he ever!"

"OK, get Mr. Bibbs to take over your 2:00 class. I've asked Eugene's mother to come in for a conference. You're about to take part in your first 'Come to Jesus' meeting," he said grimly.

Mrs. Little, Mr. Rollins, Eugene, his mother, and I gathered in Mr. Rollins's office at 2:00. I have never seen a more defeated-looking person than Eugene's mother. Her shoulders drooped, her gray hair was haphazardly combed, her eyes were sorrowful. She was not married, and Eugene apparently was as much trouble at home as he was at school. I learned later that Mr. Rollins had told Eugene's mother that she must attend the meeting or find another school for her child. And so she'd had to arrange to be absent from her job and to find transportation to attend the conference.

Mrs. Little took immediate charge of the confrontation. "Gladys," she said to Eugene's mother, "we've known each other for a long time. I realize you've had a hard time of it, but I want to say something in front of you, Mr. Rollins, Mr. Beckwith, and most of all, your son."

She turned to Eugene and with her eyes riveted on his down-turned face, she took a deep breath. "Look at me, boy. I'm about to talk to you." He looked up, but one glance at her contorted face persuaded him that that wasn't such a good idea. So he stared at his hands, which were laced together in his lap.

"You are the worst child I have ever seen in my life," Mrs. Little said. Her voice wasn't loud, but it was menacing. "You are sneaky, dishonest, a bully, and those are some of your better qualities. I'm sure everyone in this room can add some items to the list of your bad character traits. They'd sure have an easier time making that list than coming up with a list of your good ones. If I have my way, you'll never disrupt another one of my classes. Aren't you ashamed to be a person that decent people never want to see again? I can't throw you out of school—that's Mr. Rollins's job. But I'll tell you what I can do—and that is to make your life totally miserable, and I promise you if you cross me again, I'll do it in a heartbeat!"

Eugene's mother broke down in tears. "I'se had so much to bear. Ain't none of you here can imagine. I was born poor and will be poor de res' o' my life. Eugene's father gave me Eugene, but he ain't give me nuthin' else."

I felt sorry for the poor woman and also embarrassed for her as she continued to pour out her troubles to the group. None of the others seemed moved, however, and I wondered if they had heard her monologue before.

It finally ended. Puzzled, I turned to Eugene. "Why don't you behave?"

Eugene grinned, and when he did, the venom of the group erupted like the Mississippi River breaking through a levee. Mrs. Little, Mr. Rollins, and his mother took turns lashing out at him with a viciousness I had never heard expressed. No comment seemed too vile or inappropriate. Through the outpouring, Eugene hung his head seemingly ashamed. With a final warning that he would be permanently expelled from school if he didn't reform, Mr. Rollins dismissed him.

I walked behind him down the hall. A fellow student fell into step with him and asked, "How was it?"

Eugene smirked. "Not so bad. Hey, whatcha doing after school?"

16

The confrontations with belligerent students didn't abate as we left October and headed into November. One sticks vividly in my mind. The boy was Earl Wheatley, a student who had flunked a couple of grades in grammar school and was now repeating seventh grade. He was mean in his dealings with the other students, grabbing their pencils off their desks and breaking them in half, calling them names loud enough for me to hear, dropping his books on the floor with a loud bang. One day he ratcheted his rebellion up a notch by turning his back completely to me as I was teaching. Earl circled his eyes with his fingers and smirked at Eddie Watts, who sat behind him. "How're ya doin', four-eyes?" he jeered. "Can you see better with them window panes?"

At that point my patience snapped. I walked over to him and tapped him on the leg. "Turn around!" I said. "Leave Eddie alone!"

Earl jumped to his feet and clenched both his fists, challenging me to fight. I gave him a disgusted look.

"Earl, either you unclench those fists and sit down in your seat, or I am going to knock you flat on your back. I am going to do this in front of all your friends. I am going to embarrass you worse than you have ever been embarrassed. So I advise you to leave Eddie alone."

The silence in the room was complete as 7B waited for a showdown. Adrenaline pumping, I stood there, not saying a word, but making unbroken eye contact with the culprit. He was almost as tall as I, but not as robust. He was the first to look away, his fists gradually unclenched, but instead of sitting down, he skirted me and walked out of the classroom. I followed and, none too gently, took him by the arm and walked him toward Mr. Rollins's office. I didn't tell him where we were going. I didn't need to.

I gave Mr. Rollins a brief description of the culprit's defiance, and Mr. Rollins's eyes flashed fire. "Get off this campus—right now!" he said, his voice low but harsh. "And don't come back unless you bring your mother to a conference."

We watched him leave the school grounds.

"A word of advice," Mr. Rollins said as I started back to my class. "Next time use your gin strap instead of your fists. A fight with a student would leave the school vulnerable to disciplinary measures by the school board."

Through one of the other boys in the class, I heard that Earl had decided to drop out rather than bring his mother to talk to Mr. Rollins and me. The rest of the week passed with no further incidents. It was a relief to have one less troublemaker present.

Monday, however, I learned, much to my chagrin, that Earl had requested permission to return to school with his mother and have counseling with Mrs. Levison. Again the great conciliator worked her magic, and a chastened Earl reentered school. That incident gave me a renewed appreciation for the placating role that women play in our society when testosterone-driven males are more concerned with adding a notch to their holsters than with solving problems in a way that allows both combatants to save face.

My gin strap did get put to use when Stanley Gildart's disruptions turned confrontational. He asked to leave the classroom, and when I denied him permission he started shouting obscenities at me from across the room. Strap in hand, I approached him, keeping eye contact, daring him to defy me anymore. I tapped his leg with my strap, and it popped just as it had when I tested it on my own leg. Stanley jumped up, knocking his desk over. Before he could get his fists up, I grabbed him by the arm and dragged him into the hall. There I broke in my new strap, then ordered him back to his seat. He waited until he was in full view of the class, then began tearfully yelling, "I'll get you! I'll get you!"

Without saying anything, I grabbed his arm again, dragged him to Mrs. Levison's office, and left him there. Having heard the commotion, she didn't ask me any questions. When I returned to my classroom, all the students were at their desks; no one was talking. I continued the lesson as if nothing had happened. For the rest of the period, no one interrupted my lecture, and when the bell rang they shuffled out silently, no one looking my way.

School was dismissed at 2:00 that afternoon so the student body could attend a football game. Mr. Rollins had told me they wouldn't need me at the game as they had ample chaperones, and I asked if I could leave early to drive to Greenville to have my car serviced.

"No problem," he said.

When I got to school the next morning and opened the door of my classroom, it hit a solid barrier so hard I almost sprained my wrist. I peeked through the glass insert in the door and saw the problem. My desk lay upside down just inside the door. I pushed on the door until I could squeeze in and saw what looked like a revisit from Hurricane Camille. The contents of the desk and bookshelf were strewn from one end of the room to the other. The bulletin board had been slashed with scissors. A world globe that had been given to me by my parents to commemorate my teaching world history lay broken on the floor. In large letters on the front blackboard a message stared back at me: "HONKY BASTARD." Student desks were overturned and defaced with chalk scribbles; walls had been dabbed with dirty erasers interspersed with more chalk graffiti. The side blackboard contained other epithets, each seemingly building on the previous one.

"Damn you, Stanley," I muttered. "I'd get even with you by way of my grade book, except you're flunking anyway."

Then I had a second thought. "Damn it, I won't let you drag me down into the mire with you," and with that I started cleaning up the mess.

There were the class clowns—Charles Robinson and Sam Trotter—lovable and disruptive. Mrs. Levison counseled them on more than one occasion, and each time they would return to class to express heartfelt apologies for current and past misdeeds. Class would resume free of distractions and even make headway for a week, and then they would backslide. I confess that I suffered their shenanigans more benignly than I did Stanley's and Earl's offenses. This was in large measure because Charlie's and Sam's pranks were never harmful and were even funny—and because the two reminded me of myself at that age. There was a major difference, however. I had made good grades and was a member of the National Honor Society and an honors graduate, while they definitely weren't candidates for any of those designations. As a student, when I became bored in class I would attempt to compete with the teacher for the class's attention. On more than one occasion, I was given a desk set apart from the rest of the class.

One day as I was attempting to teach, Sam interrupted me on an almost continuous basis. When I finally reached the boiling point, I ordered him to stand and applied the gin strap to his legs with several good whacks. I returned to the front of the room and started to write a phrase on the blackboard that was key to our discussion when I heard snickering behind me. Sensing that it was Sam misbehaving again, I decided to ignore it. When it continued, I turned to scold him. My mouth fell open. Sam's pants were in a pile around his ankles and he was examining his legs, oblivious to those around him.

"Sam," I bellowed. "What are you doing!"

"I just wanted to see if my legs was damaged."

"But—but—" I sputtered, "people don't just drop their pants in public!"

He looked genuinely puzzled. "They didn't see nuthin' but my shorts!"

My defeat was total. I could combat impishness. I didn't know how to respond to naive unawareness of accepted rules of polite society.

"Your legs are all right. Just pull up your pants and sit down. Please!"

Order was finally restored, and I could more or less continue with our discussion of the development of early Roman civilization.

Keeping these students interested was a constant struggle. Obviously, they didn't care about ancient Rome. Their interests were in more immediate entertainment. One of the least-bright students in my 7D class was Theodo Hollins; he was in every way an object of ridicule for the other students. Even his name was different. Most people would have been proud to be named for an American president, the Rough Rider, a man's man. Instead, he was "Theodo" because when he was born his mother failed to spell "Theodore" correctly. He was Theodo with the permanently bastardized name, a name that proclaimed ignorance to everyone he met. To compound his problems, he was clumsy and mentally slower than many of his classmates. As if God had not burdened him enough, Theodo wore glasses and his health was not good.

A group of girls led by Brenda McGary enjoyed playing mean tricks on Theodo. They would hide around corners and call him names. "Here comes Dumbo! Do you know how to spell dumb? T-H-E-O-D-O." I cautioned them to behave, to leave him in peace, or bear the consequences.

The girls continued to steal his books and hide them, or steal his pencil and claim it as their own. Their meanness came to a head one afternoon when Theodo came to the front of the room to ask me a question. Brenda took his glasses off his desk and put them in his seat. Unknowingly, he sat on them, they were crushed, and he was humiliated yet another time. He sat there in tears. I was livid when I discovered their vicious trick.

"How can you be so mean," I snarled at Brenda. "What has Theodo ever done to hurt *you*?" I felt my blood pressure rise as I lashed out at her with a vehemence I didn't know I was capable of. I could now understand what Mrs. Little must have gone through when Fisheye had pushed her over the edge.

"Get up!" I hissed. "Who else was involved with this?"

Eager now to share the blame, Brenda pointed out her cohorts.

I corralled all of them and herded them down the hall toward Mr. Rollins's office. Brenda was crying—tears were always available when she had use for them—and on cue sobbed, "I bet you wouldn't be treatin' me this mean if I was a white girl!"

I angrily whirled around to her and roared, "You want to know what white folks have against black people? It's girls like you!"

I regretted my statement as soon as the words were out of my mouth. I couldn't believe that I'd let her drag me down to her level. I silently berated myself.

I delivered the quartet to Mr. Rollins and struggled back to my class. I was tired. Tired of the effort to just maintain order. Tired of feeling that I was getting nowhere, that no matter how hard I tried I couldn't reach these kids. They were indifferent to learning, unable to see the value of anything beyond the here and now. I looked ahead to seven more months of daily conflict and groaned aloud.

17

I didn't consider myself a tyrannical, sadistic disciplinarian, though some of my unruly students might have taken issue with that pronouncement. Most classes were a daily test of wills where the line in the sand had to be drawn anew and retested to see if this was the day the line could be crossed.

One day, however, near the end of October, 7C quietly filed into my room from Mrs. Hadley's English class. I was instantly wary. No one pushed anyone else or hurled insults; no feet were dragged to delay the entry of others. The students went immediately to their desks, faced the front, and waited for the roll to be called. I was dumbfounded. This hadn't happened since the first day of school. Obviously, they were setting me up for something. I began to lecture; they took notes. There wasn't a peep out of anyone for the whole period.

Am I in the wrong school, I mused. I complimented them toward the end of the period and got deadpan looks in return. When the bell rang they filed out as they had filed in. Is there an illness called politeness going around the school, I wondered. I had to find out, so I paid Mrs. Hadley a visit before the next class could arrive. In the English classroom, however, she sat at her desk, her head in her hands. Uneasily, I blurted out: "Is something the matter?"

Her face was white when she looked up at me; she blinked. "It was that Doris Brown!" her voice quavered. "She wouldn't stay in her seat, she kept saying nasty things to everyone around her, interrupted my every sentence with some smart remark. I couldn't stand it any longer, told her to come to the front of the room, grabbed my paddle and began spanking her. She knocked the thing out of my hand and it flew across the room, just missing faces by inches. The wretched paddle ended up breaking the crystal on Ruby Anderson's watch." She shook her head as if still imagining the damage it could have done.

"What's happening to me? I've never before been out of control like this." She shook her head. "The kids were stunned. Didn't say a word. Just got up and left when the bell rang."

I patted her shoulder. "I knew something was wrong when they came in my room. Congratulations! You're now a full-fledged member in good standing of 'Blow Your Stack Anonymous.' I got initiated weeks ago. It happens to the best of us. You should have been in Mr. Rollins's office the day Mrs. Little lost her cool with Fisheye. Talk about Mount Vesuvius! I guarantee you that your students were less traumatized than you are."

She thanked me for my concern. "I guess I'd better get ready for the next class," she said in a defeated tone.

By the following day, my policing activity had resumed its usual level. Life had returned to normal.

I had thought that with homecoming and Halloween behind us, we could return to full days devoted to academic subjects. Such was not the case. On the first school day in November, fifth period was abolished for a special chapel, and sixth period was abolished for no reason that was ever explained to me. During the chapel meeting Mr. Rollins announced that since he had received no reports that our students had misbehaved on Halloween night, an extra day would be added to the Thanksgiving holidays.

Abbreviated days for special events gradually became routine: one week it was for a fund-raising event; another week it was a faculty-student basketball game; another was for issuing candy to be sold to raise money for the athletic fund to install a public-address system that could be used in both the football stadium and the auditorium.

One afternoon, school let out early in order for the students to attend a play dramatizing slavery and cotton picking in the Old South. Anyone who has inadvertently worn mismatched socks and felt that all eyes were focused on this faux pas can sympathize with my feeling of vulnerability. I kept glancing around to see if I was being watched to judge my reaction to what my race had done to their race. Actually, I found that my audience was so thoroughly absorbed in watching the performance that they didn't have the least interest in me.

Still another excuse for dismissing classes early was Mr. Bigham's request to Mr. Rollins to have representatives from the Community Fund speak to the Lincoln student body and faculty. The purpose was to solicit funds. The meeting was held in the gym to accommodate everyone. Although the solicitations by the representatives were earnest, they were also long-winded. Most of the students and many teachers hadn't the vaguest idea why the fund existed and what the proceeds accomplished. Mrs. Hadley and I shared a laugh about how futile the effort had been. If I couldn't get parents to send lunch money or pay for a subscription to a student magazine, the chances of collecting anything for an intangible concept like the Community Fund were nonexistent. I found out later why scholastic endeavors had been sacrificed for a futile effort such as this: the chairman of the Community Fund drive was a member of Mr. Bigham's Sunday school class.

A similar response was given to the field representative for the Boy Scouts. The meeting of faculty and student body was held in the chapel and was opened with what was supposed to be a rousing rendition of "God Bless America." The field representative had failed to hand out lyric sheets, assuming that everyone in America already knew the words. Everyone obviously didn't, and the song progressed with Mr. Rollins and the field representative singing a duet. Daunted but unbowed, the representative launched into an earnest dissertation on the Boy Scouts' contributions to America. He had expected patriotism and reverence, but since students at Lincoln were largely unfamiliar with the Boy Scouts and became quickly bored listening to platitudes about patriotism and reverence, he got fidgeting and giggles instead. That was the last of the fund-raisers.

On Friday afternoon at the end of the first week in November, Mrs. Hadley stopped by my room after school was out.

"You got a minute?" she asked.

"Sure. Come on in," I answered. "Is this a stand-upper or a sit-downer talk?"

"Stand upper," she smiled.

"What's cookin'?"

She came over to my desk and stood facing me with arms folded across her chest, her jaw set. "I hope this shakes you up as much as it did me."

I waited.

"Mr. Woolly, the assistant superintendent at Dean, asked me to attend an impromptu meeting of some of the teachers over at the high school. When we had assembled in one of the classrooms, Mr. Woolly suggested that we 'take the necessary steps to achieve a realistic bell curve distribution of grades.' That was a polite way of saying 'dumb 'em down.' 'This is in the best interests of the school as a whole,' he said. Can you believe that!" I saw fire in her eyes.

"Uh-huh!" I nodded. "So the bean counters want to run the school. I can hear them now: 'Get those percentages in line with what it takes to make us look good. What does it matter if you have to fudge to do it.' Sooo, what did they suggest as the new grading system?"

She handed me a slip of paper on which she'd written the original grading scale and the revised version.

Old grading scale	New grading scale
93–100 = A	80–100 = A
86–92 = B	60–80 = B
78–85 = C	40–60 = C
70–77 = D	20–40 = D
below 70 = F	below 20 = F

"This is a farce," she said after I'd finished reading the lists. "We won't be giving an accurate report on the progress these children are making. An A should stand for excellence."

"We're very expensive baby-sitters," I agreed, handing back the list. "The parents want us to educate their children *and* teach them manners. They seem to feel their only responsibility is to feed and clothe them. Many of the kids in my classes shouldn't even be in the seventh grade. They aren't capable of doing the work."

"It's the same in my classes," she said glumly. "And the seven and a half months remaining, when days are shortened for any excuse that comes along, won't do anything to change that."

After she left, I mulled over what we had discussed. Even though the situation was depressing, I wasn't yet willing to throw in the towel. Since I hadn't been invited to participate in the conference or been informed through official channels about the new grading policy, I didn't feel compelled to be influenced by their decision. Instead of dumbing down the grades, maybe I could dumb down the way I presented the material.

In that positive frame of mind, I went home and spent hours rewriting my material on the fall of the Roman empire. I structured basic, simple declarative sentences using only one-syllable words. I tried to keep dates to a minimum and to eliminate minor personages. Since they'd always had trouble with A.D. and B.C., I kept to a minimum references to those time frames.

As the testing period for the second six weeks approached, I gave my students pep talks to encourage them to study the material in the book. "Let's show all the other students how well we're doing," I urged.

But two days before the test, Stanley Gildart stole another student's textbook, hoping this would cause him to fail. When I confronted Stanley with the crime, he began mouthing off at me and I sent him to Mr. Rollins. The day before the test, I had a review session that was interrupted time and again by Charles Robinson emitting gas to the point that it kept the class in an uproar. When it happened again the day of the test, I decided it wasn't involuntary and gave him a spanking. This brought the problem to a halt.

When the test results were in, I found that the number of failures was horrendous. Attitudes hadn't changed. Earning a good grade wasn't important. They still felt that I could give them good grades if I wanted to, and that the reason I wouldn't was that I didn't like them.

I admitted defeat and reluctantly revised my grade scale.

My new grading scale:

82–100 = A
69–81 = B
56–68 = C
51–55 = D
below 51 = F

Using my revised grading scale, my classes posted nine A's, fifteen B's, thirty-three C's, nineteen D's, and fifty-seven F's. This was still far from a normal bell curve, but it was probably as close as I was going to get.

I didn't admit to Mr. Rollins, Mr. Bibbs, or Mrs. Levison that I had been forced to make concessions. When they congratulated me on my classes' noticeable improvement, I kept my comments to a minimum. I did, however, admit to my classes that perhaps my grading scale had been unrealistic and that I had modified it. Rather than clapping and whistling their approval, they grumbled that the scale hadn't been lowered enough.

"If y'all are dissatisfied with your grade," I broke into the litany of complaints, "let me encourage you to bring your parents for a conference, and I'll be glad to discuss your behavior and your tests."

The response I got could be summed up by Larry Harold's comment: "If I make my parents come down here to talk to you, I'll get two whuppins instead of just one."

The day report cards were handed out, Stanley Gildart, with a flourish, signed his mother's name, walked to the front of the room, and dramatically tore the report card into pieces which he dropped one by one in the wastebasket. He then announced to the class: "I ain't gonna come here no more. I don't need you, any of you. I don't need this school neither. I'm going to the office and I ain't coming back."

He walked to his desk, picked up his book, brought it back to the front of the room, and slammed it on my desk. He departed for Mr. Rollins's office to get his drop slip.

I didn't say a word. Instead, I offered a silent prayer: Please, God, help him carry out his plan so I won't have to deal with him anymore!

Unfortunately, God must have been busy with something more important, because five minutes after I had resumed my lecture to the class, the door opened. It was Stanley.

"I changed my mind," he announced. Then he sauntered to my desk, picked up his book, and did a two-step back to his seat as if nothing had happened.

As I stood there trying to control my rage, a little girl I had never seen before opened the door and came into the room.

"Can you loan me a nickel?" she asked me.

The anger I felt toward Stanley was unleashed on this little girl. "Can't you see I'm trying to conduct a class," I bellowed. "Are you blind? Now get out of here, and don't ever again interrupt my class with such trivia!"

Wide-eyed, she backed out of the room and hastily shut the door.

Earl Wheatley in the back row got the last word. "I bet if that had a been a white girl you wouldna been so rude!"

18

As a rule, the participation of many of my 7D students in class discussions seesawed between mediocre and nonexistent. Occasionally, however, a topic surfaced that stirred their interest. One such subject was, of all things, the epic poem the *Odyssey*. Although the poem was not part of our history text, I thought it might add a bit of interest to my lecture on the ancient Greeks if I touched on it briefly. I had studied it in high school Latin classes, and I refreshed my memory of the details using my old Latin textbook. What started as a footnote to a class discussion seemed to enrapture the students. They focused on its fairy-tale qualities with an undivided attention that was unique in my teaching experience. Gratified at my unexpected success, I used the entire period to relate the story in detail.

I began the tale as Homer had, with the Greeks' use of the colossal wooden horse to conquer Troy. I talked about the saga of the trip back home. I gave sweeping accounts of the nymph Calypso, the Lotus Eaters, the Cyclops, the Sirens, and the Keeper of the Winds. I pulled out all the stops. We talked about the courting of Odysseus's wife, Penelope, by her suitors, and how Odysseus ultimately won her back with his strength and prowess with a bow. The class was mesmerized.

During lunch period, a group of those students asked me if they could come to my 7C class and hear the talk again instead of going to study hall. Amazed, I of course agreed. They stood at the back of the room and, along with the rest of the class, were spellbound. Why were they fascinated with a subject so ancient and so unrelated to their daily lives? Maybe that was the attraction: the contrast of that distant past with its tumultuous happenings to their poverty-stricken, dead-end, limited present.

Another topic on quite a different level also elicited the students' interest. This stemmed from an article in *Junior Scholastic Magazine* discussing the actions of some of the anti–Vietnam War protesters, particularly the Black Panthers, the Black Muslims, and the Chicago Seven. The Chicago Seven, who had been accused of conspiring to incite a riot at the Democratic National Convention in Chicago the year before, had recently had their day in court. The trial had been a three-ring circus. Flamboyant attorney William Kunstler had vigorously defended his clients. Defendant Bobby Seale had been gagged and chained to his chair by the judge after repeated outbursts throughout the trial. It was quickly clear that the sympathies of my class belonged with the protesters and not the police who had arrested them.

Crime actually hit our campus during the time we were discussing it on a hypothetical basis. Someone broke into Mr. Rollins's trailer one night and stole some of the lunch tokens. These red plastic discs, which were about the size of a quarter and had "Lincoln School" imprinted in white lettering, were used in place of currency at the school cafeteria. Instead of going on a fruitless witch hunt seeking the culprit, Mr. Rollins retaliated by secretly applying red coloring to part of the white lettering on the remaining tokens. If the stolen tokens showed up in the lunchroom cafeteria, they would be easy to identify. Shortly thereafter, a brown paper bag containing the stolen tokens showed up outside Mrs. Levison's office door. The culprits were never apprehended.

~

Following the stolen tokens incident, another event occurred that kept the faculty and administrators on edge. Without notice, a state auditor appeared at Lincoln to make a complete inspection of the school. The purpose of the visit was to get an accurate count of the number of students enrolled. Average daily attendance determined the amount of money the school would receive from both state and federal sources, and this money was crucial to defray the costs of subsidized lunches, sports, and academic and enrichment programs offered by the school. At times during the 1960s, the withdrawal of federal funding was threatened to force compliance with desegregation and busing. Without this threat, I never would have been hired to teach at Lincoln. It was a humbling thought that I was hired to bring the Leland school system into compliance with federal mandates.

The day the auditor appeared, I happened to eat lunch with Mrs. Hadley. We were both late getting to the cafeteria, and the other teachers had already gone. Since the beginning of school, she had eaten a sandwich at her desk. She had told me she was uncomfortable with the social implications of breaking bread with "people of color." When she had finally ventured into the cafeteria, she was pleasantly surprised to find herself not only welcomed by the other teachers but also enjoying their companionship—a restorative break from dealing with kids all morning.

"Have you met him yet?" she asked as we settled into our seats.

I didn't have to ask who. "Yes," I answered.

"And?" she probed.

"He seems like a run-of-the-mill Mississippi career government service worker. He doesn't act real happy that he got stuck with the job of auditing a black school. I think he'd made up his mind before he got here that black administrators are either cheaters or poor record keepers, or both. We know that's not true. Mr. Levison and Mr. Rollins are about as straight as you're going to find."

I got a nod of agreement from Mrs. Hadley as well as from Pearlie, who had overheard my comments as she slid her lunch tray on the table and sat down across from us. "The kids aren't helping the situation," I went on. "Running back and forth to the bathroom and raising hell in the halls. The auditor can't figure out whether he's counting the same students over and over."

"Everybody knows that a nigger's a nigger," Pearlie spoke up sarcastically. "They know they can get away with being cheats and liars since you whiteys—with your deep understanding of black culture—think they all look alike."

"Well," I drawled in return, "what's there to understand? You can't hold your liquor, and you spend your time having illegitimate children and dreaming about white women."

Pearlie gave me her patient look. "Where did you get your degree in sociology, white boy?"

Mrs. Hadley had followed our good-natured give-and-take with discomfort, but instead of leaving, as she would have done earlier in the school year, she changed the subject.

"The weather hasn't been any help to the situation either," she said, looking out the window at the rain which had fallen steadily for the past three days.

Pearlie smiled at her. "Don't worry, Mrs. Hadley. Mr. Know-It-All," she nodded at me, "and I aren't going to get at each other's throat. I'll go one step further. Whites aren't the only ones with prejudices. We blacks have our share. And talking about the weather," she frowned, "I've had a 25 percent drop in attendance."

Mrs. Hadley and I nodded in agreement. "Likewise," I said.

After three days of deluge, many of the students were unable to get to school, since they lived on rural dirt roads that turned into rivers of mud and were impassable to school buses. I suspect that some teachers and staff used the inclement weather as an excuse for a mini-vacation. We were so short of staff on the day the auditor came that Mr. Bigham's wife was brought in to serve as a substitute teacher. To add to an already disastrous situation, the ceiling in my homeroom began to leak, and to top off this nightmarish situation, a power shortage made it impossible to fully cook the dried beans that were served at lunch. The auditor left, unconvinced that we hadn't planned the whole debacle to bamboozle him, though how we managed to control the weather for three days was hard to determine.

A few days after the auditor left, Mr. Rollins called a meeting for faculty and staff to be held in the library after school.

"Thanks for helping me get through the audit," he said after we were all seated. "I don't think any of us like those guys, but we administrators know they go with the job. That's why we get paid such big bucks." He laughed. "As always, he found a few things to write us up for, but nothing major. They aren't worth telling you about."

He stuck his hands in his pockets and paced back and forth in front of us a few moments. Finally, he faced us, frowning. "What I really want to talk to you about are problems that will never make an audit report. These are major problems that need to be faced head-on. I'm not going to sugarcoat it. Student attendance is way down, and I don't mean just because of the rain. Some of you—and I'm not going to name any names—have already used up your sick days for the whole year. Mrs. Levison tells me that grades are awful. As you know, somebody broke into my office and stole lunch tokens, and David's classroom was vandalized. In my book, that means the system is broken," he said, "and I'm looking for ways to fix it. I am open to suggestions. We've got classes to teach, we don't have time for major brainstorming sessions now, but give me your ideas on these topics. My door is open. Something has got to be done."

"Mass lobotomies might help," Bill Hayes whispered to me. "At least that would make the little monsters passive."

Trying not to smile, I elbowed him in the ribs to be quiet.

"That's all for now," Mr. Rollins said, "but I'm serious as a heart attack. We can't ignore these things. They're going to get worse if we do. Ladies," he continued, "you're excused. Men, stay with me for a few moments."

Bill Hayes and I eyed each other quizzically. Mr. Rollins waited until the door closed on the last of the women, then turned to face us. His expression was grim.

"I'm not going to mention names, but I've learned that some of you in this room have secretly dated some of the senior girls. Number one, you know that policy prohibits this sort of thing, and all of you were informed of that policy at the beginning of school. Number two, it's just downright stupid. If you get accused of taking out a student, don't look to me for help. You're on your own. And you will be fired, I can guarantee you that. The next conversation on this topic will be in private as I give you your severance check—no discussion, no appeal."

There was a moment of silence, then he added, "That's all."

As we left the room, no one spoke, though each of the innocent wondered about the guilty.

As I trudged back to my classroom I felt disappointed, as I often did after a faculty meeting. How could Mr. Rollins expect teachers, who spent their time and energy in teaching seven classes of restless, disinterested children five days a week, to find extra time to come up with solutions to fixing a broken school? Wasn't that *his* job?

Mrs. Hadley was waiting for me in my room to hear my assessment of the meeting. "I don't know why Mr. Rollins is suddenly so upset," I said. "This system has malfunctioned since the beginning of the school year. It's no more broken down now than it was before. Parents send us undisciplined children who aren't ready to learn, and they expect us to work miracles."

She nodded. "All those extracurricular activities taking precedence over academic subjects, and he's surprised that their grades are so awful?"

"Right," I said. "Unfortunately, there's no quick fix. This system needs overhauling from grade one to senior high." I began stuffing papers in my briefcase. "We'll have four days to recover over Thanksgiving holidays. I don't plan to even think about the Lincoln School complex."

"Me either." She turned to leave, then looked at me over her shoulder. "Why did you men have to stay on after we left?"

I grimaced. "I think it's supposed to be a secret."

"Who do you think you're kidding?" she answered. "It'll be all over the school before you've got your briefcase packed."

I nodded. "Since you've been a teacher a lot longer than I have, I'm sure you're familiar with this topic. Some of the male teachers have been dating senior girls, which, of course, is a no-no. Mr. Rollins laid down the law. No more warnings. Next step is dismissal."

"Oh, yeah!" she said. "I guess there's nothing new under the sun. Young girls, grown men." She headed for the door. "Have a good Thanksgiving. See you Monday."

On my way to my apartment I stopped at the dry cleaner to pick up some shirts I'd left. Waiting at the counter when I entered was the girl I'd met in the teachers' parking lot at the beginning of school. She still looked as good as that first day I'd met her. She glanced over her shoulder at me, then turned around to face me.

"You're David from Lincoln," she said.

I nodded. "You're Michelle from Dean."

"How are things going?" we asked in unison, laughing at our simultaneous question.

"I haven't seen you since that first day," she said.

"I'm from the wrong side of the tracks, remember?" I said.

She frowned, chagrined. "Teaching has been a real learning experience— and I don't just mean for my students. Or should I say pupils? My high school Latin teacher always made a distinction. Students learn something— pupils are just there."

She was interrupted by the clerk who appeared from behind a curtain separating the reception area from the rest of the establishment. She put a bundle on the counter and handed Michelle a bill. I wandered over to a bulletin board to examine its notices while Michelle paid. As I stared unseeing at the notices and newspaper clippings displayed, I mulled over whether or not to invite her out.

Finished with her negotiations, she came to stand beside me. "I'd like to continue this conversation," she said.

"Well, my usually busy social calendar just happens to have an opening this very evening," I answered.

"Sounds like your social calendar is as busy as mine," Michelle replied.

"Well, we teachers from across the tracks are very much in demand, I'll have you know. It's become quite chic for Leland high society to be seen taking us places." I gave her my best sexy smile. "How about pizza at Lillo's at seven? I'll teach you how to be a social butterfly."

"Thanks, but I've never liked social butterflies," she grimaced. "Lillo's?" her eyebrows rose. "Would Mr. Bigham approve, or is it a juke joint?"

"It's a respectable juke joint. How about seven?"

"Fine! I live at the Baxter Apartments, number 4."

She was ready when I arrived and invited me into her living room. Number 4 hadn't been decorated on a teacher's salary! Expensive-looking table lamps bathed the room in a warm glow. The carpet was thick, deep, and wall to wall. The chairs and sofa were covered in colorful fabric. Two pedestals displayed stunning bromeliads. Michelle looked equally good in a flowered dress with a full skirt.

"You look fantastic," I said. "I'll have to go to that dry cleaner more often! Are you hungry?"

"Starving," she answered. "Thirsty, too."

"OK. Let's go before they run out of beer."

Conversation was easy on the way to Lillo's. I learned that she had grown up in Meridian and had attended parochial school from first grade on. She'd wanted to go to Ole Miss, but her father vetoed that because he was afraid that his daughter's higher education would be taught at an Ole Miss frat house. Instead, he'd insisted that she go to Mississippi State College for Women in Columbus.

"I sure would have loved to have been a fly on the wall there," I commented.

She smiled and nodded. "Actually I'm glad I went to MSCW. I wasn't much of a party girl, and I needed a place where I could concentrate more on the books. Where did you go?"

It was my turn to smile. "Ole Miss. I needed to hone my drinking skills, which proved difficult since Lafayette County was dry. Seriously, I wouldn't trade my four years there for anything. I'd be there right now working on my MBA, but I have to earn some money first."

"So—after this year you're going back?" she asked.

"Unless Uncle Sam decides he can't win the Vietnam War without me," I answered.

"I'm glad I'm not a boy. What a mess we're in over there." She shook her head. "You think we'll ever win that thing?"

"We are after all the mighty United States! We're bound to," I said without much conviction.

Our arrival at Lillo's interrupted our conversation. The parking lot was packed, and I had to hunt for an empty spot. The barnlike restaurant had originally been an old house. White vinyl siding covered the outside walls; the front room was now a bar with booths against the walls. Tables were placed throughout the building. A waiter seated us at a good table, well away from the entrance. The table sported a flowered plastic tablecloth and was decorated with a short, thick candle in a low glass container.

Smiling, Michelle looked around at her surroundings. "This is really neat."

"Lillo's has the best pizza in the Delta—if you believe their ad," I said. "I'm a believer."

"That's what I'll have, then," she said.

The waiter appeared as she finished speaking. "Two pizzas, hold the anchovies," I told him. "Drink?" I asked Michelle.

"White wine," she said.

The waiter looked at me. "Beer."

He nodded and headed toward the kitchen.

We had lots to talk about—speculation on the looming integration of schools; the fact that she'd been a math major, which was unusual since that field had been pretty much dominated by men; the teachers at Dean—those she liked, those she didn't. She was intrigued with my life at Lincoln: Did I mingle with the black teachers? How did the black students behave with a white teacher? Was it weird to have a black principal for a boss?

"He's a great guy. I admire him," I answered. "Was it hard at the beginning? It sure as hell was, and I'm not a veteran now. One thing I can say—it's never dull. One day you want to slit your wrists; the next, you wonder why you'd thought of that."

We progressed from school experiences to our going home for Thanksgiving holidays. "I haven't been home since school started," she said. "It'll be great to see my family again. Dad pretends to be stern—he tries hard, but we see through him. My brother and I get along great—we're so similar— but my younger sister's a real pain in the tush. I think she enjoys stirring up trouble. Funny how the same parents can produce such different offspring. Do you have siblings?"

I nodded. "A younger brother. He's artistic, I'm pragmatic; I like to be at the head of the pack, while he doesn't mind at all bringing up the rear. And when the rear arrives, it's in good shape because of his leadership."

As if to remind us it was getting late, the waiter came to suggest dessert. We both declined, and I asked for the bill. We headed out.

"Where did the time go?" I glanced at my watch. "It's a quarter to eleven. I'd better get you home. You've got a long drive tomorrow."

"It's not so bad—four hours, give or take. I'll pick up I-20 in Jackson. It'll be good to get home and not have to be at school by eight."

I nodded. "I don't plan to do anything productive."

In the car on the way to her apartment, she was silent for a while, then she turned to look at me. "When we first met, you thought I was a real snob, didn't you?"

I glanced at her and nodded. "When I told you I was teaching at Lincoln you looked like you'd smelled something bad. It kinda made me mad at first, but it's happened to me several times since then. One day I had a low tire and took the car to the gas station to see if I'd run over a nail. The attendant said, 'Aren't you that "nigger" teacher?' I made the mistake of saying, 'Yes, I am.' He refused to even look at the tire. I took it to a black gas station and they fixed it at no cost. Thank God it wasn't flat."

"You'll have to admit it was a concept that took a little getting used to," she retorted.

"It's the last place I thought I'd end up," I conceded, "but brace yourself— school integration is coming—ready or not."

She nodded soberly. Then she smiled. "In the meantime, can we do this again?"

"I'd like that," I answered. "We can try Strazi's pizza so you can have a basis of comparison."

"Are you going to ask me for my telephone number, or do you want me to hang out at the dry cleaner and wait for you?"

"A phone number would make it easier," I admitted.

She jotted her number down on a piece of paper and stuck it in my shirt pocket.

By this time, we were in front of her apartment complex. I helped her out of the car. I put my arm around her waist as we made our way up to number 4.

She dug in her purse for her keys. "This lock is stubborn," she said. "You have to push and pull and curse a little before it behaves."

"You were cursing keys in the teachers' parking lot the first time we met," I reminded her. "Have you ever considered having a locksmith look at this lock? That's what locksmiths do. They make it easier to get into your house."

"I wouldn't want to make it any easier," she countered. "If I have trouble getting into my apartment, so would a thief. Besides, it helps me keep my four-letter-word vocabulary polished."

"There!" she said, triumphant. "That was quicker than it usually is." She looked at me and smiled.

"How can I argue with that kind of feminine logic?" I pulled her to me and gave her a good-night kiss. "Have a good Thanksgiving."

"Thanks, and the same to you," she answered. "Let me know when your social calendar will let us try that Strazi's pizza."

The door closed behind me as I made my way back to the car. OK, now what? I asked myself. Logic: This is the year not to get emotionally entangled; I need to save money to go to graduate school, or be drafted. So Michelle is just a footnote; someone to enjoy being with, but easy to set aside when the time comes. Emotion: I really feel comfortable with her, and she seems equally comfortable with me. I could easily get spoiled with a few more evenings of companionship like this.

19

A 1963 song by the Essexs titled "Easier Said Than Done" summed up my situation. Over the coming weeks, memories of Michelle on our first date intruded: the light shining on her hair when she answered the door of her apartment; the way her skirt swirled around her legs when she got into my car; the laughs we shared about our first meeting in the teachers' parking lot. Having never had a sister growing up, I'd always felt that girls were a breed apart—members of the human race, of course, but seeing things from a different and less rational angle than men did. Michelle had been a math major in college, so that assumption was eliminated. The fact remained that there was no room for a serious girlfriend at this time in my life.

Thanksgiving and going home intervened. I waited several days after returning to school before I called her to suggest a movie for Friday night. "How about *Anne of a Thousand Days*, with Richard Burton?"

"I'd love to see that," she agreed. "Richard Burton is soooo sexy."

"Huh! Really? Well, I guess he is a pretty good actor," I conceded.

"I wasn't talking just about his acting," she said. "There's just something about him."

"Whatever turns you on," I said, trying to sound bored. "The movie's at 7:00. Shall I pick you up at 6:30?"

"Fine. This will be my treat," she insisted.

"Gee whiz! You really must want to see Richard! We'll run by Frostop afterwards. I know you're not a beer person, but you'll love their root beer."

"I can handle that kind of beer," she laughed. "I'll see you at 6:30."

We had a great time. Richard was impressive and the movie was good. Over root beer we compared notes on our trips home for the holiday, and I learned more about her background. Her father had gone from rags to riches with an air-conditioning dealership. He married late and became a father in his mid-forties; by the time Michelle was in her teens, he was in his early fifties and very protective.

"I never knew the hard times that he and my mom went through before I was born," she mused. "I've always taken a nice home and new cars for granted. If I've ever wanted anything it's always been there."

"I know what you're saying," I agreed. "We both could have done a lot worse in the parents department."

We had lots to talk about regarding our jobs—hers in the white school, mine in the black. She wanted to know how I was getting along surrounded by blacks.

"Two other teachers and I are the only whites in the black primary, junior, and senior high schools. At first, the black teachers had as hard a time dealing with us as we did with them. The black kids had a real adjustment, suddenly having three white teachers. But now, neither the teachers nor the students think of each other, most of the time, as white or black. We're just teachers and students."

"I'd really find it unnerving," she said, shaking her head. "I'm so used to blacks as maids and yardmen, I'm not sure I'd adjust to dealing with them as equals. And uppity black kids would really make me see red!"

"Integration is coming—ready or not," I answered. "You'll do what you have to do. The only way you can avoid it is to buy lots of canned goods and live on a mountaintop."

She nodded, grimacing. "I know. I'm still having trouble with it."

"What's the alternative?" I asked. "Having blacks continue as second-class citizens? Lincoln is in no way comparable to Dean. We get secondhand textbooks, we have beat-up classroom desks and chairs, poor lighting and lunchroom equipment—you name it. Separate but equal is a joke." I stopped. "Sorry. I'll get off my soapbox."

"I needed that," she answered. "I'm just not used to even thinking about blacks. They never affected my life one way or the other."

"I was the same way before I began teaching at Lincoln," I admitted.

"Blacks were just part of the landscape—not people you really knew or got involved with. I like to think I'm changing."

At her apartment she had the usual battle with getting the door unlocked. I stood beside her drumming my fingers on the doorframe as she mumbled an expletive or two.

Finally, she won the tug-of-war and the door opened. "Holy mackerel," I exclaimed. "I'd hate to think I had to go through that every day. Five minutes of work just to get into your house!"

"Think how frustrated a thief would be," she retorted.

"OK, I'll think about that—later. Right now, I'm thinking about something else."

With my finger under her chin, I tilted her face up to mine and kissed her.

"Hmmmm, I like that," she murmured. She backed through the door, pulling me with her into the living room. "I don't think it's proper to neck in front of the neighbors."

"Me either," I agreed, as I reached for the lamp she'd left burning and turned it off.

As she looked up at me, her eyes were luminous in the glow of a streetlight coming through the window.

"You're beautiful," I said.

As I pulled her to me, she circled my neck with her arms and we clung together for a long moment before we kissed.

Finally, breathless, we drew apart. "A lot's happened since you dropped your keys in the teachers' parking lot," I murmured.

She nodded.

"Did you do that on purpose?"

She smiled. "I'll never tell."

"Woman, thy name is deception." I shook my head, then added: "I sure am glad you did."

"Me, too," she said. "Now it's time for you to go."

I agreed reluctantly. "You don't make it easy."

The euphoria lasted until I got behind the steering wheel, cranked up the Rambler, and headed for home.

Well, smart-ass, so where do we go from here? Back off—you're getting in too deep.

But I'm not leading her on, I defended myself. She knows I'll be leaving at the end of the school year. She ought to do the backing off. Besides, we could just be good friends.

Fat chance, now!

OK, I won't call her. Besides, Christmas holidays will be here soon, and we'll both be going home. Maybe she'll meet someone else.

I flipped on the radio for distraction. What did I get—advice for the lovelorn:

> If you wanna be happy for the rest of your life,
> Never make a pretty woman your wife . . .
> ("If You Wanna Be Happy," Frank Guida)

Thank you very much for those words of wisdom, I muttered, and turned the radio off again.

~

December arrived, and on the first day of the month I got an early Christmas present when the first Selective Service draft lottery was held. The event determined the order of call for induction into the armed services during the calendar year 1970 for all registrants born between January 1, 1944, and December 31, 1950. Those of us who had planned our lives around the threat of being drafted at any time and sent to Vietnam anxiously awaited the outcome.

At the Selective Service National Headquarters in Washington, D.C., 366 plastic capsules containing birth dates were placed in a large glass container, and one by one they were withdrawn by Representative Alexander Pirnie, a Republican from New York. The first capsule he withdrew contained the date September 14, which meant that all men born on September 14 in any year between 1944 and 1950 were assigned lottery number one and would be the first to be drafted.

Mr. Cain brought a portable radio to school and put it in the teachers' lounge so that those interested could monitor the progress of the lottery during their free time. Tension had been high when the first capsule was drawn, and great was our collective relief when it was determined that none of us had been born on September 14. The drawing continued until each day of the year had been paired with sequence numbers. Even though my number was 218 and, for the time being, I would not be drafted, by no means was I permanently out of the woods. That would depend on whether the war escalated or waned.

During the first three months school was in session, I had discovered a number of things about my students: most of them were undisciplined; most of them were woefully unprepared for seventh grade work; some were vicious and seemed to enjoy hurting other students; only a few were ready to learn and really tried; and many were so discouraged by past failures that they might never try. After several frustrating days in early December, I bottomed out. What was I doing wrong? Why couldn't I inspire these children to want to learn?

I saw Mrs. Levison in the cafeteria at noon one day and asked if I could have a talk with her. She readily agreed and invited me to her office that afternoon after school.

"I appreciate your taking time to see me," I said as I sat down.

"You're welcome any time. Be assured that I'm always here for you," she answered.

We chatted a while and then I showed her a copy of the test I had recently given one of my classes. "There was one A, three C's, four D's, and the remaining twenty-six failed. Am I being too hard on these seventh graders?"

After examining the test paper, she shook her head. "No, you're not," she said decisively. "This is a good test—straightforward, not ambiguous, not too long. I couldn't have done any better myself. I think you did just fine."

"If it's a good test, then I must not know how to teach," I answered, trying to keep my desperation in low key.

As her dark eyes examined my face, her expression softened, and I understood again why she was the adult the students sought out when they most needed a friend. She did really care. "David, you are an asset to this school," she said in a tone that allowed no argument. "I know that Lincoln was probably not your first choice of schools, and that you are here because Mr. Bigham sent you. But I also know that I wouldn't choose anyone else for this job but you."

I shook my head. "How could that be, when I'm such a failure?"

"You're not a failure," she said emphatically. "Get that thought out of your mind." She leaned back in her chair and was silent a moment before she continued. "These children haven't had the advantages that you and I take for granted. Most of them don't get any support at home. Some of them don't have a father at home; others have no mother. Sometimes they go for days without seeing a parent. In many cases they're not being raised, but are raising themselves. This lack of parental supervision isn't your fault. I know your heart is in the right place. Just keep trying. These children need the example of a stable adult. They're starving for attention, and the only way they know how to get it is by misbehaving. You're influencing them whether you realize it or not. Do your best. That's all anyone can ask."

She went on talking in a soothing tone, encouraging me to keep trying. "Don't be so hard on yourself. Loosen up. Give yourself a pat on the back! You deserve it."

I thanked her for her time and her confidence in me. Her final advice when I left her office, "Don't lose hope," followed me down the hall.

I felt better. She hadn't solved the problem of undisciplined children, but she had eased my feelings of guilt. I hadn't failed them; society and their parents had. My students had survived this long despite a dearth of adult role models. I wasn't going to correct all of these inadequacies in one semester. Perhaps for some of them it was too late. But for others there was time, and for those others it was worth staying the course.

∽

During the three months that school had been in session, I had been introduced to the homes of my students through notes I received—usually from mothers. The notes were infrequent at first, but soon they became the primary avenue for communication. Some of them looked suspiciously like forgeries, but that was hard to prove, because usually the parent's handwriting was no better than the student's. The following are typical of the notes the students brought to me from home.

Dear Mr. Beckin
my son steve had to stay at home because of a bad code and so throat
                                        Sign Miss Martha Newson

This is why Randolph did not come to school yesterday. It was rain to hard.

Larry Harold was sick yesterday that's why he didn't come to school
                                        sign Mrs. Annie Harold

Dear Teacher
the reason Ruby was not at school yesterday she had to go down town
and get some medicin

Thank you
Florence Drain

Please excuse Joseph and Harry For being late from school
Miss Lonnie and Ollie

Dear Mr. Beckwich
to reason Reginald wasn't at school Thursday I had to get him some
tennis

Yours Truly
Ada Jackson

And this from the grandmother of Theodo Hollins, the sickly boy in 7D
whose life was made miserable by the four girls who taunted him:

Mr. Beckwith
Dear sir
I am letting you know why Theodo miss school Friday I taken him to
clinic & they sent him to Jackson I am leaving with him Wed. morn-
ing I can't say weather he will stay or be able to return the same day but
I hope he want to be out school long. Appointment at 10.15
(Oblige)

Mary Jones
Theodo Hollinss
Grandmother

Up to now, none of the parents had taken advantage of my invitation to
meet with me to discuss their child. Perhaps they were uncomfortable with
face-to-face encounters, or worked during school hours, or, as Mrs. Levison
had said, were indifferent to their children's welfare. Maybe they were in-
timidated because I was white. Only when the situation teetered at the crisis
stage, or when Mrs. Levison, Mr. Rollins, or Mr. Bibbs insisted, did a parent agree to meet with us in person. Most of these meetings weren't called to

discuss a child's academic progress—or lack thereof—but because of a disciplinary problem.

∼

As December progressed, school days were shortened more and more frequently for attendance at events in town, and classes were canceled for programs held in the chapel. Academic subjects took up less and less time the closer we got to December 25.

Though I was disturbed by this disregard for learning, I tried to get into the spirit of the season by remembering how excited my brother and I were at my students' age when the familiar Christmas carols were sung in churches and when school programs were devoted to the well-known themes. My parents made their annual pilgrimage to Firestone and Goodyear to buy that year's Christmas album. The anticipation of what would appear under the Christmas tree and in our stockings still gives me a twinge of nostalgia. Since the homes of my students provided little in the way of support, it was up to the school to fill the void. Academia was put on the back burner.

Early in the month, special lighting on the streets of Leland, window displays in stores, and decorated houses all added to the festive atmosphere. Crowds came to Deer Creek to admire the decorated Christmas trees attached to floats that were anchored to the bottom of the creek. The thought that Michelle would enjoy seeing them popped into my mind when the last Christmas tree was in place. Although she often intruded on my thoughts, I'd resisted the urge to call her, hoping that by waiting I would gradually forget how attracted I was to her. Then she called me.

"Are you OK, stranger?" she asked. "I've missed you."

I gave her the weak excuse that "Things got kind of piled up around here," then added, "How are you doing?"

"Not too bad," she answered. "I'd like to get together again."

"I've also been thinking that," I answered before I could stop myself. "I was just down by Deer Creek looking at the Christmas trees, and thought you might like to see them. How about coming to my apartment Friday evening? We'll have a glass of wine, then walk down and see the floats. It's not far, and they're quite a sight."

"That sounds like fun," she answered. "Where's your apartment?"

I gave her directions, and we agreed on Friday about six. I hung up with mixed emotions—eager anticipation of our next meeting mixed with the realization that this wasn't a good idea. Take it one date at a time, I decided.

She knows the score. Leave it up to her to call it quits or to continue dating. Relieved to have shifted the responsibility, I looked around the apartment and decided it needed a major clean-up job, and a few Christmas decorations would help. I made a list of items I'd need: wine, potato chips and ingredients for Mama's potato chip dip, a Christmas wreath for the door, some candles. Today was Wednesday; tomorrow I'd clean up and go to the store, and on Friday afternoon I'd put it all together.

Amazingly, everything went according to plan. My landlady even donated a potted poinsettia, saying that she had been given three and wanted to share one with me. It gave the table a festive look. Michelle arrived at six. I went out to meet her when I heard the car. She looked marvelous in a thick red sweater and black slacks, and a red tam pulled at a rakish angle over one eye. She gave me a peck on the cheek, then handed me the box of candy she carried. "I'm not used to giving men candy," she smiled, "but I wanted to add something to the festivities."

She was intrigued by the apartment. "What a location!" she exclaimed. "How did you ever latch onto this?"

"Pure dumb luck," I answered. "My landlady felt that a teacher wouldn't be giving any wild parties, I guess. I try to keep the noise level down to a dull roar."

We took the wine and appetizers out to my little front stoop and sat on the top step. The weather was a little chilly, but since we had thick sweaters on and sat close together, it was perfect. A steady stream of cars was passing, but the apartment's distance from the road muffled the noise. We caught up with each other since our last date, which had ended on such an intimate note.

At a lull in the conversation, she looked at me. "David, we always have a good time together, yet I seem to be the one who calls you. Is there a reason for that?"

I mulled over what to say. Finally, I decided to come out with it. "You're beautiful, smart, fun to be with, and ought to be arrested for excess sex appeal. Certainly you must know that you turn me on. Besides all that, I like you as a friend."

She was silent as I took a sip of wine. It helped that instead of looking at me, she gazed straight ahead. "When I arrived in Leland, I planned that it would be for a one-year stint. I came with no baggage, and that's the way I'd leave. It would either be graduate school or Vietnam. That's still my plan. But every time we go out, I have too good a time. My folks got married real young and had to do everything the hard way. They've always preached to me and my brother: get your education first!"

She took a deep breath. "You've just proven that my first impression of you was right. You're a straight shooter. I'm flattered, but I don't want to stop seeing you. I know you're going away. Can't we just be friends until then?"

"Friends?" I asked. "That a pretty loose term. What kind of friends?"

"Someone to talk to, sympathize with, understand when you complain about your job because they've been there, too."

As she'd talked, I'd leaned closer to her and put my arms around her.

"What are you doing?" she asked.

"This," I said, as I gave her a lingering kiss.

"Why did you do that?" she asked breathlessly, when I let her go.

"I wanted to prove that just because I'm a straight shooter it doesn't mean I'm dull and boring," I answered, breathless myself. "We better go see those Christmas floats before I lose interest in them."

"What floats?" she murmured, smiling.

We headed toward the road hand in hand. Traffic was still heavy, but we sidled between cars to stand on the banks of the creek. People were milling back and forth, oohing and aahing over the beautifully decorated trees. We mingled with one group and then another. "I used to drive over here with my parents and my younger brother when we were little," I told her. "It was always a highlight of the season."

"I can understand why," she said. "The trees are beautiful, and reflected in the water they're spectacular. What a lovely idea this is."

We spent about an hour walking up and down trying to decide which of the trees took the prize. Gradually, it got colder and she shivered.

I put my arm around her as we headed back to her car, then held the door for her as she slid under the steering wheel. "Do you remember how to get back?"

She nodded. "I dropped bread crumbs so I wouldn't get lost."

"Don't pick up any strangers," I admonished her. We looked at each other. "This was fun," I said. "Next time I'll call you."

She smiled, nodded.

I watched until her car joined the traffic. Then I climbed the steps to my apartment.

Just friends, I told myself. Fat chance!

20

Lincoln School soon joined the rest of the town in decorating. A large green wreath was mounted on the front of the building, and a Christmas tree was placed at the entrance adjacent to Mrs. Levison's office and was decorated with tinsel and paper chains. However, there was little danger of getting into the holiday spirit with the string of lights outside her office. Not one shone when the plug was stuck into the wall outlet, and so the tree continued to look like last year's orphan.

Mrs. Levison looked at me as we stood in the hall and commented, "Kind of pitiful-looking, isn't it? Isn't the phrase you use that it looks like a red-headed stepchild?"

Then she recalled that Eddie Watts had fixed an office lamp for her. She asked him to take a look at the lights to see if something was wrong with the cord. He inspected the cord and discovered that it was OK but that someone had bent the plug so that it couldn't connect with the electrical outlet. A simple maneuver on his part corrected the problem, and the lights gleamed. Eddie shook his head when Mrs. Levison praised him. "Anybody could have done that," he said.

"But nobody did," she reminded him.

Eddie's demeanor these days was a stark contrast to the defeated, gangling boy who had dropped by my classroom three months earlier. It was hard to believe he was the same person. His glasses had transformed his academic efforts, and the ongoing friendship he and Shirley Foster had developed through her tutoring efforts had brought him to the ranks of the achievers. A note from his mother said it all:

Dear Mr Beckwith from Eddie's mother
I usta cry over my son, Eddie. I knowed he was a good boy but he just go onto the wrong track. Now I am all smiles and we owe it to you cause of what you done for him and for me.

Ever grateful
Mrs. Watts

Students were encouraged to decorate their homerooms with Christmas scenes. Paper chains draped my room from one side to the other. My students covered part of the blackboard with a paper sleigh and reindeer. Instead of enlisting Anita's help to embellish my bulletin board, I gave the students free rein. Their cutouts of the manger and the baby Jesus with wise men and shepherds hovering nearby might not have won any art prizes, but the work was their creation, and that meant more to them than a professional effort. For some students in my classes, our Christmas celebration allowed them a wholesome, childlike enjoyment of the holiday that they might not see at home, where holiday monies were sometimes allocated to more adult purchases such as alcohol. For other students, the already overburdened family income didn't allow for purchase of these non-essentials. Once again I saw our school filling a social need that wasn't required in more affluent school districts.

"Mr. B, Mr. B, how you like my manger?"

"How you gonna fit the baby Jesus in that manger? It isn't big enough."

"My reindeer is better than your mangy manger."

"Only in your mind. My reindeer better, isn't it Mr. Beck? Mr. Beck, you ever seen a reindeer?"

"Your reindeer look like a dog with horns."

"Them paper rings look like the handcuffs they oughta put on your brother."

"You better watch your smart mouth."

The comments tossed back and forth weren't always what I would have considered in the spirit of the holiday, but what mattered was that they cared.

The Christmas season seemed to bring out the students' impulse to forgive and forget. Two of them who I thought would hate me forever, since I'd had to spank them on various occasions, gave me a copy of their school pictures.

To influence the students to think of others during this season of sharing, as well as hoping to hone their writing skills, I suggested they write letters to Santa asking him to bring a gift, not to themselves, but to another member of the class. These letters turned out to be more specific than I had bargained on:

Ross deserve a whole new body he need to rebuilt all over

Larry deserves a lesson on how to behave. He deserves a motor bike and a camera. He deserves a good lesson on how to act when in a classroom and not to play. He deserves a bunch of rubber to be shooting around like a child.

Ruby Brantley needs a father and 12 bars of soap

Ruby needs some soap and water

Robert Jenkins
I think Robert Jenkins need a new pair shoes because his shoes is smiling
I think Mr Beckwith need a new suit because I am tired or looking at that same suit.

Fanny *50* and news walk

I thank the teac her need pice and quite in class and he deserve a something good Christmas

Meanwhile, basketball games had taken over from football as the current diversion from academics. Unlike football games, many of the home basketball games were played on school nights. One day in the teachers' lounge, Tommy Seaton asked me if I was going to the game that night.

I shrugged. "I hadn't planned to."

"I think you'd like it. You wouldn't have to work. Just sit and enjoy the game. And," he added, "we'd have the best seats in the house. We can sit on the stage instead of in the bleachers."

I wasn't all that eager to spend another two and a half hours at a school activity after a full day of work, but I liked Tommy and didn't want to seem like a shirker by saying I wasn't interested. So I answered, "That sounds like a winner."

"Meet me at the door of the gym a few minutes before the game?"

"Sure thing. Thanks for the invite," I answered.

Although it was a school night, the gym was packed with enthusiastic fans. As Tommy and I watched from our vantage point on the stage, the roar in the gym seemed to shake its foundations. First the varsity girls and then the varsity boys played against their counterparts from Hollandale. Over and over, one cheer pulsated rhythmically throughout the evening. Each time it was repeated it became louder and was accompanied by stomping, clapping, and swaying bodies.

Humpty Dumpty sat on the wall
Humpty Dumpty had a great fall
Humpty Hump Hump Hump
Humpty Hump Hump Hump

For me it was a very strange spectacle, almost eerie, as if the participants were in a trance.

During halftime, while Tommy and I were talking with some of the other teachers at the game, one of my 7G students, Charles Robinson, came over to me. After we'd chatted a few moments about the game, he looked at me and said, "Mr. Teacher, my friends and I was wondering: have you got mixed blood?"

I tried not to show my surprise. "No, Charles," I managed. "I have several nationalities in my family history, but as far as I know they're all white. Why do you ask?"

"We was just wondering," he answered vaguely.

As we chatted, another student, Louise Beasley, who'd also been watching the game, joined Charles and me.

Her question set me back a bit. "You don't have any children, do you?"

"No, I don't," I answered. "You know I'm not married."

"If you did have children would you send them to a private school?" asked Charles.

"No, I wouldn't," I answered. "What made you ask?"

"Oh, nothing," Charles replied. They exchanged glances and with no further conversation quickly disappeared back into the stands.

Halftime ended and the game resumed. By then, however, I was tired from the day's events and the incessant cheering, which seemed to grow louder with every hour that passed. When the game was finally over, I was relieved that I could escape. The shoes I'd been wearing since early that morning were starting to feel as if they were stuck to my feet.

21

It was 8:00 when I arrived at the front entrance to Lincoln Attendance Center the next morning. Mrs. Levison was in her accustomed place standing in the hall outside her office. Though she greeted me in her usual affable manner, her eyes darted back and forth as she watched for pranksters and troublemakers among the incoming students, ready to head off any disturbance they might cause. As was my habit, I stopped to exchange a few words. Her calm and benign demeanor was always a welcome antidote to the bedlam that I knew awaited me in the classroom.

"How was the game last night?" she asked.

"Loud!" I jiggled my little finger in my ear.

She smiled. "I know what you mean. I heard that we won."

"It was a good game," I answered. "I got a surprise at halftime."

Her eyebrows rose as she momentarily took her eyes off the hall to look at me.

"Two of my students came up to me at and wanted to know if I had any children. I told them no, that I wasn't married. Without blinking an eye, they asked if I did have children would I send them to private school. Again I said no. I don't understand my students' fixation on whether I have children or not."

"You've had other inquiries?" she asked.

"Yeah, I had a funny encounter with Stanley Gildart the other day about the same subject. Do you know him?"

She sighed. "I'm afraid I do. What's good ole Stanley up to now?"

"He stayed after class one day. That was a major surprise. Usually he's running over somebody trying to be the first one out the door. Asked me how many children I had! When I told him none because I wasn't married, he explained that obviously I wasn't ripe yet!"

I recounted his suggestion that I invite Anita Yarbrough and the two of us could go riding with him and one of his girlfriends. "When I pointed out that Anita was a married woman, he asked, 'Is her husband around?' Then he smirked and said that one of his friends already had two children, and added that 'When I gets to be your age, I'll have kids running all over the state of Mississippi.'"

By the time I finished my tale, her expression had shifted from affable to angry. Her eyes narrowed and her mouth was grim. "That may seem like a funny incident to you, but that attitude has led to very serious social problems in the black community. The name of that friend of Stanley's is Johnny, and what Stanley didn't tell you is that the poor girl Johnny knocked up twice had to drop out of ninth grade and is living with her parents, who could barely feed themselves before two more babies arrived. He also didn't tell you that neither Johnny nor his parents have ever given that girl or her parents a red cent to help them out. I also bet Stanley didn't mention that Johnny's sister, Mary, had to turn a baby boy over to child welfare a couple of years ago because she couldn't afford to keep it."

She paused and shook her head. "It's not the least bit funny—it's a pitiful tragedy—and it keeps on happening! Ignorance and misery begetting more ignorance and misery. You wonder why those on the bottom rung of the economic ladder stay on the bottom? It's this kind of crap," she said, spitting out the final word with uncharacteristic vehemence.

I looked at her grim expression and wished I could erase my "funny incident" remark, which now sounded so trivial in the face of such harsh statistics. For the first time, I fully perceived the many facets of Mrs. Levison's personality. I had known her only as the soothing presence who allayed fears and anxieties, but she was also a stern critic of the apathy that kept members of her race trapped in a cycle of poverty.

The interchange had lasted only a few minutes, yet it had been an eye-opener for me. I apologized for making light of such a serious matter. She patted my arm, acknowledging that my "funny incident" description was made from ignorance. I was reminded once again of how shallow my knowledge of the people I worked among was. I still had so much to learn.

~

The school's focus on Christmas grew each week. It became commonplace to cancel classes for a program related to the holidays. Some programs were morally based; others had biblical references. At a chapel meeting after lunch one day, an insurance salesman gave a testimonial about what the moral principles we live by, based on Christian teachings, had meant to him. However, his "Do unto others as you would have them do unto you" message must have gotten lost in the shuffle. When I got back to my class, I found that someone had slammed the door on Brenda McGary's hand. Brenda was wailing and holding her hand. Robert Rayford couldn't wait to tell me what had happened and identified the culprits as Louise Beasley and Dorothy Myers. Without warning, Louise jumped on Robert and started pounding him with her fists.

As I was trying to break apart the combatants, Mr. Bibbs happened to come along and heard the melee. He exploded and threatened to expel Louise from school. Mrs. Levison intervened, and relative calm was restored. So much for peace and goodwill to all.

~

Mr. Rollins decided that Christmas was a fitting time to have an open house and invite parents to visit the school. The open house was scheduled for an evening so that more parents would be off work and able to attend. The first part of the get-together was arranged so that parents could visit their children's classrooms. The decorations that the students had created would give the rooms a festive air. Mr. Rollins and members of his staff would be available to answer questions.

The second part of the occasion was to be held in the gym, where punch and cookies would be served and teachers and parents could mingle. It seemed like a good plan to me. Without the bleachers in place, the gym seemed cavernous. Only about twenty parents of the entire junior and senior high schools were present.

A wispy little figure in a clean, ironed, but faded blue dress came up to speak to me. "I'm Shirley Foster's mother," she said shyly. "My daughter loves school. She loves being in your class."

"I'm so glad to meet you." I held out my hand, and she hesitantly extended hers. "Your daughter is a model student," I enthused. "She is so smart, she's a delight to teach."

Mrs. Foster's eyes shone, her thin face beamed with pleasure. "She does love to learn."

"You've done a wonderful job in raising her. I wish the parents of some of the other students could take lessons from you."

Just then, Eugene Watson's mother came over to speak to me. Mrs. Foster thanked me again and left me and Mrs. Watson together. She was tall, had her son's somewhat belligerent expression, and unfortunately had the same protruding eyes that gave Fisheye his nickname. "Good to see you again, Mrs. Watson." After we'd exchanged a few remarks, I decided to put my feelings about her son on the table.

"If Eugene would sit in his seat and behave, he could learn a lot more in class," I said, "and wouldn't keep other students from learning."

"Then why don't you make him behave?" she asked.

On the tip of my tongue was the angry question, "Why haven't you!" Instead, I tried reason. "Mrs. Watson, I'm a teacher, not a parole officer. I really want to teach your son, but I need some support from you. You've got to make it clear to Eugene why he's in school—that he's here to get the best education we can offer. If you demand results from Eugene, I'm convinced you'll get results. You're not going to get more until you expect more. Please, let's make this a team effort."

This novel idea seemed to have escaped her up to now. "I feed him, I get him clothes, and give him a place to live. I ain't got time to teach him manners," she said in a truculent tone. "That's what the school is suppose to do. I got other children to deal with. I can't spend all my attention on Eugene."

It's a shame there's no Mr. Watson in the picture, I thought. I found myself wondering how much of a difference he would have made if he had been part of their family's life. "That's what he wants—attention," I said, quoting from my talk with Mrs. Levison. "That's why he misbehaves. If he would apply himself in class and study his lessons at home, he could do very well."

I could see by the look on her face that this wasn't what Mrs. Watson wanted to hear. "I can't make him study if he don't want to," she said. "That's what the teacher suppose to do. Make him study in the class."

We both concluded that our conversation had reached a stalemate. As she wandered off to join a group of friends at the punch bowl, it seemed to me that she felt that in giving birth to Eugene she had done her share: the rest was up to the school. With thirty students in each of my classes clamoring for my attention, I could do only so much to make up for what one child lacked at home.

On the whole I didn't think the gathering of faculty and parents had been a total success, but at least I'd met Mrs. Foster. As I drove home I found myself wondering how my brother and I would have turned out if our home life had been as deficient as Fisheye's appeared to be.

22

By now, many barriers separating black and white faculty members had fallen. Mrs. Hadley ate lunch regularly in the school cafeteria, enjoying the give-and-take that took place around the table. She even made a joke to the group about entering her classroom to find a group of the boys sitting in a circle on the floor unrolling prophylactics to examine them. She was amused at the interchange between the physical education teacher, Theresa Hinds, and me over the fact that I had playfully pinched her in the teachers' lounge and that to retaliate she had hidden my briefcase behind a pillow. There was a point, however, beyond which neither she nor Anita would travel—social get-togethers in which the school wasn't involved.

Earlier in the month, some of the younger black teachers had met to plan a faculty Christmas party. The gathering was to be held at the black Elks club on Thursday, December 18. Since the following day was the last day of school and was an abbreviated day devoted to class parties, our only responsibility would be to monitor our class parties before everyone scattered for the holidays. A paper was passed around for each of us to initial if we planned to attend the faculty party. A follow-up planning meeting was scheduled after school one day later that week.

I initialed the paper indicating I would attend the party, but because I had to grade test papers, I couldn't attend the planning session. Later that day I asked Mrs. Hadley and Anita if they planned to go to the faculty party. Both said emphatically that there was no way they would go.

The morning after the planning meeting, Mr. Bibbs stopped me in the hall on my way to class.

"Sorry you weren't at the meeting yesterday," he said.

I explained the need to grade test papers.

"You coming to the party?" he asked.

Of course," I answered. "Wouldn't miss it."

"Glad to hear that. I'd hate to think you weren't coming because you're prejudiced." His eyes bored into mine. "By the way," he went on, "we all agreed to throw three dollars in the pot for refreshments. Is that OK with you?"

"Sure. It should be a fun party. Is it casual?"

He nodded and went on his way.

I later heard from Mrs. Hadley and Anita that he had blindsided them with the same comment he'd thrown at me: "I'd hate to think you weren't coming because you're prejudiced."

It had caught both of them momentarily off guard, but both had come up with the excuse of having previous plans. None of us could figure out what his motive was in accosting us in such a manner.

Faculty members were soon buzzing not only with the excitement of the party but with the fact that its organizers had managed to get a local blues singer, Boogaloo Ames, to play for the gathering. Boogaloo was a celebrity on the black music scene around the Delta. He played a variety of instruments and billed himself as "the one-man band." Though he now eked out a living playing mostly juke joints and clubs throughout the Delta, he was as close as most blacks in the Delta would ever come to associating with someone who had been involved in the "big time." Boogaloo had played with Louis Armstrong and had provided backup for Nat King Cole and Errol Garner. His nickname came from his eclectic boogie-woogie style of piano playing, which he had been known for since his days in Detroit during the Depression. Boogaloo's piano style has been described as straddling the lines between blues and jazz. He came from Caribbean lineage. He had been taught the piano during his college years, when he developed the amalgamation of jazz and rhythm and blues that became his trademark.

I had become familiar with Boogaloo when, as a ten-year-old child, I badgered my parents into finding someone to teach me to play a musical instrument. They borrowed a tenor banjo from a friend of theirs and somehow found Boogaloo Ames, who, for five dollars a week, came to our house two evenings a week to teach me to play. I'll never forget Boogaloo puttering up to our house at less than ten miles per hour in his ramshackle pickup truck.

The truck's engine emitted unusual thumpings and pings as if some vital component was loose and rattling around inside. We deemed it sheer luck on every visit that he had made it one more time. He would amble up to our house, his famous lopsided grin on his face, knock, and patiently wait to be invited in.

My talents were not as remarkable as I had led my parents to believe. I found the banjo chords difficult to master. Boogaloo tuned the four-string banjo to a guitar so that I could use the simpler guitar chords to learn to play. Despite my limited talent, he patiently coached me on the rudiments of playing. Boogaloo was a fixture at our house for about six months, never missing a lesson. Eventually, I became more interested in other teenage pursuits, and my contacts with the kind and patient teacher came to an end.

When I mentioned to a group of the teachers in the faculty lounge that I had studied under the now-famous musician but that none of his talent had been transferred to me, they laughed.

"Old Boogaloo couldn't find the soul in you," Tommy Seaton said, shaking his head. "Some things you white boys just can't seem to do—play the blues or shoot a basket."

December 18 finally arrived. After school that afternoon I rushed around town buying the food I needed for the students' party the next day. By 5:00 I had purchased several gallon jars of giant kosher dill pickles, two cases of ice cream sandwiches, jumbo-sized bags of potato chips, and two cases of canned soft drinks. Back at school I put the soft drinks and the ice cream in the cafeteria cooler. I couldn't imagine kosher pickles with ice cream, but the students had assured me that the combination was absolutely delicious.

By 5:30 I was home and had fixed a bourbon and water, which I sipped while soaking in the tub. When I arrived at the faculty party at the Elks club, festivities were already in full swing. A room had been reserved for our group, and Boogaloo was playing the old Charles Brown standard on the piano.

Merry Christmas baby, you sure have been good to me.
I haven't had a drink this morning, but I'm all lit up like a Christmas tree.
("Merry Christmas Baby," Johnny Moore and Lou Baxter)

Boogaloo didn't confine our entertainment to Christmas music. Soon we heard the syncopated beat of his arrangement of Tommy Dorsey's "Boogie Woogie." As Boogaloo entertained the revelers, we drank, we danced, we drank some more. We played a card game called Whizz. The music got louder, we drank some more. Soon there wasn't a sober person there.

When Boogaloo took a break, I approached him. "I wonder if you remember me?" I asked.

He tried to place me through his alcohol daze but finally shook his head.

"You used to come to my house and try to teach me the banjo."

The light went on in his eyes, and he grinned. "You're Mr. Bobby and Miz Chris's boy. You has really growed up. Whut you doin' here?"

"I work at Lincoln with these other teachers," I answered.

"Lawd amighty," he shook his head. "This world is really changin'." Then he looked at me with his lopsided smile. "I sure hope you is a better teacher than you was a banjo player." He gently patted me on the back and went back to his piano.

Mrs. Little and I were sitting at the bar when she surprised me with a revelation. "My good friend, David," she said in a slurred voice. "If I hadn't had a few drinks I probably wouldn't tell you this, but you're a pretty good fella so I think I will."

She had my full attention.

"I knew who you were when you came to teach at Lincoln. You didn't realize that, did you?"

"Sure didn't," I responded. "How's that?"

"My cousin, Kitty, used to work as a maid for your grandmother, Mrs. Black. Mrs. Black is your grandmother, isn't she?"

"Yes," I nodded, amazed. "Boy, it's a small world."

"My cousin used to change your diapers and wipe your butt. I never would have thought that you and I would be working here together." She turned and looked at me. "That wouldn't have happened a few years ago. It's a changin' world, isn't it?"

"It sure as hell is," I agreed. "For the better. I hope I haven't disappointed you."

She shook her head. "You haven't. Kitty did a good job of raisin' you."

Bill Hayes had stumbled up to where we were sitting and heard the last part of her revelation. He gave me a whack on the back. "See, I told everybody, David. You is a white nigger."

The next morning I woke up with the king of all hangovers. I limped to the bathroom looking for a breakfast of aspirin and made it to school with my head throbbing, dreading the day ahead. As I ran into my colleagues in the halls, we eyed each other, each thinking, "You couldn't possibly feel as rotten as I do."

The kids turned up the record player to its loudest while I tried not to think about throwing up. Chuck Berry's voice and gritty guitar playing blared out of the speakers:

Out of all the reindeer you know you're the mastermind.
Run, run Rudolph, Randolph's not too far behind
Run, run Rudolph, Santa's got to make it to town
Randolph he can hurry, he can take the freeway down
And away went Rudolph a whizzing like a merry-go-round.
("Run Rudolph Run," Chuck Berry)

That last line really struck home. I longed for a cool, quiet place—Deer Creek flowing gently by, and me with eyes closed lying on the banks. Instead, I donned a Santa Claus suit, and one after another the students sat on my knee and I tried to come up with a sufficiently jovial "Ho, Ho, Ho" and listen to what they wanted me to bring them for Christmas. After that valiant effort, I distributed gifts that they had bought for each other based on drawing names. Arguments arose immediately about who got the best gift, and there was a great shuffling of presents from one to the other. Mary Bishop, who had drawn my name, gave me a Tally-Ho cologne and after-shave set.

When I went to the cafeteria to get our soft drinks and ice cream, I found that someone had stolen eighteen of our drinks. Mrs. Curtis, who supervised the cafeteria, felt so bad about the theft that she gave me eighteen cartons of milk free. While I was in the cafeteria, Fisheye snuck out to a nearby convenience store and bought several bottles of beer. He and a group of friends sat at the back of the room and, during the melee resulting from the swapping and opening of presents, surreptitiously drank the beer. I felt so sick, I didn't even try to stop them. In my queasy state I was more alert to the nauseating sight of kosher dill pickles being eaten with ice cream bars.

23

Finally, the party wound down. After enduring Chuck Berry and "Run, Run Rudolph" for the twentieth and hopefully last time, I enlisted the students' help in straightening the room. With "Happy New Year!" shouted back and forth they straggled out into the hall, jabbing and poking each other as they went. I wished I could siphon off some of their energy. When the last of them had finally departed, the silence soothed my tortured head. I gathered my books, notebooks, my new world globe, and other items vandals might attempt to destroy during the two weeks the building would be empty and made my way out to my car. Back in my apartment I slept around the clock and woke up feeling almost normal.

The next day I did some Christmas shopping of my own. Despite the crowds, shopping was a relaxing experience compared to a day at Lincoln. After another good night's sleep, I headed back to Greenville to spend the rest of the holidays with my family. It would be a time of renewal and re-charging my batteries, touching base with high school and college friends, and being lazy. I vowed that I wouldn't give Lincoln another thought until January 5.

After a couple of nights catching up with the home folks, I called Sally Stein. She was home from Indiana University for the holidays. I hadn't seen her since Labor Day weekend, when we had gone to the movies.

"David! How good to hear from you! I was hoping you'd call so we could plan a get-together while we're both home."

"Well, how about a beer and pizza at Strazi's tonight?" I asked.

"Sounds cool. What time?"

"Seven o'clock?"

"You're on. Can't wait to see you," she said.

Sally answered the door when I arrived at her house. She looked very pretty with her dark hair shorter than I remembered and bobbed in a becoming fashion. She had left off her glasses and added some kind of eye makeup that made her brown eyes look large and shining. She always dressed very well and looked preppy tonight in a sporty jumper outfit. Her parents lived in one of Greenville's wealthiest neighborhoods. Their home was bigger and much more expensive than my parents', as well as those of most of her friends, but never in any way did I or anyone else detect any snobbishness on her part.

Her parents greeted me warmly, inquired about my teaching experience, and asked to be remembered to my family. I could see that Sally was eager to get going.

"Man, am I glad to see you." As soon as I pulled away from the curb in front of her house, she slid across the seat, put both arms around me, and gave me a kiss. Then she settled back on the seat. "Whew!" she breathed. "I've only been home two days, and already I'm getting cabin fever. My parents treat me like a child. And Bobby is driving me nuts!"

"I always thought he was a pretty neat kid," I said.

"He's not your little brother!" she retorted. "But enough about them. God, it's good to be back in Greenville. I've missed this place. I can almost taste that pizza. We have a lot of catching up to do."

"Yes, ma'am! Miller time is almost here," I said.

"And after that I'd like to see your apartment," she suggested. "You were just moving in when I saw it last."

"Definitely a good place to catch up," I said, keeping an eye open for a parking space in Strazi's jammed lot.

Sally and I knew the occupants of some of the other cars, but there were lots of new faces—kids younger than we. They're displacing us, I thought, just like my age group displaced the generation that preceded us. As always, Mr. Strazi patrolled, his eyes darting back and forth like an eagle's.

"Hi, Mr. Joe!" we called to him as we headed for the taproom. He smiled and waved to us but was too preoccupied to acknowledge us further. Inside we lucked out on the last empty booth, thankful we wouldn't have to sit at the bar.

As we sat down, Sally sighed and leaned her head back against the partition separating us from the adjoining booth. "Hallelujah! I feel like I'm home!"

A cute little waitress in a short skirt came and took our order for a pizza and a pitcher of draft beer. "I'll bring the beer now; the pizza will take a few minutes," she said and left us to ourselves.

"Well, Sally," I sat back, folded my arms on my chest. "You look great. Tell me about your semester."

She was quiet a moment, staring at her clasped hands. The thought that she was getting prettier as she grew older flashed through my mind as I examined her features. It's comfortable being with her since we've known each other such a long time. Neither of us is trying to impress the other—we can relax and say what we think.

"I love Indiana U, but life in the Midwest is"—she frowned—"different. I feel so Jewish there. I never felt that way here in Greenville—growing up, going to school. We were just another family in the neighborhood; I was just another kid in school—a rich kid, but no different from the others. At IU there are Jewish fraternities and Jewish sororities, and people seem to want to run with their own kind. I never knew I was a 'kind' until now. But," she frowned again, "you wouldn't know what I mean."

"Before I taught at Lincoln, I probably wouldn't," I agreed. "The only difference I was aware of back then was that you went to a different church than I did. We went to the same school. So did the Baptists and the Presbyterians for that matter. Jews in the Delta were just people. The main difference in our families was that your dad owned a store and mine didn't."

She smiled.

The waitress appeared and set the beer and glasses on the table. I poured each of us a glass. We clinked them together and toasted each other's health.

"If you feel set apart at IU, you can imagine what it was like when I began teaching at Lincoln," I offered. "Remember the ugly duckling story of the goose that ended up in a family of ducks? I'm the goose. I always knew that black kids went to a separate school from us, but I never gave much thought as to why. They lived in a world that was totally different from yours or mine. Now suddenly I have to care about that world, since I'm a part of it."

"I've wondered about you going into that snake pit," she said, "and what it was doing to you."

"I wouldn't call it a snake pit, but at times I panic wondering how to deal with situations so different to me. My reaction was pretty mild, though, compared to that of the white English teacher from Florence, Alabama. She still wonders if she died, went to hell, and someone forgot to tell her."

I paused to drink some beer. "Are you really interested, or do you want to talk about something not so depressing?"

"I am interested. Makes my problems at IU seem really petty," she answered.

"If you get bored, raise your hand and you may be excused," I smiled.

"OK, teach!"

"At first I thought I had a communication problem—they didn't understand my accent, I was using words they weren't accustomed to, whatever. Then, like a bolt out of the blue, it came to me that most of my students have different aspirations and expectations than we do. Their circumstances have molded them to see life from a different point of view. Reality to them is being so short on food that they eat lard sandwiches. We take for granted finishing high school and going to college and getting good jobs. Yet those are goals they can't visualize in their wildest imagination."

My monologue was interrupted by the arrival of the waitress balancing a large tray. She deposited plates and the hot, fresh pizza in front of us.

"Y'all need anything else?" she asked.

"We should be good for a while, thanks," I answered. In the next few minutes I refilled the mugs while Sally helped our plates to slices of pizza.

"Good stuff," Sally said. "I was starving!" After a few bites, she urged me to continue my tale.

"Where was I?" I asked.

"Goals," she answered.

I nodded. "In rare cases they've dared to think about goals. In many cases it seems unrealistic that anything better can happen, and few have role models in their families to dispute this assumption. These children imitate their peers—friends and relatives who also have accepted mediocrity as their destiny. We teachers have the children six hours a day, five days a week, and try to convince them that we are the ones who are right. The people in their neighborhoods have twice as much time to undo everything we've tried to accomplish."

When I paused, Sally frowned and leaned against the back of the booth.

"While you were talking I tried to think of a black person I know who I could talk to one-to-one without them nodding their head and agreeing with everything I said because they're supposed to. I came up with a zero."

"You're not real to them. I'm not real to them. I'm a white guy wearing a necktie telling them they can be something that their parents and friends tell them they can never be. They don't resent my being there, they just don't understand why I keep telling them things that are irrelevant to their daily existence and will only bring disappointment if they dare to hope for them."

Sally nodded. "After I'd been home a couple of days from the university, for some reason, I was thinking that I don't ever remember hearing my parents say 'If you go to college.' It was always 'When you go to college.' I hadn't realized until then how our lives are shaped by our parents' assumptions."

I nodded. "My dad always told me that the only thing he would hold my feet to the fire over was not reaching my potential. It was one thing if I wasn't capable of achieving something, but there'd be hell to pay if I was capable and didn't. No one's telling these black kids that."

Someone must have put a coin in the jukebox, for the sound of a Beatles song rose above the clatter of dishes and the loud voices.

He say "I know you, you know me"
One thing I can tell you is you got to be free
Come together right now over me.
("Come Together," John Lennon and Paul McCartney)

"I never paid much attention to those lyrics until now. My kids can't get free of themselves. It's like their role models are trying to do them in— especially their male role models. My kids may never identify with what I'm teaching. Maybe as far as they're concerned I'm just saying what I've been paid to say, but for reasons that are difficult to understand until you've been there, I feel like I've got to keep trying! Mrs. Levison has sure reminded me of that before. And you know she's right."

"Do I hear a conservative southern white boy turning into a liberal?" she said with a smile.

"I don't think so," I said, smiling in return. "It's just that for the first time in my life I'm not looking at blacks in a one-dimensional way like I used to.

I've stopped seeing stereotypes, and I'm starting to appreciate them as individuals with good sides and bad—like us!"

The waitress came and ask if we wanted anything else.

"Just the bill, thanks," I said.

After I paid it, Sally nodded toward the crowd at the door. "There's going to be a stampede for this booth. We'd better get out of here."

We made it safely out of the building to the parking lot. I put my arm around her as we walked toward the car. "I hope I didn't bore you with all that white/black talk."

"You know better than that," she answered. "I found it real interesting. It's going to take longer than our lifetimes to work the thing out so everybody gets a fair deal."

As I slid onto the seat beside her, I gave her a sideways, come-hither look. "Do you want to see my apartment now?"

"Are you trying to proposition me?" she asked in an exaggerated tremulous tone.

"I sure as hell am," I answered.

"In that case I'd love to see it," she answered. "Let's go!"

24

On Monday, January 5, 1970, school opened again. Getting back into the routine of classes after two weeks without structure to their days wasn't easy for the students or the teachers. Most of the students' parents worked, leaving the kids to their own devices for the day. Often, that consisted of roaming the streets with their friends, pilfering items from stores when a wary owner had momentarily turned his back. Spray-painting cars was also a favorite pastime. Getting into a fight with whoever happened to be the current enemy kept some of them occupied. Whatever they'd done during the Christmas recess, it didn't lend itself to the discipline of being in class on time, behaving, and most of all, studying.

Remembering my success with Homer's *Odyssey,* and since we had just finished studying the Greeks, I asked my classes to draw and describe an ancient Greek house. The dwellings they drew and described might not have been recognized by an ancient Greek as his home. What they lacked in authenticity, however, was balanced out by imagination.

1. The house had 25 rooms
2. It have a women room
3. A open den, were ther ate.
4. In the room ther they cook had hold on the top
5. The home cost about $18.00

The Athenian house was brikage It was mak out of brikage and the house cause 1800 dollars at they was chief but they are a pretty buckat there was round about 21 rooms in and the people was go out in the street and do number 1 and number 2 in the road.

The Athenian house has 24 room with a hall for eat with coast in table in it with no roof. The savel live in the forins and of the house the lady stay in the back the kichen was full of soot they ketchen had not chimney so the suon go all over the room the little chickener. It have a lost of room. They did have any bathroom.

What I herd yesterday was how the Eugyth house was made and how they ate their food and the lade and man had one big bed and the prative room. And the children live in one room by there shelp. And open room they had a big barthroom when they barth at they all barth and one barth doned.

Athenian house had 25 room onto it and it had a spertrate room for each people aroom for girl and aroom for boys and mens and for husband and wife. and they did not have a base room in it and they had to go out side to use the do whatever they had to do they had a pool to take a bath in one pool. for mens and womens, they was not ashame because they was use to that

On another day I attempted to get a discussion going about unusual customs practiced by people in other countries during ancient times. I had someone in the class read a passage from the text, and then we would attempt to discuss and clarify it. Sam Trotter read a paragraph which stated that it was an ancient Chinese custom to wear furs in the winter but to go naked during the hot summers.

Mary Bishop, without raising her hand to be recognized, and not trying to be disruptive, asked: "Does this cause the Chinese men to rape the Chinese women all the time?"

As I was trying to frame a proper response, Mary blurted out her next concern: "Does this mean the Chinese make love in public all the time instead of doing it at home?"

While I continued to fumble for a reply to the first question, Mary changed directions. "We got a custom I bet the Chinese don't know about. If you gets poisoned, you pee in your hands and then drink it. This kill the poison."

Several students nodded in agreement.

At a loss for a reply, I attempted to move on.

～

From trial and error I had learned that lecturing to the class on the subject we were studying was not productive. The students soon became bored, and boredom always led to misbehavior. The more I could involve them in the subject matter, the more interested they became. John Dewey encouraged educators to involve the learner, reminding his students that experience is education. Instead of lecturing about law and order, crime, and punishment in the various cultures we covered, I made up a crime and let them take the part of the perpetrators as well as the police and the judge hearing the case. I called for volunteers, and everyone wanted to participate. I picked Fisheye as the ideal perpetrator, appointed Shirley Foster as the judge, and made Larry Harold the policeman. I motioned for the three to come to the front of the class.

"OK, Eugene," I said, "you've gone into a grocery store, and while the owner's back is turned, you steal two loaves of bread, run out of the store and down the street. You know you can get away, because the owner can't leave the store unattended in order to chase you. But someone in the store saw you escaping and pointed you out to a policeman who happened to be driving by. The policeman caught you, and now you've been brought before the judge. Shirley, what would you say to the thief?"

She thought a moment, then looked at Fisheye. "You know that it's a bad thing to steal, don't you?"

Fisheye answered, without hesitating, "What's two little old loafs of bread to him? He never would of missed them if that good-for-nothing in the store hadn't told him."

"Stealing is wrong. It's against the law."

"But that store owner is a whitey. He got a lot more money than we have. And that policeman riding by so high and mighty, he just waiting for somebody like me to come along so he can arrest them. There ain't no reason for them to be fair—they got us. Y'know what I mean? They got us."

There were murmurs of approval from the class; heads nodded. Mary Bishop chimed in, "Yeah, they push you around, man. They always checking on you and telling you that you is past your curfew. Who is they to tell us about curfew if your parents don't care if you are out."

"You should see how they push my cousin around," added Eddie Pittman. "The 'man' tell him that he in violation of his terms. He didn't show up to see his probation officer one time, and they issue a warrant for his arrest."

"They just don't respect us, man," said Sam Trotter. "That's the problem. They just looking for the chance to kick you around."

"But," I interjected, "was it wrong for Eugene to steal two loaves of bread? That store owner will now have to pay to get two more loaves to replace those that Eugene stole."

Frowning, Mary turned on me. "The store owner is white! They got a lot more money than the blacks got," she said, as if explaining a well-known fact to someone a little dense.

"If you were white and he stole money from you, would you think that was OK?" Shirley asked Mary.

For the first time in a long time, Mary could think of nothing to say.

"Judge, what should be the punishment?" I asked Shirley.

She looked at Eugene. "I sentence you to earn the money for the two loaves of bread and take it to the store owner. You will also maintain a curfew for two weeks."

"Court dismissed," I said.

$\sim$

Whatever euphoria remained from the Christmas holidays was replaced by grim reality when Mr. Rollins sent around a notice announcing a faculty meeting after school. We gathered in the library. Mr. Rollins stood in front of the group and held a *Delta Democrat Times* article in each hand. The headlines made it clear why we were there: "U.S. COURT TO HEAR ARGUMENTS ON SPEEDING AREA INTEGRATION" and "PUBLIC GETS TO HEAR LELAND SCHOOL STATUS." One article showed a white mother picketing with a sign that said "We'd rather fight than switch."

"Second semester promises to be chaotic," Mr. Rollins said without a preamble. "Judge Orma Smith in Oxford has ordered us to begin preparing for complete desegregation of all schools—immediately." Head shakings and muttered exclamations greeted this bombshell. Although we knew it was coming, it had always been somewhere in the future, and there were too many other things to be concerned about without borrowing trouble.

"Our school board submitted a plan to Judge Smith to establish a dual school system," Mr. Rollins continued. "That plan was to have two separate, desegregated systems: one for vocational training, and one for academic training. Judge Smith threw out our plan."

A collective murmur rose. When it subsided, Mr. Rollins went on. "The superintendent, Mr. Bigham, had hoped that we could have a unified system until third grade when the children would be tested. Those who showed an academic aptitude would be directed in that direction; those who seemed to benefit from a basic education with a higher emphasis put on vocational training would have that option available."

"Bull! That doesn't sound like 'our' plan," announced Leroy Cain. "Sounds like the white man's plan. They're just trying to re-create a segregated system. I know what those white SOBs are up to."

"You don't know what you're talking about, Leroy!" Mr. Rollins answered sharply, "because you don't know what's been going on behind the scenes. There's a train leaving the station, and you can either get on or get off right now. This is bigger than any of us."

The rebuke silenced the audience. This first controversy that had erupted during a faculty meeting caught us by surprise. "I've been to meetings that I couldn't discuss until now," Mr. Rollins continued. "The plan was not to try to re-create a new segregated system, but to provide children, black or white, who are not college material, with job skills they can use when they get out of school. That way, they won't end up in low-paying jobs like most of their parents. And," he went on, "every child would have the option of being re-tested every year."

He shrugged. "But that's neither here nor there. The school district didn't win on appeal. Judge Smith threw it out. The social agenda is obviously more important to him than practical considerations."

The room began to buzz with side conversations.

"You now know as much as I do," Mr. Rollins said. "I guess we just wait to see where the appeal leads. We'll be going through difficult times. There's no use in pretending in front of your classes that this situation doesn't exist. It's in the newspapers and on the radio. This controversy may put us in the national spotlight. I'm asking you as friends to stay calm and not add to the chaos with inflammatory statements. Don't spend your time worrying about something none of us can do anything about. Nothing endures but change, as my mother used to say. First, we've got semester exams to get through. That's what's important right now."

Unlike most faculty meetings, which ended with a hurried mass exit, today's meeting fragmented into smaller groups to discuss this new development. Since we didn't know anything other than what Mr. Rollins had divulged, all we could do was hash over what he'd said.

During the first week after the Christmas recess, absentee rates soared. On average, nine students were missing in each of my classes each day. The culprits were the weather and sickness. We had our first snowfall the day school opened; the rural roads froze, and it was dangerous for the buses to travel them. Coughing and sneezing spread cold and flu germs around. Even with these disruptions and absences, we had to review for semester exams.

Studying for exams, however, was not uppermost in everyone's mind. One day a student in my second-period history class wrote "white brother" on the hall pass I had given him. When Sam Trotter brought it to my attention, a discussion of the desegregation plans ensued:

Earl Wheatley: "I don't want them white kids at Dean over here at Lincoln."

Charles Robinson: "Those white boys come over here and mess with me, I'm going to have to hurt one of 'em."

Brenda McGary: "Mr. B, why do they call y'all white? You're kinda pink, you know."

Doris Brown: "Those hotsy totsy white girls think they better than we are."

Bobby Ann Washington: "Mr. Beck, you be colored—like we are." She frowned. "Only you jes' a funny color."

Velma Davis: "I just wish those whites would stay at Dean. We don't want 'em here."

Samuel Ross: "My mama works for a white woman. She say they don't want to come here. She's gonna send her girls to the Academy."

Eddie Watts: "Why don't we have a black history class? Black people have a history, too."

And on and on the discussions went. Each time I tried to get the class to return to reviewing for the exam, the students became sidetracked on desegregation.

"All right," I said finally. "No more discussion of desegregation. I'll make you a promise. If desegregation doesn't go through, I'll teach a unit on black history during the second semester."

The promise was made partly as a diversion, but partly because I had realized for some time that there was a need to make history relevant to them. Yet even as I made the promise, I inwardly groaned. That unit would require time-consuming research on my part—since I knew absolutely nothing about the subject—and I hadn't the vaguest idea when I'd have time to sandwich that into my already tight schedule.

The conversation over coffee in the faculty lounge centered on the changes desegregation would bring, and the sentiment there mirrored what my classes had expressed.

Band leader, Mr. Birks: "I don't know why they have to do this in the middle of a school year. My band is finally starting to sound good."
Science teacher, Mrs. Little: "I can't imagine what they're thinking about!"
English teacher, Mrs. Britton: "This is gonna be pure hell."
History teacher, Bill Hayes: "As if we didn't have enough problems already!"

Pearlie looked at me over the rim of her cup, then put it on the table beside her chair. "A few months ago, I bet the last thing you thought you'd be doing now is having a discussion like this in the teachers' lounge of a black school," she said.

"I sure didn't," I said, "and, on top of that, not feeling uncomfortable about it." I circled my coffee cup with both hands. "This is the first time I've ever been a minority. I can't lie well enough to say that I didn't feel like a fish out of water when I first walked through the door at Lincoln. But you guys have made it a lot easier for me to adjust than I probably would have made it for you if you'd integrated my school. Now, I think I'm beginning to understand. You're just people. The system here might not be like the one we had when I was going to school, but it's not broken. It's just different, with a different set of priorities. But we're both working with the same aim in mind—raising productive future members of society."

I leaned forward and rested my elbows on my knees. "I've learned a lot—not to be as judgmental as I used to be—and believe it or not, it's rubbed off on my parents. I thought they would be disapproving about my teaching in a black school, but they've been remarkably understanding."

"Hallelujah!" Pearlie exclaimed. "We knew we were getting a pig in a poke when we got you, and speculated about how much we would dislike you.

Turns out we like you—but don't get the big head!" she chastened me. "Just because you're getting more accepted and sure of yourself doesn't mean you'll ever be black. There's more to it than just working on the wrong side of the tracks!"

"Don't take this wrong, but I wouldn't want to be black. As Popeye used to say, 'I yam what I yam.' As long as we're laying our cards on the table, Pearlie, what really pleases me is that the kids are increasingly accepting me."

That got some grins, an "Attaboy," and applause from some of the others.

"Things aren't yet as black and white for them as they are for adults," I went on. "Life hasn't made them cynical. What scares me, though, is that some of the white kids coming over are vicious, vindictive—just like their parents."

"No more than some of the black ones we already have here," Bill Hayes answered. "You've been insulated from some of the really bad ones because you're white and they're still scared of you."

"I hope it stays that way." I held up a hand with my fingers crossed.

With that, the gathering broke up and we went our separate ways.

Tensions continued to mount. Charles Robinson in my second-period history class verbalized an old fear: "You know why all those white folks don't want us to go to school with them? My daddy tell me that they're scared we gonna date their daughters."

Heads nodded.

Even with desegregation looming, the everyday challenge of maintaining order continued. Oscar McAdory and Charles Murray, two of Lincoln's football players, decided to test my control of the high school study hall. Maybe they were setting out to prove they weren't scared of me because I was white. This extra chore of monitoring the study hall had been added to my various other duties because none of the female teachers were willing or able to stand up to the group of male high school malcontents led by Oscar and Charles. Most of these kids had failed grades along the way and, although they were high school freshmen, were now pushing sixteen and as tall as I was.

Because of maintenance problems in the room usually reserved for study hall, we had to move to the library. As the others filed out of the room to tramp to the library, Charles Murray announced: "I ain't going to the library."

Rather than having a showdown in front of the class, I sent one of the girls to the office to summon Mr. Bibbs to come and use his power of persuasion.

With that, Charles and Oscar ducked out the door and, in order to cause as much disturbance as they could, sashayed up and down the hall, kicking lockers and slamming doors. Since Mr. Bibbs hadn't arrived yet, I was forced to give them the confrontation they wanted.

"Oscar, Charles, either you come into the library, sit down, and behave or I will arrange to have your Christmas holiday extended indefinitely," I said icily. "Do you understand me, or do I have to embarrass you in front of everybody?"

"You think you tough, Mr. White Man," Oscar yelled. "You don't show no respect for me and my friends. I'm gonna run you outa this school."

"If you keep behaving like you are, I'll be here longer than you will," I answered. "Either you come in the library like the others, or you're out of here."

With that, the two turned, ran down the hall, and into Mr. Bibbs, who was hurrying from the other direction. I watched in admiration as he corralled them without seeming to exert much effort, and with no change of expression. He spoke quietly to each of them, and they, subdued, went with him down the hall to his office.

～

Caldwell M. Bibbs, Lincoln's assistant principal, was respected by both races and all ages. Light complexioned, mostly bald, physically strong, and outwardly unemotional, he led by sending an unspoken message that he cared but that he would not put up with misbehavior. I never heard anyone call him by his first name—even his boss, Mr. Rollins. He was the first in his family to graduate from high school and obtain a college degree. He put himself through school by working as a manual laborer in the concrete business.

Mr. Bibbs never flaunted leadership; he simply led. He had distinct ideas of right and wrong, and students knew that these ideas were not negotiable. Should any tough student challenge Mr. Bibbs, he was treated to a dose of Black Power. That was the name Mr. Bibbs gave to his gin strap, folded up in a small case, which he kept with him wherever he went. Newcomers quickly learned about Black Power. Mr. Bibbs reminded malcontents that true black power was gained from education, hard work, economic success, and respect.

He was innovative in his punishment. One day he caught two students shooting dice on the school grounds. He approached and stood silent, sizing up the situation.

"I see you boys like to gamble," he said in his low-key manner.

"Yessir, we sure do," one of them responded in a smart-aleck tone.

Mr. Bibbs surveyed their game as they continued playing. He stroked his chin. "I guess you know that gambling on school grounds is not permitted," he said.

"We just shooting a little crap," the other said. "We ain hurtin' nobody."

"Well, since you enjoy gambling so much, I think it's only fair that you shoot your punishment," he suggested.

"Wha' zat mean?" the first boy demanded.

"It's very simple," Mr. Bibbs answered. "Each of you gets a throw, and whatever you shoot on the dice is the number of licks you receive from Black Power."

The boys angrily eyed each other, joining the ranks of those who had tried but failed to get ahead of Mr. Bibbs.

～

To prepare students for the six-week exams, I began reviews of the material we had covered. On the last day before exams, Mr. Rollins announced over the loudspeaker that the students and faculty would meet in the gym as soon as school was over. Finally, I thought, we'll find out something definite. When we had assembled, however, he repeated to the students what he had told us at our faculty meeting. By then, of course, everyone had heard that desegregation of the county schools was under consideration.

The next day, Mr. Rollins announced over the loudspeaker that the teachers' monthly reports were due at the close of the school day. I halted my review of the past six weeks' material and told the students that they would have to study for exams by themselves. Enlisting the help of Willie Mae Jackson, I started on the attendance records. We worked on them for over an hour, but we kept getting different answers. Finally, when our frustration had reached its peak, Willie Mae discovered the problem.

"We've been basing our figures on twenty school days. It should have been nineteen," she said.

"Bless you, Willie Mae," I said. "We might have been here all afternoon if you hadn't found that!"

She smiled, pleased with the compliment. Compliments didn't come to these children often enough.

We discovered that attendance during December averaged only 76 percent.

On Thursday, Mr. Rollins announced that the integration hearing in Oxford had been delayed because of a criminal trial. The delay created more speculation and gossip—mostly that the whites were causing problems to delay integration. On Friday, Mr. Rollins announced that the integration hearing in Oxford had been delayed until Monday. By now everyone was sick of speculations and recriminations.

The following Monday I gave the students what should have been the dream review for final exams. I read aloud the questions on the exam, word for word, along with the correct answers. I also told the classes that I was going to delete all unexcused absences (of which there were many) from grade calculations and would use my revised grading scale:

82–100 = A
69–81 = B
57–68 = C
51–56 = D
0–50 = F

Early Monday afternoon, Mr. Rollins announced over the loudspeaker that Judge Smith had ordered complete and immediate faculty integration in Leland, but was reserving his decision on complete student integration until the U.S. Supreme Court could rule on that topic. Uncertainty continued to reign.

On Wednesday, judgment was rendered. The Supreme Court repudiated the *Brown* language of implementing school desegregation "with all deliberate speed" and ordered that it be accomplished "at once." As a result, this case was sent back to the lower court for the specifics of implementation. The Fifth Circuit Court of Mississippi set February 2, 1970, as the deadline for complete desegregation of staff, faculty, and students of the Leland Consolidated Schools (see Appendix 1). Setting the deadline for desegregation had been easy. It would be another matter entirely for the schools to accomplish this in twelve working days.

25

On January 14, after a seeming eternity of review sessions, semester exams began. My first-period class took forty-five minutes to complete the test, and despite the days I had spent reviewing the material with them, even giving them the questions and the answers, most of the students failed. On succeeding days, my four other history classes took the semester exam. The final tally for all my classes: five A's, seventeen B's, forty-two C's, twenty-two D's, and forty-nine F's. My morale hit a new low. When I shared these figures at lunch with Pearlie Brantley and Theresa Hinds, they sighed and nodded. Their test results mirrored mine.

That being Friday, I called my mother and asked if I could come home for the weekend. She, of course, welcomed me. I threw some clothes in an overnight bag and set out, arriving in Greenville about the same time my parents got home from their office. My brother joined us soon after. Heading down the home stretch of his last year in high school, Bill was eager to measure himself against me. Though he was inching up to my height, we had a good-natured tussle to prove that it would still be a while before he could get a half nelson on me that I couldn't break. We all pitched in to get supper on the table.

Although they'd kept up with the integration brouhaha in the papers, my parents were eager to hear about specific problems the faculty and students faced. "Nobody wants desegregation," I said. "The blacks and whites dread it. Most white parents who can afford it are going to put their kids in private schools. That means we'll get rednecks, white trash, troublemakers, and the ones who don't care about school. The blacks kids who will be transferred to the white schools will, with few exceptions, end up at the bottom of the class academically. This is a foregone conclusion, since many were at the bottom of their classes in all-black schools."

"The judge who hands down these orders doesn't have a clue about what this will do to the communities involved," said my mother.

I nodded. "But in the long run, this has got to be. Lincoln is 'separate,' but it is in no way 'equal' to Dean. The ones I feel most sorry for are the black faculty members who will be sent to Dean. They'll have a rough time of it—with both the white faculty and the white students."

"I wonder how integration is going to change the social order of the South," Mom mused.

"It already has," I said. "At the teachers' Christmas party I had an interesting talk with the science teacher, Mrs. Little. She was a little tipsy, or she probably wouldn't have told me, but her cousin used to be Nana's maid. 'Now, here we are,' she said, 'you and I, fellow teachers in what will be an integrated school system.' I don't know the science teacher at Dean who will be coming to us, but I do know that white parents at Dean don't have to worry about Mrs. Little teaching their kids. She knows her stuff!"

"I'm sure the white kids at Dean are going to find out that she's not the only qualified black teacher," Mom replied.

The rest of the weekend was relaxing, enjoyable, and tension-free. I returned to Lincoln on Monday to find that school had been suspended because of an unexpected snowstorm. On Tuesday the bad weather continued, but faculty members were required to report to work to finish the students' cumulative folders and report cards. While we were working in the teachers' lounge, someone turned on the radio and we listened to a crowd of white parents and teachers demonstrating outside the courthouse in Greenville against the judge's ruling on the desegregation of Washington County schools. There were chants, angry shouts, bullhorns. It sounded wild and disorganized. Governor John Bell Williams was on television often, and he left no doubt in listeners' minds that he disagreed completely with the judge's decision.

After listening for a few moments, Bill Hayes shook his head, looking puzzled. "My, oh my, hit do sound like de guvnor an' dem white folks is kinda upset 'bout de white chirren comin' to school wid us black folks," he parodied. "I jes' don't understand dat."

"Hit do seem dat away," Gwen Stewart agreed, "an' iffen I wuz a black parent, I sho' wouldn't want my chirren going to school wid dos no-count white trash."

Bill Hayes, sitting beside me at the table, nudged me with his elbow. "Present white trash excepted," he said, smiling.

As we were finishing up our work, Mr. Rollins called over the loudspeaker for us to come to the school library for an informal meeting. Once we had assembled, he told us that he had received a phone call from the office of John Woolly, the assistant superintendent of schools.

"The court has ruled," Mr. Rollins said. "Beginning with the new semester, grades one through three and ten through twelve will be attending Dean. Grades four through nine will be enrolled here at Lincoln." He paused, awaiting our reaction to the fact that the system as we knew it would no longer exist, and that in a matter of two weeks many of us would be teaching in a totally different world. The reaction wasn't long in coming.

From the front row, Gwen Stewart's "God almighty, what a mess" seemed to sum up the faculty's reaction.

"Integrating the high school is a major mistake," Pearlie Brantley said. "They ought to start with the little kids and every year add another grade and reach the high school last."

"That's where most of the trouble is going to start," Theresa Hinds spoke up. "But since when have teachers been consulted about what's good for education?"

Nods of approval greeted this statement. More objections followed. Mr. Rollins listened for a time, then glanced at his watch. "I agree with everything you've expressed, but we either give up our careers in education or go along with the ruling. We have no say-so in the matter." Above the murmur of dissatisfaction, he announced that all books must be collected when the students returned to school on Wednesday.

After he left the room, we continued to discuss our new circumstances. Then we heard a shuffling noise in the hall. Our conversation subsided as Mrs. Little peeked out the door, listened a moment, then reported to us.

"Mr. Woolly is giving a tour of Lincoln to the white teachers from Dean who will be coming here on D-Day"—the name we'd adopted for the first day of desegregation of the schools.

We waited silently while the library door opened again and the assistant superintendent ushered a group of white teachers into the room. The group included a couple of middle-aged women, four younger women (including

Michelle), and two middle-aged men. Michelle and I looked at each other, uncertain if or how we should acknowledge each other. She'd telephoned me on the day that she'd been told of her transfer, and she'd been terribly upset. "I know I shouldn't be as mad as I am, but I can't help it. I worked so hard to get my math degree, and at Lincoln the students won't even know what I'm talking about!"

"Making judgments before you get here isn't a good idea," I had cautioned. "I know it's a shock, but don't borrow trouble. They're kids. You could be a really good influence on them. I'll be here for you."

"I *know* I'll need help," she'd answered.

It was an awkward moment for everyone in the library. Instead of introducing all of us individually, Mr. Woolly just said, "These are the faculty members from Dean who will be coming to Lincoln." No one smiled . . . a most inauspicious beginning. He herded the group back into the hall.

"Well!" Gwen Stewart huffed as the door closed, "so much for getting started on the right foot!"

Befitting the occasion, Wednesday, January 19 was a damp, cold Delta winter day. Clouds blanketed the sky, turning the landscape a depressing gray. Students reported to school and went through an abbreviated schedule, ending at 2:00 p.m. We attempted to collect schoolbooks from the first semester, but the day ended with as many books missing as had been found. There was nothing to keep the students occupied, and they spent a lot of time milling about in the halls, where no one was in charge. Bells rang erratically; papers and books littered desk tops. Just after the 2:00 dismissal, I saw an angry Mr. Bibbs marching in long strides toward his office.

"What's happening?" I asked. "Do you need me? Is somebody hurt?"

"Not someone—something!" he retorted. "Damn it to hell, somebody's put sugar in the gas tanks of six of the buses. The other twelve buses will have to make double runs to get the kids home." He paused. "Yeah, there is something you can do. Come with me and try to keep order with the ones who are stranded until the driver can get back here to get 'em. If the ones who did this believe in God, they'd better pray I don't find out who they are. God may get their souls; their ass is gonna be mine!"

"Give me a second to lock my door and I'll be with you," I answered. "I guess the fun is just beginning. With these roads iced over, all we need now is an accident to make the day a total loss," I yelled back.

He didn't acknowledge my comment. He'd turned the corner and was gone.

On Friday, the students reported to school to register for the second semester.

"I don't wanna come back to this school," Doris Brown said to me as I wrote her name in my book. "I wouldn't have come to register except my mama made me."

"Me neither," Brenda McGary chimed in. "Those white kids goin' to ruin this school for the rest of us."

"I wish there was somewhere else we could go," Samuel Ross added.

"Hey, suck it up, guys," I said. "Let's look at it as a challenge. The white kids don't want to come here any more than you want them to, so we'll all have to try extra hard to get along."

Their eye-rolling spoke louder than words. What else should they expect a teacher to say other than the company line?

None of us knew what to expect from the new semester. The here and now, however, was a meeting of the faculties of Lincoln and Dean in the auditorium of Dean High School. When Lincoln teachers arrived, Dean's white teachers had taken up the seats at the front of the middle section of the auditorium. Instead of sitting in the back, behind the whites, Mr. Bibbs led our Lincoln group to the front seats of the right-hand section. Of course, Anita, Mrs. Hadley, and I sat with our fellow Lincoln teachers. As we seated ourselves, we overheard snatches of conversation from our white counterparts. Little effort was made to keep these comments quiet and discreet.

"I hear these colored have absolutely no discipline."

"I've been told we're really going to have to dumb down everything we do to even have a prayer of communicating with them."

"They tell me that Negro children have absolutely no respect for authority."

"Harrumph. It's dangerous to even drive through that part of town."

"And they expect us to leave our cars parked out there for a whole day? I'd better take the hubcaps off and hide them."

"My husband said if it gets too bad that I can just quit."

The stream of derogatory comments subsided when the superintendent of schools, Mr. Bigham, appeared on the stage and took the podium. He braced a hand on each side of the lectern, as if seeking something solid and dependable while everything was changing around him.

"Thank you for coming," he said. "We are going through difficult times, and the method by which change is being brought about will be hard for all of us to deal with, but God will see us through."

"I was hoping he'd tell us something we didn't already know," Anita muttered to me.

I gave her a nod in response.

"I do want you to be aware," Mr. Bigham continued, "that officials of both schools as well as members of my staff and I tried to intercede with Judge Smith to postpone the order to desegregate the schools until the end of the school year, but he would not agree to grant our request. There will be no postponement. So we must abide by his decision. Both races will be inconvenienced, and so I'm asking you to be patient, and do your best for the sake of the children." He pushed himself back from the podium.

"Good luck," he said and walked off the stage.

As Anita and I made our way out of the auditorium, we heard bits of conversation of our black colleagues:

"An' he's talking about asking the judge for a postponement when there's already been a fifteen-year postponement since Little Rock!"

"John Bell Williams claims that he's the governor of all the people of this state. Bullshit! His constituency is those white voters. You listen to him on TV—he practically told those white folks to set up private schools. They didn't bring those fifty federal marshals down here to Leland for a winter vacation. Freedom of choice, my ass!"

"Lord willing—I just want to get through this school year!"

"You gonna need more than just the Lord . . ."

I looked at Anita. "Let the games begin."

26

On Monday we were required to report for work—ostensibly to collect un-collected books, but actually just to provide a presence on campus, I suspect. Since buses were not running, none of the students in the county could get to the school, but I was pleased that several who lived in town stopped by and delivered their books. When that trickle of visitors ended, I cleaned out my cabinet, then helped Pearlie Brantley finish her cumulative folders. Pearlie was telling me about this wonderful new show she'd seen on TV called *Sesame Street* when an unexpected visitor poked her head in the door. She introduced herself—Mrs. Bradham—and said she was one of the newly arrived teachers from Dean.

She gave me a bright smile. "I thought I'd come by and invite you to lunch in my new room," she said, looking all the while directly at me, completely ignoring Pearlie. "I've just finished decorating it."

I was disconcerted that Pearlie was obviously not invited. I recalled that my parents and the Bradhams had done business together through the years. They were considered Mississippi blue blood—aristocrats. I had always equated "blue blood" with class, and equated "class" with good manners. My parents had taught me to be civil and to show respect for the feelings of others, even if their station in life might be different. That Mrs. Bradham could be this rude suggested that the Bradhams didn't have the "class" that I'd assumed they possessed.

I gave her a cool acceptance, and when she left I looked at Pearlie and raised an eyebrow. "Wanna come?" I gave her a fixed smile.

"Not on your life!" she answered. "I hope she'll run into a post somewhere with her nose stuck up so far in the air."

"I think it would be kinda fun to see her face if you showed up," I said.

"Well, I'm not going to give you that pleasure," she answered.

I expected Michelle to be among the group, but when I arrived in Mrs. Bradham's room Michelle wasn't there. I did discover that Mrs. Hadley, Anita, and I had been invited for a reason. As we ate our sandwiches, each of the former Dean teachers, who had also been invited, took a turn telling us horror stories involving blacks, meant to impress upon us where our future loyalties should lie.

"I saw a colored child sneaking down the hall this morning," Mrs. Black, one of the new elementary teachers, began. "I confronted her and asked where she was going. She said one of the Lincoln teachers had asked her to come down and scratch her head! Can you believe that?"

Mrs. Hadley, Anita, and I exchanged glances, having never heard of anything like that. We suspected the episode had been dreamed up for our benefit.

Anita smiled sweetly, then replied: "One day a first grader in my class came up and asked if she could feel my hair. A boy student in the back shouted at her, 'You're not supposed to do that.' I told him there was nothing wrong with being curious. It's how we learn. So, the whole class came up and felt my hair, and I felt theirs." Her expression was guileless as she looked around at the white teachers who were trying hard to conceal their looks of distaste. "They're so cute—really harmless. They've just never been around us. You'll see." She glanced at me, and I read her "tit-for-tat" message.

The teachers weren't amused. One after another, they related horror stories. "I've heard that a third grader has already had a child."

Other stories followed, equally far-fetched.

"Don't believe everything you hear about your students," I advised. "Probably 90 percent of it isn't true."

I received disapproving stares as our new colleagues tried to size me up.

Lunch seemed to last an eternity. When Anita, Mrs. Hadley, and I left, we were of one mind—we didn't want to join their clique. "Can you believe these people?" Anita asked. "David, please tell me I wasn't as bad as that when I first came here."

"Whew!" I said. "Well, maybe not quite that bad, but you didn't have the luxury of a group of co-conspirators."

She poked me in the ribs with her elbow.

By Wednesday, January 21, staff members from both schools had been switched and students from both schools had been registered. There was no socializing between the races. There was also no mischievous playing or maneuvering for advantage, at least on the surface. We hoped this peaceful interval was not the quiet before the storm.

It soon became apparent that the limited vocabulary that I had come to expect from my students was not confined to products of the Lincoln system, and there seemed to be little difference in the educational level of some of the students from Dean and Lincoln. Referring to the registration card, one of the white students asked, "What does 'occupation' mean?" Another asked me to explain "nationality."

After all the students had been dismissed and those Lincoln staff members who were transferred to Dean had left, the rest of us counted and alphabetized registration cards. We found that seventy of the Dean seventh graders who had been assigned to Lincoln had made arrangements to attend seventh grade in private schools that were popping up all over the Delta. These schools, for the most part, had little in the way of resources. Many were makeshift one-room schools sponsored by churches. With little funding, a staff of sometimes questionable qualifications, a bare-bones physical plant, limited extracurricular programs, and no accreditation, their only advantage was an exclusively white student body. The children were being used as guinea pigs as these private schools groped to try to quickly become legitimate educational institutions. Some would make it; more would not.

There was nothing for us to do after lunch. A group of us played solitaire, then whizz until we got bored. Then I decided to trade my old desk, whose drawers stuck and were hard to close, for one in much better shape from Mrs. Cathey's room. I talked Tommy Seaton into helping me in my nefarious plan.

"Since she's been transferred to Dean she won't need this desk," I rationalized aloud as we slid her desk toward the door.

Tommy's eyebrows rose innocently. "And that means that one of the teachers from Dean will be assigned this room?"

"You got it."

"That's sounds like a very judicious use of school equipment," he said.

I was trying out the drawers on my new desk, marveling that they slid in and out as they were designed to, when Mr. Rollins announced over the loudspeaker that there would be a meeting of Lincoln staff in the library.

John Woolly presided at the meeting and told us that the time was at hand to transfer thirteen of Lincoln's staff to Dean to replace those sent from Dean. I really felt sorry for those thirteen Lincoln teachers, remembering the icy reception we had received from Dean's teachers at the combined faculty meeting.

"This has been a difficult time for all concerned," Mr. Woolly continued. "We need to meet the challenge presented to us with an open mind. Nothing will be gained by bad-mouthing the situation confronting us. With that in view, we would like all of you to pick up one of the bumper stickers on the table as you go out. It says 'Evolve or Dissolve.' I hope all of you will take that suggestion to heart. And now Mr. Rollins has a final word for you."

Mr. Rollins stepped forward and in a very serious voice said, "I got an anonymous phone call this morning. The caller warned me that Dean was sending some white thugs over to Lincoln, and if they were antagonized they could cause trouble, so we'd better watch our step." He paused a moment and looked out over the crowd. "So I told the caller that we already have plenty of black thugs of our own, so we didn't need to borrow any from Dean."

That got a good laugh.

After the meeting, I approached Mr. Rollins to see if I could swap my noisy room next to the cafeteria for one in a more tranquil location. I reasoned that as I was no longer low man on the totem pole, I deserved a more prestigious site. I didn't actually verbalize that we could foist my old room off on one of the unsuspecting Dean teachers and no one would be the wiser, but his half-smile while I stumbled through my request made it clear that he got the message.

A short time later, I was delighted when Mr. Rollins informed me that I had been assigned Tommy Seaton's old room, number 39, as Tommy had also managed to upgrade. Tommy helped to transport my new desk to room 39—to the victor belong the spoils—and I in turn helped him move his desk to his new digs.

My new schedule gave me a homeroom and five classes of history, just like the previous semester. The good news was that I had the fourth period vacant, which meant no study hall duty during my lunch hour.

On Tuesday morning, seventh grade teachers assembled in Mr. Rollins's trailer and examined the registration cards of seventh graders in order to group them according to ability. Two hours later, we had ten sections of twenty-eight students each. After we'd finished, the band leader, Mr. Birks, stopped by the trailer to see how the distribution was going.

As he flipped through the cards, he said, "But you haven't put members of the band in a single section so they'll all have a free period every day to practice."

With some effort, I restrained the urge to shout: "Why in the hell didn't you point that out to us *before* we began?" We had to start over, separating the band members from the rest of the students and then rebalancing the classes. When we'd finished the second time we had placed eight white students and twenty black students in every class. Each class was 72 percent black and 28 percent white.

My next task was to collect the set of encyclopedias I had used during the semester. Wondering how books could travel so far, I ended up retrieving odd volumes from classrooms in the grammar school and high school as well as the junior high. That took a while, but I was glad to have it done, and I returned the entire set to the owner, Mr. Cain.

Since we were required to stay on campus and I had nothing else I needed to do, I decided to check on Michelle; she was in Bill Hayes's former room. When I got there and tapped on the door, no one answered, so I stepped into the room to find Michelle practically upside down with her head and upper body buried in a cardboard carton. Hearing my second and louder series of knocks, she pulled her head up, shook her hair out of her eyes, and gave me a feeble smile.

"I am not a happy camper," she announced.

"It'll get better," I promised.

"That's the only way it can go," she grumbled.

"What can I do to help you?"

"First you can tell me that it's not going to be as bad as Mrs. Bradham and the other white teachers say it will," she answered.

"When Mrs. Hadley, Anita, and I came here we said the same things Mrs. Bradham is saying. We don't say them anymore. You learn to roll with the punches." I stuck my hands in my pockets and wondered about pontificating. I decided to say what I thought and let the chips fall.

"We learned that our biggest enemy was our own attitude. Remember what Pogo used to say, 'I have met the enemy and he is us.' Once we went through a period of attitude adjustment, everything got better. You need to trust me on that one. If I hadn't had a group meeting with myself on this topic, I'd be one miserable SOB right now. I guarantee you that if Mrs. Bradham doesn't have that group meeting with herself real soon she's going to have one very long semester."

Then, thinking I was getting a little too serious, I went on, "Of course, you get a few razor and knife scars along the way." I rolled up my sleeve as if to show her. Her face had a look of horror until she saw I was kidding. "You'll survive, and then you'll laugh about it to the next rookie who shows up. Remember what Mr. Rollins says, 'Evolve or Dissolve.' Now, what can I do to help?"

"You can tell me what you think of my bulletin board," she answered.

I looked at the bulletin board on the wall beside the doorway. In the center of it, Michelle had pasted a large photo of football hero Joe Namath. She'd inscribed his jersey with mathematical symbols and was in the process of creating a robot out of geometric shapes. "Hey, that's neat. The kids will love it," I said. "You're very creative. Even if he is a white boy from Alabama," I added.

She smiled, pleased with my praise, and her shoulders relaxed a little.

"You'll do fine, Michelle," I said. "Remember, the kids will be just as leery of you as you are of them. Give 'em a chance. I'll be here if you need to unload on somebody."

"I may take you up on it. I appreciate your offer to help, but," she looked around the room, "I think I'd better do the unpacking and putting away myself, so I'll know where everything is."

I nodded. "When things settle down, we could go to a movie, or bowling or something."

"I'd like that," she answered. "Thanks for stopping by."

The lunchroom was closed, and I was hungry so I went to the nearest store for some takeout food. I bought hog's head cheese and a box of saltines. On returning I ran into Mr. Bibbs, and after I showed him my purchases he decided that he, too, was hungry. We went to his office, where he made a pot of coffee, and the two of us had a glorious lunch. I told him about my talk with Michelle.

"Now, aren't you the pot calling the kettle black?" he asked with eyebrows raised. Then he smiled. "I guess you're entitled—as an honorary brother. Are any of our new recruits brother material? Some of them look pretty hopeless right now."

"Yeah, they do," I agreed, "but who knows. There might be a couple of white niggers in the bunch. We'll have to wait and see. Remember: 'Evolve or Dissolve.'"

We shared a good laugh.

Wednesday, the seventh grade students came in for a brief period—ostensibly to get their schedules, but primarily so we could get an accurate head count. No one knew how many white students from Dean would actually show up. After the students had been dismissed, Mr. Birks informed us that he not only wanted all band members in one section but that he wanted that section to have third period vacant. It took three hours of rescheduling to accommodate him. Then, after lunch, he advised us he'd changed his mind. Since the academic abilities of band members were so diverse, he didn't want them all in the same section. By then we were numb and wanted to throttle him. At afternoon's end and one final try, we brought the classes back to some semblance of grouping by ability. With the final reshuffling, I ended up with a homeroom and first-period history class with twenty-six students: twenty black, six white. There was only one white girl in the class. This caused considerable discussion, but we finally decided to let the distribution stand. We were too tired to make any more changes; we felt that no matter what we did, someone would be unhappy.

As I had volunteered to work as an ongoing member of the core group that was responsible for arranging schedules, I had gained the reputation of being unusually magnanimous—a Vince Lombardi team player. Actually, I had a more nefarious motive: by being in on the ground floor, I was able to rid my classes of as many troublemakers as possible. I was sure that last year at this time another group of "self-sacrificing" teachers had had the same motive, which explained why I had so many students like Fisheye in my classes. I laughed as I tried to imagine Mrs. Bradham trying to cope with Fisheye or Stanley.

The cafeteria was closed for lunch Wednesday, so I invited Mrs. Hadley to my apartment for a sandwich. She rode with me, and I parked in front of my modest abode. As we stood a moment on the little stoop, I pointed in the direction of Deer Creek.

"You can't actually *see* the creek from here," I said. "If I could see the creek my apartment would be considered creek-front property, and I couldn't afford it. But at least I know it's there and can walk over whenever I want to."

"It's a lovely location," she said. "How lucky for you it was available."

Despite being somewhat dismayed by my bachelor housekeeping, she was good-natured about it. "I'd say your place needs a keeper," she mused aloud. "A female keeper?"

"Not yet," I said. "Unless she happens to be self-supporting."

While I made sandwiches, she found glasses and fixed the spiced tea she'd brought. Then we sat at my little kitchen table and, as we ate, had a good chat about how amusing it was going to be to watch the unfolding drama. We agreed that, so far, our new colleagues were doing little to make the transition easier on themselves.

"They need a wakeup call," I said. "Have you ever heard the story about the farmer who dealt with his stubborn mule with a two-by-four? He said that first he needed to get the mule's attention—then he could teach him something."

"I guess we had to be hit with a two-by-four, didn't we. On the whole, I think you, Anita, and I did pretty well," she said. "I had further to go than you two. I'm just as glad not to be new and have to go through it again."

"Yeah, we got thrown to the lions and survived, and we did learn something. Like Caesar said to the gladiators: let the games begin. I'm sure glad we know how to play the game."

"I hope we do!" she answered.

Thursday was spent finishing schedules for eighth grade. Again, students were brought in to get an accurate head count. Scheduling the eighth graders turned out to be more difficult than seventh graders because we had fewer whites to distribute throughout the section. There were eighty for seventh grade but only thirty for eighth grade, and many classes ended up having only two or three white students. Ranking by ability was discarded in order to comply with the mandate that we create racial balance. Schedules were changed again and again, and finally we established a distribution that pleased no one but which none of us had the energy or will to object to. Shortly before I went home, Mr. Rollins gave me a key to my new room. For me it was proof that there really would be a second semester, and that I would be a part of it.

On Friday, January 30, the ninth grade came to enroll. There were 66 white students and 192 black students. Since ninth grade teachers worked on the scheduling, the rest of us were free. After lunch, faculty members were called to a surprise meeting in the auditorium at Dean, where Mr. Woolly gave us a stern lecture.

"It behooves all of us to be aware of what we say to outsiders concerning any problems we face," he said in a serious voice. "This has been a difficult time for everybody connected with the school system, but we need to be circumspect in our comments out in public. Above all, be wary about talking to the press. There is enough gossip circulating without our adding to it. Don't be part of the problem." He concluded with an exhortation to do the best we could under trying circumstances. As I was leaving, I happened to be behind Mr. Bibbs, who was giving a dressing-down to one of the new white faculty members.

"I heard you refer to one of our teachers as 'colored,'" Mr. Bibbs said. "Many of us take offense at that term. If you must use a color designation, it would be more acceptable to call us 'blacks.'"

The white teacher listened to this piece of advice while staring at the floor as he walked along. He didn't answer, but his red face indicated that he resented the reprimand. He felt helpless and subservient. I was surprised and somewhat disappointed at Mr. Bibbs's bluntness. If there was anything we didn't need at this juncture, it was fostering the antagonism between Lincoln's black teachers and the white newcomers.

27

Monday, February 2, was the first day of the new semester, and we had met the court's and Mr. Bigham's deadline for school desegregation—something that even the most optimistic among us had considered doubtful. Now desegregation would be accomplished when school started at 8:00 this morning. Joe Tex's "Show Me" blared from the radio of the car next to mine as we waited for the traffic light. Oblivious of me and anything else around him, the young, black male driver beat time to the music with his hand on the steering wheel. When the light changed, he zipped in front of me. He looked old enough to be a senior in high school. If he was a senior, he would find that his upcoming semester at Dean would be different from the one he would have had if he hadn't been uprooted from Lincoln.

The drive from my quiet apartment along tranquil Deer Creek was no preparation for the bedlam that greeted me when I entered Lincoln Attendance Center. Students by the dozens milled about the halls, ignorant of the location of their assigned homeroom. We should have posted monitors to direct traffic, but that was one detail we overlooked. When I entered my own homeroom, thirty smiling faces greeted me, but only two of them actually belonged there. Twenty-eight made their exit to join the confusion in the hall, while others drifted in. The usual twenty minutes allowed for homeroom had stretched to two and a half hours by the time all the students had found their assigned rooms.

After my students had seats to match my chart, I issued their books. As the white students came to get books, I concentrated on matching names and faces. I already knew the twenty-three black students.

"And now," I beamed when all had settled down, "would you like my short sermon on good behavior in my classes, or the long version?"

That drew a blank. "OK," I continued, "good behavior means that you hold up your hand for permission to speak, that you do not disturb students around you, and that you come to class ready to work." What a pipe dream, I thought to myself.

"For tomorrow's lesson, read the chapter on the start of the Middle Ages, which begins on page 187 in your textbook." I waited a few moments while they wrote the page number in a notebook. "Since we only have a few minutes left, I'd like to have some suggestions about how you think we should decorate our bulletin board."

Twenty-three black and seven white faces switched from me to the bulletin board and back to me. No one spoke.

"Well," I said, "I guess we can decide on that later. How are you new students liking school so far?"

Silence.

"Does everyone have lunch money?" I was starting to feel a little edgy.

Silence.

"I bet you had fun being out of school for the last couple of weeks. Did any of you go on a trip or do anything unusual during the holidays?"

Silence.

Enough already! Give me a break, kids!

"How about sports? Anybody here play on a team? Basketball, football?"

Silence.

Ring, bell! Ring! I pleaded.

The twenty minutes usually allotted to homeroom had always passed so swiftly, I could never get everything done that was necessary. Now, when there was nothing to do, I had all the time in the world to listen to my students but was confronted by silence.

"Let's talk about our favorite historical character," I said, trying to keep the rising frustration from turning my voice into a squawk. "Anybody got a suggestion?"

I was saved by the bell! Never had that discordant clang sounded so heavenly. Now it was time to teach history again.

Mr. Rollins called a faculty meeting in the library after school that afternoon. Michelle was already seated when I got there, and white teachers were occupying chairs on either side of her, so I sat a few rows behind. "We need to come together as a group, and each of us needs to work harder than ever to make this merger a success," he exhorted us. As his pep rally continued, I saw some of the white faculty members making eye contact with each other. You could almost read their minds: "Who does this black so-and-so think he is, lecturing us like this?"

Michelle waited for me after the meeting, and we walked down the hall together.

"Are you getting to know any of your black colleagues yet?" I asked.

"I was hoping some of them would stop by my room, but no such luck," she said. "I can tell you that the Mrs. Bradhams of the lot are griping about everything."

"Integration is a done deal," I answered. "They'd better get with the program. If not, they'd better leave teaching. Can I give you a piece of advice?"

She nodded vigorously.

"Don't get tied in with that bunch. Reach out to some of the black teachers. You may discover you really do like them."

She looked at me with eyebrows raised in disbelief. Then seeing the set expression on my face, she sighed, then nodded. "I'll try, but they've got to meet me halfway."

"Good. I think you're going to find they will." I patted her on the back. "Let's do something Friday night. Movie?"

"Are you only going to ask me out if I behave like you think I should?" she grumbled.

"No. That invitation had nothing to do with your behavior."

"In that case, OK. Seven?"

I nodded.

For the rest of that first day and for the next couple of days, the halls often had more students than the classrooms. Several of the buses were still out of commission while mechanics tried to repair the damage caused by the anonymous thug who had put sugar in the gas tanks. The buses that did run had to make several trips back and forth to gather all the children. The weather during this period was rainy and cold, causing the dirt roads to be either muddy and slick or icy and slick. This slowdown in busing meant that children were arriving at school at different times of the day and didn't know where they ought to be, so they milled about in the halls. Before lunch one day I found myself with two classes filling my room at the same time.

One group was supposed to go to study hall, but that room hadn't yet been assigned. Therefore, they had nowhere to go. I guess I should have been flattered that they picked my room to invade. The two groups were surprisingly well behaved, finding the novelty of sitting two to a seat to be fun.

This pleasant hiatus was short lived. In the class that followed there were two poorly dressed, loud-talking white girls. When I called the roll after the bell rang, a Vertis Ethridge appeared to be absent. The other two girls poked at each other knowingly. Ten minutes into the class, Mrs. Levison came into the room, trailed by a rebellious-looking white girl. She was thin and had stringy, dirty-looking blond hair. Her skirt was too short, her top too tight. I indicated a vacant seat for her to take. Her eyes darted around the class before she decided to sit down. Mrs. Levison motioned for me to step out into the hall.

"David, I just wanted to warn you. This girl was in my office because she walked out of her last class complaining that some black boy was winking at her and making suggestive remarks."

I did a double take. "Really? I doubt that I would wink at her if she and I were stranded together on a desert island!"

Mrs. Levison nodded. "She wishes she could be so lucky! This one is going to be trouble."

"Just what we need!" I sighed. "A fourteen-year-old tramp with a bad attitude who thinks she's twenty-five."

"Good luck," Mrs. Levison said.

When I reentered the classroom, the newcomer, Vertis Ethridge, was holding court with some of the other white girls, ignoring my presence.

"I guess I showed them," she maintained. "I'm gonna make these coons sorry they ever saw Vertis Ethridge, and my daddy told me if they give me any trouble, he's coming up to this school and whup some ass."

Pretending not to have heard her comments, I walked over to my desk and took up the lesson where I had left off.

This didn't deter her. "My daddy owns a gun, and he'll use it if he has to," she muttered.

As I continued to ignore her and bore down on the lesson, her comments became directed at me.

"He's not one of us. He was here first semester before they made us come," she muttered aloud. "He likes these people."

Vertis became irritated that I didn't acknowledge her. "You saw this teacher talk to that jungle bunny counselor. I think he likes that type. I hear he's a nigger lover."

Our contest continued through the rest of the period. I was determined to teach; she was equally determined to annoy me. When the bell rang, I was glad that she hadn't had the satisfaction of disrupting the class.

I saw Mrs. Levison later. "You're right," I told her. "That girl's middle name is spelled T-R-O-U-B-L-E."

"I found out who the student was that set her off to begin with," Mrs. Levison answered. "Charles Robinson."

I shook my head. "Up to his childish antics trying to impress the new girl." I told Mrs. Levison about his efforts in the first semester to impress Gloria Hampton when she had transferred into school two months before.

"That was cute when he was trying to impress a black girl, but his innocent prank with Vertis could create a white backlash that none of us wants," she said.

I heartily agreed.

Between classes I got a visit from my old friend, Eugene "Fisheye" Watson. "It sure is good to be back in school, ain't it, Mr. Beck?" Without waiting for an answer, he hurried on. "I need to talk to you about something. All my teachers is recommendin' I be promoted to the eighth grade. You know I been in the seventh grade before."

"Yes, I remember that," I said, straight-faced.

"The only teacher that ain't recommended me for eighth grade is you. If you will, they got to let me go."

It took some effort for me not to strangle him. I did manage to purse my lips and nod in a serious manner. "I'll think about it, Eugene," I promised.

"Thank you, suh!"

After lunch, I dropped by the teachers' lounge for a few minutes and joined several of the teachers who were sitting around comparing notes. "Guess who paid me a visit?" Tommy Seaton tossed into the give-and-take.

"Who?" we chorused.

"Fisheye," Tommy answered. "Looked me straight in the face and told me that all of his other teachers were recommending that he be promoted to the eighth grade. 'You is the only holdout,' he said, 'and that's what's keeping me from being promoted.'"

Mrs. Little, Mrs. Hadley, and I hooted with laughter. "I thought I was the only holdout!" said Mrs. Little for all of us.

Gwen Stewart, who'd popped in and heard the end of the discussion, said, "At least Fisheye is awake. Ruby Drain went to sleep in my class and snored so loud I had to stop my lecture and wake her up."

"Your class must really be a doozy!" Pearlie Brantley said, giving Gwen a friendly whack on the back.

The following morning I received my second visit from Fisheye.

"You give any thought to what we talked about yesterday?" he asked.

"Yes I have, Eugene. You didn't do too well in the seventh grade, and I don't think moving you up the eighth grade would be a good idea." I didn't see the need to mention my knowledge of his visits to the other teachers. "So I guess I'll be seeing you in my history class. OK?"

"Geez, Mr. Beck. You're the only one keepin' me back," he grumbled, and shuffled out of the room. He didn't show up for my class, and I heard that he didn't put in an appearance for the classes of the other teachers either. That afternoon I saw Charles Robinson in the hall. "Have you seen Fisheye?" I asked him.

"Yessir, Mr. Beck, I sure did," Charles answered. "He says he's not going to any class again 'til he gets promoted to eighth grade where he belongs. He told me to tell you that."

The next day I saw Eugene loitering in the hall. "I missed you in history today," I told him. "You can't just come to school every day and hang around in the hall. I'm going to have to report you to Mr. Bibbs."

With no reply, he turned his back and walked off down the hall and, I heard later, left the school. His boycott lasted a week. Then, Eugene appeared in my class and took his seat as if he'd been there since the semester started.

The following week, Mr. Bibbs told me that Fisheye and a cohort, Earl Wheatley, would not be in class for a while.

"Has his boycott resumed?" I asked.

"No, this is a different problem," he said grimly. "He and Earl were caught extorting money from some of the white students—threatening to hurt them if they didn't pay up." He shook his head. "That boy will come to no good end."

Later I heard that Fisheye and his sidekick were caught stealing lunches from kids in the grammar school. Both were expelled for two weeks.

28

Problems with blacks extorting money from whites weren't limited to Lincoln Attendance Center. At a faculty meeting, Mr. Rollins told us of a telephone call he received from John Ward, the white principal at Dean.

"Mr. Ward told me they had a big problem over there. Black students at Dean are extorting money from the white students—a dollar seems to be the going rate—threatening violence if the whites don't pay up. I told him that we had had the same problem here and that we took very quick action. The guilty students were expelled.

"He objected that this sounded pretty extreme, but I said if you let those students get away with that kind of behavior, you're asking for more serious trouble down the line. I told him that firm accountability right at the beginning of school heads off trouble in the future." Mr. Rollins shrugged. "Maybe that was out of line, but I was telling him like it is."

In the midst of these problems, a flu epidemic hit the schools, laying low both teachers and students. Teachers who were still able to stand up in front of a class took up the slack for those too sick to teach. I had ten extra students in each of my classes. And since troubles come in threes, we waited for the third disaster to occur. Occur it did. Someone broke into Mr. Rollins's trailer and stole all the lunch tokens. The door to the safe had been pried open, and the contents were scattered over his office and down the hall. Since the theft might have been racially motivated, Mr. Rollins called investigators from the Leland Police Department.

During dinner-table talk on a weekend home, I described for my parents the detective who came to investigate the crime. "White, overweight, middle-aged—a parody of the redneck, southern police officer. He reminded some of us of Obie, the policeman whom Arlo Guthrie satirized in *Alice's Restaurant.*"

I went on to describe how the detective spent the morning investigating every inch of the office trailer with a magnifying glass and his fingerprint kit.

"Did they find the culprit?" my mother asked.

I shook my head. "Never did."

Daddy shook his head. "Isn't it a shame so much time has to be spent on things like that instead of teaching kids how to read and write!"

After we'd cleaned up the kitchen that evening, I decided to visit my old haunt, Strazi's drive-in, and see if anyone I knew was there. Since this was Greenville and not Leland, Mr. Bigham wouldn't be driving around to police the parking lots, so I felt relatively safe from his watchful eye. Although it was winter and too cold for people to eat in their cars, I sat a moment in the parking lot recalling a typical summer scene that was a staple of every small southern town: cute girls in short skirts bringing trays of food and beverages out to the parked cars; friends jawing with each other through open car windows; neon signs blinking on and off; car radios blaring; boys trying to impress dates with how sophisticated they were. Joe Strazi, called "Mr. Joe" by the regulars, encouraged the local police to drive by from time to time to spot underage drinkers or troublemakers. Life had been pretty simple then.

The taproom was crowded, over-warm, and the Rolling Stones' rendition of "Honky Tonk Women" blared from the jukebox in the corner. I ordered a beer at the counter and, while looking around for a place to sit, heard above the din someone call my name. A waving hand helped me locate the caller. I made my way to a corner table and hailed two high school football players who had been classmates of mine.

"Son of a bitch!" Dennis exclaimed. "Where you been hidin'?"

"C'mon, pull up a chair," Ronnie said.

I borrowed a chair from the next table and sat down. "Didn't expect to see you guys," I said. "I didn't know who I'd find here."

"We're here every Saturday night," Dennis said, "just like the old days in high school."

"How 'bout that State football team this year?" I asked. "You guys just don't know how lucky you are to play in the big leagues. I can't tell you how bad my dad wanted me to get a scholarship like y'all got."

"Wasn't no big deal," Ronnie said, his gray eyes evasive.

"A four-year scholarship! The hell it wasn't!" I countered. "It gave you the springboard to all kinds of jobs."

In looking from one to the other, I noted that the muscular physiques that had been their hallmark in high school had changed subtly. Weight had been added to midsections, and the lean, chiseled faces that had been the envy of the rest of us were fuller than I remembered.

"You must have had your choice of job offers when you finished," I said enviously. "What are you doing now?"

Ronnie's shoulders hunched defensively. "I'm working on one of Bilbo Williamson's towboats. Dennis is over at the oil mill."

"Really?" I frowned, puzzled. "But you had a ticket to do anything you wanted," I blundered on.

"Only if you finish college," Dennis said in a flat voice. He sat back and stuffed his hands into his pants pockets.

"We both flunked out, but," he winked at Ronnie, "we had a hell of a time doing it, didn't we?"

That stopped the conversation for a few moments.

"Geez, I'm sorry to hear that," I answered lamely, wishing I could think of something to say that wouldn't sound patronizing or phony. Instead, I drained my glass and suggested another beer.

They readily agreed. I turned and signaled the bartender to bring three more.

"You're the one who always made the grades," Dennis went on with a touch of belligerence. "The best jobs always go to guys like you. By the way," he added, "whatcha doing now?"

"Teaching school," I answered.

They both nodded. "That figures—not bustin' your butt like we are." Ronnie smiled.

"You always were into that academic shit. You teachin' at Greenville High or the Academy?"

"No," I answered, "I'm teaching in Leland. Lincoln Attendance Center." I waited for what I knew was coming.

Their mouths dropped open. "You teachin' in that nigger school?" Ronnie was incredulous.

"Sure am," I answered matter-of-factly. "Seventh grade history."

Dennis looked at me with pity. "And that's what your college degree got you?" He shook his head. "Can't say that's much improvement over the oil mill."

While drinking our second beer we made several attempts to keep the conversation going with questions about what some of our classmates were doing now, but it was uphill work. Their disbelief—and scorn—that I was stuck teaching in a black school was so obvious that I decided it was time to end the uncomfortable encounter. On the way back to my car, I compared those two with some of the black teachers at Lincoln that I had come to know and like, and these former football players came out way down on the list of people I wanted to engage.

~

I had hoped that the first week of school was a shakedown period, that the kinks had been worked out. Not so. The theft of the lunch tokens complicated all the lunch periods. Teachers were required to stand at the head of the cafeteria line and indicate to the cafeteria attendant who had paid for lunch and who was entitled to a free lunch. It was interesting to note that in my classes only one white girl applied for a free lunch. Mr. Rollins told me privately that many of the white students had had free lunches while attending Dean but were reluctant to let blacks see that they lived as close to the poverty line as the blacks they ostracized.

I was shocked at the level of poverty of some of the white families. After rebuking Marvin Broussard for wearing his hair long and unkempt, I was in turn rebuked by another white teacher, who told me that Marvin's family couldn't afford a haircut for him. Another white teacher informed me that Joyce Bancroft, an slovenly white student in my 7B class, lived until recently with her family in a shack so dirty and decrepit it had been considered an eyesore. Some of Leland's wealthier citizens, motivated by a desire to rid the town of this disgusting shack, had built another house for the family. I soon discovered, however, that Joyce would most likely continue to perpetuate this cycle of poverty; she read at about a second grade level.

~

Some of the black students were making genuine efforts to be friendly to the new white students. James Hurse, in particular, went out of his way to take up for whites when his black friends criticized them. They retaliated by calling him an "Uncle Tom." The whites thought James was patronizing.

Puzzled and disheartened, James came to me and asked, "Why don't the white kids like black people?"

His dilemma presented me with a challenge—one that had little to do with formal education, but one that needed to be addressed with honesty. It was education about life.

As a new teacher a few months earlier, I would have been embarrassed to respond. Now, my comfort level to speak out about race had increased and I could discuss the topic without distress.

"James, there are ignorant people on both sides of the fence. Prejudice is never rational. You must form your own self-image in your mind. That image is the one that's important, not the image these ignorant people thrust on you. You know who you are—that you're a fine student and a good person. Be proud of yourself, and make your parents proud of you. Don't pay attention to these people who try to pull you down."

James looked at his feet, stuck his hands deep in his pockets, and mumbled, "That's what my mama told me too, but what those white people say hurts. It hurts bad. I haven't done nothing to them to make them not like me. I was trying to be friends, but they keep backin' off and being mean."

That gave me pause. How could I explain that poor whites felt threatened by blacks who were trying to better themselves? Education was the key to advancement, and with education it would be the blacks who would take away the jobs reserved presently for whites on the lower economic scale.

I hurt for him, but my hurt was a fleeting emotion. I hoped James wouldn't let his hurt color his feelings for all whites from now on.

About a week later I got a letter from James that expressed his feelings about his life.

7C

James Hurse
Feb. 27, 1970

If I had three wishes

If I had three wishes thing I will wish for is a good house to live in so that when I married my wife would wish for a pretty house. All wives should have a good hard working husband. That was what I had plan to be. I want my wife to be happy. with lots of good thing to wear. I hope I will be married when I'm about 28 years old.

The second thing I wish for is to finish high school and go to college. When I finish college I want to be a doctor and have lots of friends to work with white or black. Help people with some of there problems if I could.

The last thing I would wish for now is a little Mini Trail to ride on, to go hunting with, and let my friends ride it. I can go up town when I want to. I would make lots of friends. Then I would be happy.

That's all I wants.

Another example of white bigotry erupted soon after James's experience. Debra Philips, a white student, publicly called Earl Wheatley a curly-headed monkey after he tried to befriend her. I witnessed the exchange and knew that Earl had done nothing to provoke this attack. With the other students looking on, I spanked her hands.

She, of course, burst into tears, which seemed to be available whenever she needed them.

I ignored them. "We do not call each other ugly names!" I said to her, then looked around and added, "That goes for everybody in this room."

As soon as the class was over, Debra made a beeline for Mr. Rollins's office. She demanded to call her parents. They drove over to the school, at which time I was summoned to Mr. Rollins's office. The parents and I confronted each other, and I explained what had happened. Debra's parents' dress, speech, and chip-on-the-shoulder aggressiveness immediately identified them as low class. Her father had that long-haired, Brylcreem look that had been popular in the fifties. It was obvious that they had come prepared to verbally let me have it. Their attack on me had just begun when Mr. Rollins intervened.

"Name-calling is not allowed in this school," he said in a determined voice. "That is the school policy. Debra knew it, and yet, in front of the whole class, she called the boy a spiteful name though he had done nothing to offend her. Mr. Beckwith witnessed the whole incident."

Although Debra dredged up more tears, her mother had obviously been down that road before and said they would withhold some privileges from their daughter to punish her. To save some face, she added: "I think it would have been better to have sent her to the office instead of punishing her in front of the class."

I should have reminded her that Debra had called Earl an ugly name in front of that same class.

Mr. Rollins and I parted with the parents on what I thought were even-tempered terms, but not so. John Woolly in the administrative office at Dean High School told me that Debra's parents had called him immediately upon arriving home to demand that I be disciplined by the school board. Having tamped down that brushfire, Mr. Woolly decided that, from now on, Mr. Rollins or Mr. Bibbs would handle punishment of white female students. I was told that Debra's parents were livid that they had lost face in a verbal battle with that "nigger principal" and that "nigger-loving history teacher." Their daughter's transgression, it seemed, was of secondary importance to them.

～

Neither the academic level nor the conduct level improved at Lincoln with the introduction of white students. Many of the incoming white students seemed to have the same second or third grade reading ability that I had encountered with many of my black students. As far as differences in behavior, for a period right after the integration of Lincoln the black troublemakers seemed to conduct themselves better, perhaps playing a waiting game to see how the white students would behave. By the second week of the new semester, however, it was business as usual.

Up until then I had never seen mean, vicious behavior to equal that of three white girls, Vertis Ethridge, Debra Philips, and Joyce Bancroft (the Unholy Triumvirate, I called them). Joyce matched the intelligence level and behavioral patterns of the other two. As if it were a curse, the unholy three were inflicted on me every day during homeroom and first-period class.

The thought of facing these girls cast a pall over me when I woke up every school day, and as I drove to work I had visions of being rescued from them. Maybe a traveling band of gypsies would kidnap them and they would never be seen again. Maybe white slavers would take them to some foreign land or they would join a carnival passing through town. Maybe the three would be diagnosed with some untreatable malady that prevented them from coming in contact with other human beings. These fantasies danced in my head every morning as I drove to work, but each morning when the bell rang there they were, eyeing the room, looking for an opportunity to cause disruption.

Alas, the Unholy Triumvirate didn't even have the common decency to get sick occasionally. They were the healthiest kids in the class. I decided that their strength and good health came from tormenting others. They spread malicious gossip about each other, and when they tired of that they spread the same lies about anyone else against whom they had a momentary grudge. They would then concoct lies about every girl in the class.

For example, Joyce started a whispering campaign that students were re-questing transfers out of my first-period class because of Marvin Broussard's evil past. Hearing one of these rumors, I went to Mrs. Levison's office to check Marvin's file. I learned that Marvin's picture in his file had been taken at a California reform school, that his brother had been incarcerated in the same reform school, and that his sister had been arrested for streetwalking. I never found out how much Joyce had actually learned of his troubled past. I suspected she took a very sketchy bit of gossip or knowledge and then em-bellished it to suit her purposes. Whichever it was, Marvin was not reformed in reform school, and soon he was expelled for chasing a black boy across the football field, threatening him with a knife. With his record of violent be-havior, if he had found out that Joyce was spreading malicious gossip about him, her life really could have been in danger.

For the members of the Unholy Triumvirate it was one petty offense after another—showing up at school with a skirt so short that she had to be sent home, accusing another student of stealing her fountain pen, opening the textbook to find the answers during a test, walking out of class and reporting to Mr. Rollins's office that I was allowing fellow students to write malicious notes about her—these three cried "Wolf!" so often that no one paid any at-tention to them.

29

It was a beautiful, cloudless Saturday morning, and I had the whole weekend to look forward to—no papers to grade, no chores that needed to be done. I slept late, made coffee, and went out to get the paper, still barefoot and in my gym shorts. I picked up the paper and paused to look at the azure blue of the sky and take a deep breath of the crisp clean air. Nothing, I decided, could put a damper on such a perfect day. As I gazed toward Deer Creek, a pickup turned the corner and came slowly down my street, the driver peering out as if looking for the number on a house. The truck was heavy, moderately old, with a gun rack showing in the back window. It wasn't the kind of truck a weekend warrior like me would buy.

To my surprise, the driver of the truck pulled into my driveway, cut the engine, and got out. Bemused, still half asleep, I stood there watching him.

"You David Beckwith?" he said, walking toward me.

I nodded. Involuntarily, I stuck out my hand. "Anything I can help you with?" I asked.

He was a wiry man, not as tall as I. He had thinning gray hair, wore wire-rimmed glasses, and was dressed in khakis and a clean but somewhat rumpled striped shirt. What struck me was the severe cold look in his soulless blue eyes. The thought that this wasn't a guy I want to be on the wrong side of flashed through my mind.

"I'm De La," he said.

I frowned, trying to remember where I'd heard that name. Then it hit me.

My God! Byron De La Beckwith, the notorious white supremacist who had made national headlines a few years earlier when he had been unsuccessfully prosecuted for the murder of the civil rights leader Medgar Evers, was now standing at my front door.

Our family had spent years denying any kinship to Byron. The facts of that famous case had been national news in 1963. Prominent black NAACP field officer Medgar Evers had pulled into his driveway in Jackson, Mississippi, after a long day's work. As he stepped out of his car, gunfire shattered the late-night silence. Evers was shot in the back. Bleeding from his wound, he'd dragged himself onto his front porch, where his wife, Myrlie, and his three children hovered over him, helplessly watching him bleed to death. The authorities had arrested Byron as the suspected assassin despite the fact that no one had actually seen him pull the trigger. The murder weapon found at the scene of the crime was registered to Byron De La Beckwith. He was well known in the Jackson area for his militant racist beliefs and his affiliation with various white supremacist groups such as the Ku Klux Klan.

The case became a media circus. Two highly publicized trials occurred in 1964 before all-white juries. Both ended in mistrials as a result of hung juries. Reports circulated that De La, feeling he was invulnerable, would boast at Klan rallies that he had killed Evers. He was even quoted as saying that killing Evers had given him "no more inner discomfort than women endure when giving birth."

Now here I was, face to face with this murderer. Just minutes before, I had rejoiced in this lovely Saturday morning, thinking that nothing could go wrong! Now I was worrying why this hero of racists had sought me out.

"Mind if I come in?" he asked.

"Sure," I answered shakily. "I just made a pot of coffee."

He gave my place the once-over as he stood inside the front door. "I heard there was a Beckwith living in Leland, and I thought as long as I'm here on business I'd stop by and see if they was right."

"Who is they?" I asked tentatively.

"Al Karls at Moeller," he replied.

I breathed a sigh of relief. Moeller Manufacturing was owned by the father of my best friend and college roommate, Dick Peterson, and I had dated Al Karls's daughter from time to time. Maybe this was a social call, not a "business" appointment stimulated because of my job at Lincoln.

"Y'know, all us Beckwiths are kin to one another," he went on, "so I thought I'd stop by and see you for myself. It never hurts to know another Beckwith. I'm a good person for you to know, too. You can't ever tell when you might need me or my friends in the cause of freedom. We have to protect our way of life at all costs from the mongrel nigger aggressors."

I remained speechless. Please, Lord, let him forget to ask me what I do for a living, I silently implored.

"I know our way of handling problems isn't for everybody," he continued, "but if you could ever see your way clear to help us, we'd sure appreciate it. Your money would go to a good cause. We're fighting for white people everywhere."

At this point I attempted to explain to Byron that I was just starting out with my first job. I was careful not to mention what my first job was, that I barely made ends meet as it was, or that I probably wouldn't be in a position to be much help.

He didn't press me and finished his coffee, "I need to get on down the highway and head for home. I have a family history book with me that I'll loan you to read. I'll pick it up from you the next time I'm up this way," Byron volunteered.

I went out to the truck with him to fetch it, more to get him out of my house than because of any interest I had in the book. As he pulled out of my driveway, I thanked God that I'd been able to avoid disclosing my being a teacher in an all-black school.

As soon as his truck disappeared around the corner, I ran into my house and called my mother.

"Mama," I almost yelled into the phone. "You won't guess in a million years who has just had coffee with me." Without waiting for a response, I plowed on. "Byron De La Beckwith."

"David," she exploded. "You stay away from that man! He's dangerous! Do you hear me? My God! Why did he go to your house? You didn't encourage him to come back, did you? He's called me at my office, but I wouldn't return his calls! What did he want?"

"He said we were kin, and that us kinfolks have got to stick together. He left me a family history book to prove it. He threw out feelers to try to find out if I supported his cause. Don't worry, I think I managed to stay on the fence and not make him mad."

"I hope so," she answered, her voice shaking. "Those people are psychos. They make chills run up and down my spine. Bring me that book, and I'll give it to Dick's dad so Byron can pick it up at Moeller. I don't want him over at your house again!"

I called Dick's father myself. He offered me the use of the copier at his office to make a copy of the book. Mr. Peterson promised that the book would be returned to Byron.

So much for my carefree weekend!

30

Toward the end of the second week of school, two members of the Unholy Triumvirate, Joyce Bancroft and Vertis Ethridge, stayed after class one day to report to me that they were being forced to drop out of school. I managed to control my elation sufficiently to ask: "Being forced? How?"

"There's some nigger boys that keep comin' on to us in the hall. They keep puttin' their arms around us."

"Who are they?" I asked.

They shrugged. "We don't know their names. They all look alike," Joyce said. "We just can't stand for them to put their nasty hands on us."

I found it hard to put credence in their complaint. Neither of them was attractive by any stretch of the imagination, and both were slow on the up-take and overweight.

"Why don't you try ignoring them," I suggested. "They'll soon lose interest and move on to something else." Then I snapped my fingers as if I'd just thought of another good solution. "How about studying your lessons and getting involved in class discussions, and then you won't have time to think about those boys bothering you."

That wasn't what they wanted to hear. They rolled their eyes in a "we ought to have known he wouldn't understand" expression and meandered on down the hall.

As I watched them disappear into a crowd of students, I knew their threat to drop out was an empty one. Why? Because their parents wouldn't allow it. Was it because their parents longed for the girls to better themselves by staying in school? Not exactly.

As long as a child stayed in school until the age of sixteen, a family meeting the criteria for poverty-level income was eligible for free school lunches from HEW (Health, Education and Welfare Department); dependent Social Security; dependent stipend from the Welfare Department; dependent access to the County Health Department; and welfare commodities such as flour, cornmeal, cheese, sugar, rice, butter, dried beans, dried eggs, lard, and dried milk.

Parents had an economic interest in a child's maintaining attendance, even if that child learned nothing and spent his or her time disrupting the class. Did our founding fathers envision that public education would come to this?

～

Racial discord wasn't confined to the school environment. One Sunday morning I stepped out to pick up the morning paper and found taped to my door a note from a group calling themselves the Leland Chapter of the Americans for the Preservation of the White Race, which claimed to be a "legal chartered organization" with more than five hundred local members. The message was a venomous account of the supposedly skyrocketing crime rate in integrated schools. It urged all members of the "White race" to band together against the "limousine liberals" who live in "high rise downtown apartments" and "owe their high living to the labor of the White working man." These liberals, it claimed, sent their own children to private schools instead of giving them the "social enrichment" of "associating with Blacks in Mixed schools." It then predicted the horrors of "blackboard jungles of rape, gang beatings, extortion, dope, and senseless vandalism" that we as a society had to look forward to if we didn't join their organization and actively oppose "these warped and fuzzy minded creeps" who were promoting school integration (see Appendix 2).

I was really irritated that these people knew where I lived and were brazen enough to pay me a visit on a Saturday night. Could they be connected to De La? And did he instigate the planting of such a note on my door? I took the note to school Monday and made sure it received wide distribution among my peers in the faculty lounge. This action distressed the newly transferred white teachers and served to push me further from their camp. Although they might not condone what the note said, they were outraged that I, a white person, would show a black person how venomous and narrow minded members of the white race could be. Mrs. Hadley and Anita vocally supported my efforts and emphasized their own separation from that group which, just a few months ago, they would have joined.

The following Sunday morning I found another typewritten note on my door, this time from a group that identified itself as the National States Rights Party (NSRP). Based in Birmingham, Alabama, the NSRP was a neo-Nazi organization and Klan alternative whose beliefs were based on anti-Semitism and the hatred of African Americans. The note called the struggle of "White Christian America" a "racial civil war" and warned that the Jews intended to "murder our White race by pumping the animal jungle blood of Africa into the veins of God's specially created White race." Moderates, which it called "lukewarm cowards," were said to have been condemned by "Our Lord Jesus Christ" in the book of Revelation as being guilty of "treason to the White race," while white racists were "patriots" who were fighting "Black ape radicals" in a war that would determine "the survival of our race." It warned that "negroes only have contempt for Whites who are so degenerate as to betray their own kind and join the Black camp." It concluded that "lukewarm people" were being "forced to choose between the righteousness of White racism on God's side or the evil of the Jews and Negroes with their Satanic Black degeneracy, on the other side" (see Appendix 3).

This second note alarmed me even more than the first and brought home to me that the risk of teaching at Lincoln had escalated to a level that I never could have imagined. The last thing I wanted to do was spend the day alone in my apartment; I was grateful to have an escape. I ate a hasty breakfast, dressed quickly, and headed for my parents' home in Greenville. There, I hoped, routines and normality would offset the lurid images those two notes had planted in my mind. I didn't mention the notes to my parents. The threats would worry them extremely; anyway, they couldn't do anything about them.

Despite the pleasant interlude in Greenville, on returning to my apartment Sunday evening I couldn't repress certain memories of Klan activities. At the abandoned drive-in theater on Highway 82, the Klan had erected a burning cross during their rallies. And in 1961 my friend Donald Hayden had had a close call while visiting his grandmother in Philadelphia, Mississippi. Don had been mistaken for a Freedom Rider (Freedom Riders were activists who employed nonviolent strategies to challenge Jim Crow laws concerning buses in the South) and was abducted by the Klan. After a harrowing interrogation session, he was finally released.

On Monday morning I took the second scrawled message to school and showed it to my fellow teachers. This act alienated my white colleagues even more than my passing around the first one. Tuesday, before school began, Mr. Rollins approached me as I was about to enter my classroom.

"These notes are disturbing you, aren't they?" he asked.

"They sure as hell are," I answered. "These people are nuts. Now you understand why some of their children act the way they do."

"Keep this to yourself," Mr. Rollins said. "I don't want to make more out of it than it is, but I've got a black friend who's a patrolman at the police department. He owes me a couple, so I asked him to cruise by your house at night to keep an eye on things. He's circulated the word in the department."

"I really appreciate that. Makes me feel a hell of a lot safer. If I told you those thugs didn't worry me, you'd know I was lying through my teeth," I added.

"I know you would be," he answered. "But trust me, you'll be fine. I really think they're too yellow to pull something in the middle of town. I wouldn't put some sneaky vandalism past them, however," he nodded. Then he smiled. "And now, I've got something else to tell you, and you can tell as many people as you want to: I'm the father of a brand-new, nine-pound baby boy."

As I babbled my congratulations, he reached into a pocket and brought out a cigar.

"You've had more on your mind since school started than I suspected," I said, shaking my head.

He nodded. "I take this as a sign. Things are looking up."

∾

My power struggle with one of the Unholy Triumvirate was upped a notch one morning in February when Debra Philips came to class without pencil or pen to take a prescheduled test. Instead of taking the pencil offered by a classmate, she decided that the lack of a writing instrument excused her from taking the test. After I'd handed out the papers and the test had begun, she pulled out a book and began to read, murmuring the words aloud. This lasted until the period was half over, and she was furious that I had ignored her.

"I can't take the test because I don't have nothing to write with," she said aloud in a petulant voice.

"Good," I replied pleasantly. "That means that I'll have one less paper to spend time grading."

Realizing that I had the upper hand—temporarily—she accepted the offer of a pencil from Joyce Bancroft, another member of the Unholy Triumvirate. But she could not, of course, finish the test by the time the bell rang, and demanded additional time.

"Nope," I said. "You had your chance. You blew it."

The moment class was over, she streaked down the hall to Mrs. Levison's office and tearfully demanded that she be allowed to call her mother. Mrs. Levison complied, and she overheard Joyce's tearful account that Mr. Beckwith had not allowed her to take the test because she had no pencil.

During lunch, Mr. Rollins notified me that I had a call from Mrs. Philips. I rolled my eyes, and he shook his head in sympathy.

The call in his office began with a high-decibel scream. "I bought Debra a pencil. Why can't you keep up with it? This wouldn't be happening if it weren't for this goddamned integration, and people like you who are scared of those damned niggers."

"Mrs. Philips, may I—" I tried to interject.

"Liar!" screamed Joyce and Debra behind me, practically deafening me.

"Mrs. Philips, as I was about to say—" I tried again.

"Liar! Liar!" came the scream again.

Livid, I whirled on the two. "Shut up!"

I interrupted the tirade Mrs. Philips was dishing out by saying in a loud, carrying voice, "Let me finish! Debra never asked to borrow a pencil. I am a teacher, not a pencil salesman. It is not part of my job to follow your daughter around the building all day and make sure that her pencils are not lost or stolen."

Mrs. Philips became hysterical and slammed down the phone. As I turned to my tormenters, they scurried out of the office and down the hall, almost colliding with Mr. Rollins. "What's going on?" he asked, frowning.

I gave him a summary of what had happened.

"Whew!" he grimaced. "And here it is only February. What'll they think of next."

An hour later, Mr. Philips arrived at the school with his fists clenched and a pistol in his belt, determined to defend the family's besmirched honor. Mr. Bibbs, always on the lookout for troublemakers, spotted Mr. Philips before he entered the building.

"Sir, may I help you?" he asked politely. "You can't take a gun into the school building. I'll have to ask you to give it to me and come to the principal's office."

He spoke quietly but authoritatively.

Surprisingly, Mr. Philips complied without comment.

Once he had Mr. Philips in the office, Mr. Bibbs summoned Debra and me. Debra retold her version of the morning's events; I repeated mine. Since they differed substantially, I suggested asking two independent witnesses to give their accounts.

She insisted that white students be chosen. I went along with that. She picked Marvin Broussard and Gloria Hampton, believing they would lie to support her agenda. Much to her chagrin, the two agreed with my version of the morning's events.

Red-faced, disgruntled, Mr. Philips sat in a chair listening to their repudiation of his daughter's testimony. He seemed to deflate like a leaking balloon. He leaned over, defeated, frustrated, and rested his head in his hands. Without a word to his daughter, he got up and walked out of the room.

The rest of us resumed our daily routine until after school, when Mr. Rollins, Mr. Bibbs, and I rehashed the day's events. We all agreed that we'd had a narrow escape.

The day following her defeat, Debra was extremely polite and contrite. The sign of what she really thought, however, was a drawing that mysteriously appeared on my desk. I could never prove that it came from her, but we both knew this was her way of getting the last word.

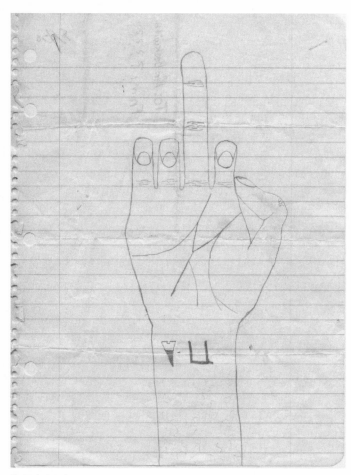

Debra's drawing

31

I wish I could say that racial tensions had abated as February came to a close, that all was sweetness and light at Lincoln between the newly trans-ferred white students and the entrenched blacks, but such was not the case. A minority—black and white—with extreme attitudes caused the ongoing problems that plagued the school. One day a white girl screamed at the top of her lungs all the way down the hall to Mrs. Levison's office. As a result, the hall filled with people thinking a crime had been committed. It turned out that the girl had imagined that some of the black boys were winking at her. Mrs. Hadley attempted to establish rapport by asking class members to write on a piece of paper the names of their classmates that they knew. It was reported to white parents that Mrs. Hadley was mandating that all students in her class associate with every other student in the class.

On another day Debra Philips dropped her lunchbox and broke the ther-mos, almost hitting a black girl on the foot in the process. She then went to the office during her study hall and called the dime store where it had originally been purchased to demand that the salesclerk replace the defec-tive thermos. Her next phone call was to her mother, who took her out of school to return the thermos to the store and get a new one. When Debra re-turned to campus she promptly slammed the replacement thermos against the school wall, stalked down to the office, and called both the dime store and her mother again. Her mother returned to school, picked Debra up, and returned to the dime store to get yet another thermos. They returned empty handed. The store manager told them that the store had sold out of thermos bottles and refunded their money. Debra tried to become the center of attention for the rest of the school day by bragging to the other white students that she had created an abbreviated school day.

Court challenges to judicial orders to integrate continued. Mr. Bigham, the superintendent of schools who had hired me and had exhorted me to keep an open mind and work for the betterment of the school, threw in the towel and announced his resignation effective June 1. The assistant superintendent, John Woolly, was named as his successor.

Our sports program was mangled. We were forced to reschedule basketball games because other teams refused to play Lincoln on our campus. Integration's impact on every aspect of school life was not just noticeable but dramatic. In a desperate effort to comply with the court mandate, Mrs. Levison, our counselor, and Heno Head, Dean's counselor, rotated daily between the two schools so that each would have both a white and a black counselor.

The racial issue came to bear on class lectures. At first I wasn't sure how to play to both white and black audiences simultaneously. My first few lectures were dreadful and appealed to neither. Before administering a test, I had to submit it to an independent, unbiased educator for review to ensure that it contained no racial material to anger either blacks or whites. After giving a test, I had to sign a statement declaring that I had reviewed all the questions with each class after the tests were graded. Mr. Rollins was ordered to file the test papers permanently in his office in case there were challenges from disgruntled parents or students. If this weren't enough, we were ordered to follow to the letter the suggested grade scale and not to curve grades in an attempt to establish a normal grade distribution. "Let the chips fall where they may" was in force.

~

Early in the semester, perceptions of who should be society's leaders and who should be followers hadn't changed. Despite the court mandate and the fact that my homeroom had only eight white students and twenty-two blacks, white students were disproportionately represented in the leadership ranks when class officers were elected. White students were elected president and treasurer, while blacks were elected to vice president, secretary, and sergeant at arms. If elections had been held a month later, after racial tensions had kicked into high gear, the outcome of the elections probably would have been the reverse. At this juncture, however, the black students were deferential to the whites simply because they were white, not because they deserved respect.

~

The many forms that racial sensitivity took was driven home to me by an incident I witnessed one morning before school. I was a short distance from the front entrance of the school when I saw ahead of me Shirley Foster, who, during my first semester, had been a beacon of light in my homeroom and first-period history class. She was always prepared, never misbehaved, and was a joy to teach. Yet here she was in an altercation with her black friend Samuel Ross. Their voices were loud and strident, and neither cared who overheard their heated discussion. As a final blast at Samuel before opening the front door, Shirley said triumphantly, "Well, at least I'm not as black as you are!"

I had never known how significant skin tone was to many blacks, yet seeing Samuel's hangdog look as he followed Shirley inside persuaded me that indeed shades of black did matter. The incident made me better understand how "light," "bright," or "high yellow" blacks were considered elite to other blacks—a new definition of "white nigger." I wanted to comfort Samuel, but I didn't know what to say. Besides, was there anything a white outsider such as myself could say that wouldn't send his self-esteem reeling to an even lower level?

As Samuel disappeared into the milling crowds, I didn't have time to reflect more on the endless grief the black/white issue had delivered to us. I had a problem of my own. In yesterday's mail I had received the notification that my draft deferment had been changed to reflect the results of the lottery. Deferments were now meaningless. My future would be totally dependent on the number assigned to my birthday by the lottery. Now I could possibly apply to graduate school. Despite my uncertain future, should I consider a second year at Lincoln? This was a thought I certainly wouldn't have entertained a few months previously. I felt that I needed someone to talk to, but I decided not to bother Mr. Rollins this early in the morning. He had enough on his mind just synchronizing the gears to get the school going for the day. So the problem took its place along with others at the back of my mind. Of more immediate concern was my homeroom and the first-period history class I was about to face.

Our lessons had covered the rise of the Roman Empire. We had discussed Rome's centuries of flourishing, and now, because of the breakdown in their defense system, we were approaching Rome's demise. I tried to make the attacks by the Persians from the east, by Germanic tribes from the north, and by Goths and Visigoths from the west as realistic as possible. I spoke of the stirring scenes of the Roman Legions trying in vain to stem the tide of invading barbarians, the loss to the Romans of Emperor Valens, and the final debacle when all was lost.

Were they interested? The boys seemed intrigued with the battle scenes and the uniform of a Roman Legionnaire. I had brought to class artists' renditions of things that I thought were pertinent. No one in the class seemed intrigued that the Romans gave us a Latin alphabet, the basis for all the Romance languages. They were indifferent to Roman numerals, the upright style of printing types used in modern texts. They ho-hummed to discussions of Rome's many architectural innovations, such as semicircular arches and domes. Probably few saw any connection to these people who lived so long ago.

~

Mrs. Hadley, Anita, and I called one group of teachers the Bradham Group. They were white teachers from Dean who had pretty much ignored us and stayed to themselves when they'd discovered that the three of us were on good terms with our black colleagues. Members of the Bradham Group were now calling upon us frequently for advice on how to deal with problems in their classrooms. I was shocked to discover that an active member of this group was Mrs. Woolly, the wife of our new superintendent. I had somehow expected her to remain politically neutral, since I thought her husband's career depended on this conversion being successful, but she took every opportunity to try to manipulate both factions at Dean and Lincoln by telling what she thought they wanted to hear. I sarcastically told Mrs. Hadley in private that Mrs. Woolly would have made a good southern politician.

"You know, David, our occupational designation as teachers is a misnomer," Mrs. Hadley said to me one day in the hall. "We should be listed on the syllabus as counselors. I think I'll start charging fees."

"I'm with you," I agreed. "Suddenly the Bradham Group wants us to be best buddies."

"My whole lunch period yesterday was spent listening to their complaints and handing out advice," she grumbled. Then she gave me a sidelong look. "I shouldn't be criticizing them, should I? They're no worse than I was five months ago. You listened to my gripes then, so I guess it's time for me to listen."

"You, Anita, and I have learned to be tolerant," I answered. "Maybe they will, too. I just wish the white students could see that behaving themselves is more productive than going out of their way to cause dissension and trouble."

~

Michelle and I were seeing each other more often—not only when our lunch periods coincided, but also at least once a week when one of us would invite the other to go out to a movie or come over for a meal. With my plans to go to graduate school fixed—I had been accepted at Ole Miss—we tried to keep each other at arm's length, but below the surface of good-natured joking and verbal give-and-take, sexual currents sometimes bubbled to the surface. One such occasion was her twenty-third birthday. We made a date, and I brought her a bottle of her favorite wine. When she opened the door to her apartment, I handed her my present and pecked her on the cheek. Michelle smiled with delight at the considerate gesture.

"You're so thoughtful," she murmured. "What have I done to deserve you?"

I shrugged. "Just your lucky day, I guess."

She looked at me, her eyes shining, then put her arms around my neck. I ignored my brain's "back off" signals. We clung to each other, then lingeringly kissed. It was so spontaneous, neither of us had had time to prepare. Finally, I let her go and she backed away. "I could get used to that," I said, my voice a little hoarse.

"I guess I was being a tease." Then she added: "I only do that on my birthday."

"Thank goodness," I sighed. "I wouldn't want this to become a habit."

We were back on the safe ground of verbal jousting.

When I had invited her out for her birthday, we'd decided to go to the restaurant where we'd eaten the first time after we'd met at the cleaners. And so we set out in the Rambler for Lillo's. Lillo's, a Leland institution, was an old white barnlike building with a steep-pitched roof. The front room, the bar with booths lining the wall, was crowded, so we headed for the dining room. We ordered the trademark pizza. I had a beer, Michelle ordered white wine.

It was always easy to find things to talk about, even though we mostly talked shop. It seemed that there was constantly some off-the-wall happening at school.

She confessed that teaching at Dean and Lincoln had opened her eyes to a new world, one that her overprotective father hadn't wanted her to see. The experiences she was having in the teaching profession had been the hardest of her life. "You never know from one day to the next what calamity or victory you'll encounter."

"How are you and the Bradham clique getting along?" I asked.

"We're polite, but at arm's length," Michelle answered. "I let it be known I wasn't going to join in their criticisms and put-downs, so they probably consider me a traitor." She shrugged. "Who cares? I don't."

"Good girl!" I smiled. "You having any trouble with some of the boys in your classes?"

"Making passes, you mean?" she asked.

I nodded.

"Oh, sure. I tell them they have a choice: sit down and behave, or I'll arrange an introduction to Mr. Bibbs's Black Power. That usually gets their attention real quick."

"You're a fast learner. Gee." I winked at her. "If I was sixteen and lucky enough to be in one of your classes, I'd fantasize about making a pass at you."

"I'd give you a choice. Sit down and behave, or you'll get introduced to Mr. Bibbs's Black Power."

My eyebrows rose. "I'd better watch my step!"

Giving me a sidelong look, she purred: "But we're not in class, are we."

"You got that right!" I exclaimed.

Because we had school the next day, we called it quits at 10:30 when I took her home. At the door, which I unlocked this time, I dropped the key into her hand. "As much as I like to come in, I'd better get going," I announced.

"I understand," she said sympathetically.

"That doesn't mean I can't kiss you good night, does it?"

"That sounds like a double negative," she smiled. "I'm confused."

"This will clear things up," I answered as I tilted her face up to mine. We kissed, gently and without urgency. "Happy birthday," I murmured.

"It's been a perfect evening," she answered. "Every minute of it."

And so we went from one encounter to another, trying to keep each other at arm's length but becoming more and more aware of what a large part we were playing in each other's life.

After school a few days later, she came to my room as I was trying to bring order to the day's clutter on my desk, which, despite my efforts, seemed to accumulate exponentially as the day progressed.

"You look frustrated. What's wrong?" she asked from the doorway.

"Do you know how to throw things away?" I asked.

"I'm an expert," she said. She walked over to my wastebasket and peered into it. "It's only half full. You've got a long way to go."

I handed her the latest directive from the office; I had already received three that day. She eyed it. "Looks familiar. Are we supposed to keep all these?"

"If we did, we'd have to move out into the hall. Chuck it," I said.

She crumpled it into a ball then tossed it like a basketball toward the wastebasket. It bounced off the rim.

I shook my head. "You'd never make the Lincoln team. But," I leered, "on my team you'd be first string."

"And what do you play, Mr.? Forward? Hey, you'd have been proud of me today," she hurried on to cut off my smart reply.

"How come?" I asked.

She crumpled up the next sheet I handed her.

"You know Sam Trotter, don't you?"

I groaned a positive response.

She planted her fists on her hips. "I gave my class a math test, and with me watching him, he copied the answers to the test from the book! Instead of going berserk, I didn't say a word. I waited until he was finished, then picked up his test paper and, in front of the class, tore it into pieces and deposited them in the wastebasket. 'You get a zero,' I said. For once, he didn't have some smart remark."

"My oh my, how you've changed since I stopped by your room and you were unpacking those boxes," I said. "Congratulations."

"I owe much of it to you," she said. "Having someone to talk to—understanding what I'm going through. It's meant a lot to me."

"Aw shucks, hit wadn't nothin'," I said, becoming even more southern than usual.

In reply, she tossed a piece of crumpled paper at my head.

I ducked just in time and it landed on the floor beyond me. I gave her a stern look, pointed at the paper, and then jerked a thumb at the waste-basket.

Scuffing her feet, she shuffled over to the paper, picked it up, then deposited it in its proper place.

"That's better," I said sharply, as if speaking to one of my students.

She smiled. Then her face got serious. "That business with Sam wouldn't have happened at Dean. One thing I really can't get used to is the flagrant cheating."

"I had a problem with that, too," I agreed. "I had to confront 7I about cheating on their homework. On top of that they lied, claiming they hadn't cheated. Finally they admitted they had. It's not a racial thing, however. Those white girls in 7I behave as badly as any black students I've ever seen. I had another incident with them just a few days ago. You know that sweet little black girl Irma Jean Fox, don't you?"

"Oh, sure! Ed Allen's sister. Nice kid!"

"I was trying to catch up on my lesson plans during study hall, so I told her to take names of people acting up so I could focus on what I was doing. Some of the names she took were white kids. When class was over, I spanked the boys and Mrs. Hadley spanked the girls on Irma's list. And, believe you me, the people on the list were guilty as sin. The white girls started pouting. They had the gall, right in front of Mrs. Hadley and me, to threaten to gang up on Irma after school and beat her up. They justified it by claiming that they were upset because Irma purportedly didn't put Leon Wilson on the list because he is black. I'm convinced that Irma tried to be fair. There were as many black kids on the list as white kids."

She nodded. "You're right. By now I should know better than to jump to hasty conclusions. The trouble is that so many of these children, black and white, come to school without any sense of values. We're expected to teach them values and educate them on top of that."

I nodded. "Welcome to Parenting 101. Oh, I almost forgot to tell you, guess who's getting moved from 7I to 7C? Vertis! It has been decided by the powers that be that 7I doesn't have a prayer to ever advance unless Vertis and Debra are separated."

"But Vertis can barely read! 7C is for real students. She'll totally be a fish out of water."

Michelle crumpled up the last paper I'd given her and dropped it straight into the wastebasket.

"I guess I know one way to get promoted around here. Just be a big enough nuisance! The only good thing about this whole arrangement is that Vertis has to spend every activity period and study hall in Mrs. Levison's office," I returned.

"Maybe there is some justice in the world! How about a movie tonight?"

"What's tonight?" I asked.

"How could you forget! TGIF! No more school until Monday."

"Let's do it, then," I answered. "I'll pick you up about—hmmm. When?"

"7:30." She headed for the door.

~

Every faculty member had an amusing story about race—something they had said or had overheard. One of these was something Mr. Bibbs heard Mrs. Woolly say while they were talking in the hall. Mrs. Woolly was not only a teacher but also the wife the new superintendent of schools. "We were discussing some school matter," Mr. Bibbs continued, "when she glanced down the hall and saw Marvin Broussard walking toward us. Mrs. Woolly broke off our conversation and said, 'Mr. Bibbs, do you black folks know what pore white trash is?' As I was pondering what would be an acceptable answer, she went on with, 'That, Mr. Bibbs, is a living breathing example of what pore white trash looks like.'"

Another time, he was accosted in the teachers' lounge by a group of disgruntled black teachers. "Mr. Bibbs," one of them said, "they say that you favor the white teachers."

"Tell me, who is 'they?'" he asked.

"They are saying it all over the school," came the reply.

"I asked who is 'they'?" he said again.

"Some of the parents, they say you favor the white teachers," came the complaint.

Mr. Bibbs ended the conversation by saying, "My grandmother always told me that whenever 'they' say something and nobody knows who 'they' is, 'they' is a damned liar."

Mr. Bibbs was even-handed in his humorous criticism of racial bias. On one occasion he was asked to escort the Lincoln boys to a basketball game in Philadelphia, Mississippi. As the game progressed, fans from the home team's section of the stands continually chanted "Redneck! Redneck! Redneck!" at the players from Lincoln.

Finally, Mr. Bibbs turned to one of the white officials and asked, "Why do those Philadelphia fans keep yelling 'Redneck' at my boys? They all look black to me."

The uncomfortable official looked back quizzically at the deadpan Mr. Bibbs, who prolonged the official's discomfort by letting the uneasy silence continue.

Later, observers said that you could almost hear the official's thought: "Is this guy for real!"

～

Racial sensitivity appeared in various guises. After getting to know the students in my new homeroom, I appointed what I hoped was a reliable child to take names of misbehaving students so that I could catch up on grading tests and homework. I chose these monitors randomly among students who had not recently been a discipline problem themselves. Students considered it an honor to be chosen, since it was my silent vote of confidence in their reliability and judgment. It also temporarily gave a student a certain amount of power that he or she didn't normally enjoy. On this particular day I chose a black student, Ada Ware, for the duty as name-taker. It was understood that at the end of the period, anyone whose name was put on the list would be punished accordingly. Ada put the name of Doug Conlee, who is white, on the misbehavior list. When time came for his punishment, Doug refused.

When Doug reported to me after school, it became apparent his problem wasn't that he denied behaving in a rowdy manner but that he didn't like having a black student determine his fate. After a brief negotiation, he grudgingly capitulated and accepted the penalty.

This wasn't the end of the matter, though. A week later, his mother filed a formal complaint and I was called to a meeting in Mrs. Levison's office.

An angry Mrs. Conlee claimed that I was using name-taking as a method to give black students leverage against vulnerable whites. Further complaints followed. A week later, after a lecture from me on his continuing bad behavior, Doug made a beeline to Mr. Rollins's office, claiming he had been manhandled. This time I was summoned to Mr. Rollins's office; a heated meeting with Doug, his parents, Mr. Rollins, and me ensued. After I explained my difficulties with Doug's behavior, his parents finally acknowledged, without apologies, that Doug did indeed have behavioral problems. They claimed that these problems were intensified by Doug's being uprooted from his familiar surroundings and abruptly transferred to the unfamiliar

Lincoln environment. As far as they were concerned, 99 percent of Doug's problems were related to the system, and they should not be expected to offer apologies.

By then I wanted to yell, "For God's sake, just try to give a little bit and meet us halfway. I didn't create these surroundings or this environment. We're doing the best we can under very difficult conditions, and your son is adding to our problems!"

What a relief it would have been to let that out—a small payback for the distractions, the wasted time, my efforts and trips to the office to try to make things work.

But, of course, I didn't say any of these things. As usual, I gritted my teeth and kept my thoughts to myself.

32

By April, every attempt at disciplining misbehaving pupils became mired in the white/black issue. Students of each race accused teachers of singling them out for retribution solely because of the color of their skin. Mrs. Levison was on call continually for counseling. She could almost always defuse potentially explosive confrontations. After letting both sides air their grievances, she would ask each to switch roles with his or her antagonist and tell those grievances from the other's viewpoint. Often, she was able to get them to laugh at the similarity of their accusations. But, to everyone's frustration, this fungus continued to pop up and would have to be eradicated again and again.

One confrontation contained no humor at all. James Hurse, a black student, had come to my desk to ask a question when white troublemaker Doug Conlee threw a piece of chalk at James. He saw it coming and ducked. I, not seeing it coming, did not, and the chalk scored a direct hit on my left eye, breaking a contact lens. It shattered into so many small pieces that I was unable to flush the final shards out until the next day. Miraculously, my eye was not injured.

I sent a note to Doug's parents politely requesting that they pay to have the lens replaced. Two weeks went by with no voluntary payment on their part. I called his father and repeated my request in person. His father's response was, "If you'd learn to control them niggers and not let them pick on innocent white boys, things like this would never happen."

"Mr. Conlee, your son, Doug, threw the chalk, not the black kid," I answered.

"But he never acted like this when he was at Dean. Y'all are just out of control," he countered.

This back-and-forth continued for several minutes, until finally he grudgingly agreed to pay for replacing the lens. I thought the matter was resolved until I saw Mr. Rollins waiting for me in the hall as I arrived at school the following morning. He nodded for me to follow him to his office.

"David, I just got a phone call from Mr. Conlee reading me the riot act," he said when we were seated.

I sighed. "I guess I should have told you about it, but I thought it was all settled."

"I've heard his side," Mr. Rollins answered. "Tell me yours."

I did, to which Mr. Rollins replied: "He said you strong-armed him into paying for the lens, and he's not going to stand for it. He's calling Mr. Woolly."

I shook my head. "I haven't seen a dime yet. He ought to be glad I'm not suing him for the loss of the sight in that eye. It was a miracle I could flush all the pieces out before they caused any damage."

Mr. Rollins was sympathetic, yet he had to face reality. "David, let's save our fight for bigger things," he said. "I've a gut feeling that we're going to need all the energy and ingenuity we can muster for problems that will arise before this racial thing is settled—if ever!"

The next racial incident was not long in coming. It concerned the state's two professional associations for teachers. The membership of the Mississippi Education Association (MEA) was exclusively white, and that of the Mississippi Teachers Association (MTA) was black. A teacher was expected to join whichever organization suited his or her race. However, since Mrs. Hadley, Anita, and I were teaching in a black facility, we had joined the black organization. Membership in the MTA seemed so logical and was of so little concern to any of us that we had never thought to mention our choice to other staff members or even to each other.

This laissez-faire attitude had worked well the first semester and into the beginning of the second. Our white colleagues from Dean assumed that we had joined the white association. That assumption changed, however, in March when school was dismissed for the MEA's annual meeting in Jackson.

When our white colleagues asked if we were going to attend, we replied that since we belonged to the MTA, we would not be participating.

At first the white faculty members applied subtle pressure for us to switch. When we resisted, pressure increased. We knew it would be a slap in the face to our black colleagues if we yielded to demands of white teachers. Each of us, individually and without informing the others, refused to withdraw from the MTA to join the MEA. The white teachers at both schools considered this a deliberate snub of "our kind," a way of ratifying and dignifying what they considered the whole abhorrent concept of integration. The more pressure they applied, the more insulted we became. What had begun as a matter of little importance mushroomed into an "us and them" issue. An interesting aspect of Mrs. Hadley's, Anita's, and my line of reasoning was that each of us, without consulting the other two, had arrived at the conclusion that we would not be bullied into submission by the white teachers.

I thought this was a local problem, but much more was at stake. In 1966 the National Education Association (NEA) had ordered all state education associations to desegregate and to merge the separate teacher groups by 1968; only Louisiana and Mississippi had failed to comply with this mandate. The 1968 deadline came and went, and no action was taken. The NEA suspended the Mississippi organizations and threatened expulsion if the MEA and MTA did not reach a compromise at the MEA's March 12, 1970, convention in Jackson. After much debate, with measures and countermeasures being tendered and rejected, the NEA severed its ties with the MEA on April 19, 1970.

∿

The racial divide had begun to dominate every facet of school life. Students in my classes reacted to racial situations in varying degrees of intensity. Charles Robinson's behavior became extreme. During first semester I had found him to be a harmless clown. He was never a good student, and he could and did irritate me, but I always found myself forgiving him and laughing at his antics. However, his efforts at the beginning of the second semester to get the white girls to pay attention to him were ridiculed by Vertis Ethridge and her cohorts. They told anyone who would listen that Charles's efforts disgusted and amused them.

This rejection had a marked effect on his personality, and Charles was transformed from the class clown to the class troublemaker. This change also affected his schoolwork. Claiming that a smaller white student, Doug Conlee, had called him a "nigger," he started fights with Doug and picked on him mercilessly. To defuse the situation, I moved Doug to the other side of the classroom.

I continued to teach by asking questions that involved all the students. Whenever I asked Doug a question, Charles would shout at him from across the room: "If you open your mouth, white boy, I'm gonna eat you alive!" Doug's response was to scrunch down in his seat and remain silent. Although I reprimanded Charles, a few days later he started a fight in class with a former ally. That did it. I'd had my fill of Charles and bodily dragged him to Mr. Rollins's office, where both Mr. Rollins and I gave him a tongue lashing. The fracas attracted Mr. Bibbs's attention, and he came in to see what was the matter.

"Everbody's always botherin' me. I don't do nothing and they still bother me," Charles complained.

Within a week, as if the previous incidents had never occurred, Charles popped into my room bubbling over with plans to go out for spring football practice. In his mind's eye, he was already the star player on the team. He asked if I'd put a picture of him on the bulletin board when he made the team. From then on, all he could talk about were his sports aspirations. He desperately wanted to be respected. Being limited academically, Charles felt that if he could become a sports star, all his problems would dissolve; his success would supply the respect and adulation he desperately craved. Sadly, when Charles failed to make the team, he slipped backwards once again— into serious trouble, this time. He brought a knife to school and threatened a teacher. He was suspended.

The next day, Charles's mother came to my room before the school day began. She was a single parent, an uneducated maid with limited income. "Mr. Beckwit, I really need your help," she said, all but wringing her hands. "I don't know what to do with Charles. He's really a good boy. You knowed him before this integrating started. You was good with him. He always like you. Other people pick on him, and when that happens, Charles got to fight back."

I slowly shook my head. "Ms. Robinson, I'm going to be truthful with you. Charles stays in trouble because he starts the trouble. Charles has a giant chip on his shoulder. I see the old Charles peeking out every once in a while, but most of the time he's looking for a fight. Charles has got to *want* to get along, and right now he doesn't want to."

That isn't what she'd come to hear. I was supposed to work my magic, and her son would suddenly become the model student she wanted him to be. She left unsatisfied, and Charles continued his downward spiral. This time he called a group of Italian students "a bunch of Dagos." Although he bitterly resented being called a "nigger," he didn't expect the Italians to be turned off by his offensive epithet. These outnumbered white boys dared not retaliate for fear of being beaten up.

∼

This racial turmoil took place against the backdrop of my efforts to continue our lessons on European history. Many of the black students wondered aloud why our textbook never talked about blacks in European history—especially since, as Charles maintained, it was really a Negro who discovered America. That set off a spate of questions.

"Mr. Beckwith," Velma Davis asked, "how can I trace my family's history?"

"You may be able to trace your family history back to slave days," I answered, "but it would be difficult, maybe impossible to trace it beyond that point, because you wouldn't know which country in Africa your ancestors came from."

Again I pondered how relevant the history I was teaching was to my students. The history they could relate to began when their forebears were sold by their tribal chiefs in Africa to shipowners who brought them to America and sold them again to plantation owners. Our textbooks gave but cursory treatment to blacks' early history in this country. The historians seemed to assume that there was little legacy of greatness and identified only a few black historical heroes.

In order not to leave them with the notion that they had no one in their race to admire, I spent one class extolling some blacks of more recent history who had made major contributions to society. "Let me give you some names, and see if they ring a bell for you," I said. "Dr. Booker T. Washington, Dr. Martin Luther King Jr., Joe Louis, Nat King Cole, Jackie Robinson." As I mentioned each name, recognition dawned in their eyes. "All of these people made a contribution to the society in which we live today," I went on. "You have every reason to be proud that you all belong to the same race."

The discussion continued with Sam Trotter's inquiry: "What makes George Washington so great?"

Relieved to have the subject matter revert to a topic I could explain, I told the class that the Revolutionary War was fought to gain our freedom from Great Britain, and that George Washington being a great military leader as well as the father of our country and the first president. They seemed intrigued that the relatively few people of the thirteen colonies could defeat a great power such as England, and I entertained a slim hope that some of them might even read the chapter I assigned for homework describing some of the battles.

~

As March wound down, racial discord began an upward spiral. Bomb threats at both Lincoln and Dean became frequent. As always, the schools had to be evacuated to let bomb detectors determine if the threat was real or just another hoax. Then it was back to the classroom to try and pick up the lesson where we had left off. Black and white gangs exchanged warnings. I was shocked to learn that some of the black teachers who had been transferred to Dean were refusing to salute the flag or recite the Pledge of Allegiance—the same teachers I'd been comfortable around in the teachers' lounge less than two months earlier. Boys of both races were being routinely searched to discover knives and other weapons. One afternoon after school, a group of black boys stood hand-to-hand across the street leading to the school, blocking all traffic. Police broke up the protest, but as soon as they left, the group reassembled and blocked traffic again.

The day after that episode, Mr. Rollins called a student-faculty meeting in the gym. His message: the administration was not going to tolerate bullies and would deal with them harshly. He pleaded for tolerance on both sides. His talk had no effect. Bullies still preyed on the defenseless. I caught two black students hitting a smaller white student and sent both of the boys to the office. Later that day I confiscated a knife from another black student.

Mrs. Little had her own way of dealing with bullies. When a black boy from Dean showed up at Lincoln and started hanging around the boys' bathroom, accosting whites who went in and out, she sent someone to tell him to leave the campus. He sent word back that he would leave when he felt like it. Her solution was to barge into the boys' bathroom holding a Coke bottle poised as a weapon, and threaten to bash the boy in the head if he didn't leave. When the boy saw she meant it, he decided he suddenly felt like leaving, and promptly did so.

Some disagreements were settled in a more organized manner. When two white students got into an argument, I allowed them to settle it after school by trading licks with my strap while I acted as referee. They hit each other on the hand and on the behind for about five minutes before deciding to call it a draw and go home. I never had any more trouble from those two.

~

April 4 was the second anniversary of Martin Luther King Jr.'s assassination in Memphis. I had been on the outskirts of Memphis the night of the murder. It was a Thursday. My friends and I had been studying for tests all that week. We had reached a point where we wanted to get away from the books for a few hours. Since my birthday was approaching, someone suggested this as an excuse for a road trip to a small beer joint in Southaven, a town just south of Memphis right across the Mississippi line. Four of us piled into a car to make the hour's drive from dry Lafayette County to wet Southaven. A local came into the establishment, and soon the bar was buzzing with the breaking news: Martin Luther King Jr., in town to support striking sanitation workers, had been shot at the Lorraine Motel in Memphis as he leaned over a second-story balcony to talk to Jesse Jackson.

Everyone in the bar talked at once, speculating on what had happened and who had done this. Before long a highway patrolman came in and told us that Mayor Loeb had issued a curfew and we had to leave. The Memphis police with the help of the National Guard were instructed to prevent rioting, burning, and looting.

The next day we monitored the fast-moving events on TV as the story continued to break. A rifle had been found. The suspect was an unidentified white man. Rioting had broken out in Memphis and the surrounding area as soon as the news circulated about Dr. King's death. Violence continued the next day and spread from the black section throughout the city.

Two years later, this tragic event still caused civil insurrection and was very much a part of my life. During my second-period class I heard noises coming in the window that overlooked the street. Loud chanting and singing filled the air:

We shall overcome
We shall overcome
We shall overcome someday.

As my students and I watched from our classroom windows, we saw a full-fledged demonstration of black students who had left Dean and were now marching toward Lincoln. The demonstrators had demanded that the flags at Dean and Lincoln be flown at half-mast and that they be given a holiday in remembrance of King's assassination. Over the loudspeaker, Mr. Rollins announced that Lincoln would not be dismissed, that buses would run on schedule, and that students were not to join any demonstration either during or after school.

Mr. Rollins's announcement was followed by one from Mr. Bibbs: "Listen carefully. Lincoln students will not be allowed to leave school for any reason. With Mr. Rollins's support I am announcing that if any student leaves our campus and joins the demonstration, I will lock the door behind you. You will not be allowed in this building again until both your parents bring you back and we have a conference. You will receive a zero in every class for every day that you miss."

To challenge this threat, several black eighth graders left the school and joined the demonstrators. After they left, Mr. Bibbs did indeed lock the entrance and stood guard over it. When he heard the bolt slide into the lock, one boy hesitated on the lawn, reconsidered his decision, and turned to re-enter the building. He rattled the doorknob, pounded on the door. Mr. Bibbs stood inside, dispassionately eyeing him through the glass panel. The boy pleaded to be readmitted—to no avail. Finally, frustrated and enraged, the boy stood back from the door and screamed words that, in his eyes, constituted the ultimate insult: "You . . . You . . . You white man!" This condemnation elicited the same stoic stare from Mr. Bibbs. It was as if the boy were yelling at a cigar-store Indian. Dejected, defeated, the boy went home to contemplate his fate. A week later, he and his parents participated in a session with Mr. Bibbs to negotiate his return to class.

33

When the second six weeks arrived, it was time to administer the dreaded Otis-Lennon exams, from which a student's intelligence quotient—better known as IQ—was derived. The test would also reveal the subjects—English, history, math, and so forth—in which the student might have a weakness. In order to get standardized results, no matter whether the school was in Mississippi or Vermont, it was important that conditions under which the test was given be as uniform as possible. Thus, the students should be tested at the same time of year in every locale, and the test should last three hours in the morning and two and a half in the afternoon. Because of space and controlled acoustics, the test maker suggested the school auditorium as the preferred place to conduct the test.

Lincoln had no auditorium, so we had to use the gym, where noise of any kind was amplified and reverberated in the scaffolding overhead. Trying to keep students with a limited attention span focused on a test for five or six hours seemed an impossible task. However, the state of Mississippi required that the test be given, and we had to comply.

Two days before the tests were scheduled to begin, a faculty meeting was called to iron out any questions the teachers might have concerning the event. We all agreed that time should be set aside the day before the tests for students to fill out the answer sheets calling for name, date of birth, date of the test, school grade. This completed, on the day of the test, students could immediately begin work on the tests.

It sounded so logical when we discussed the matter in the faculty meeting. In reality, though, the project did not take the few minutes I had allotted for it, but the entire first period. Even then, the majority of the answer sheets hadn't been filled out correctly. Some had no name, others had the first and last names out of order, and many students had incorrectly computed their age in months. Numbly, I stared at the jumble of sheets dumped on my desk, knowing it would be futile to return them to the students to complete. So that I wouldn't have to repeat this fiasco with every class, I didn't hand them out to my other classes and stayed after school to finish all the forms myself.

The next morning, before the school opened, the janitors carried desks from some of the classrooms to the gym for the students to take the test. Mine was one of those classrooms, so I conducted my homeroom with everyone standing. Mrs. Hadley's car had broken down on the way to school, so I had my class and hers. The novelty of having so many kids standing around the room seemed to overcome their natural inclination to poke and scuffle with each other. Or, since homeroom lasted only twenty minutes, those natural inclinations didn't have time to blossom into mischief.

The students behaved well for the morning's testing. Three hours was a long time for that age group to maintain self-control. Right after lunch, they were due back in the gym for another two and a half hours. We weren't far into the afternoon session before the tedium of the testing began to take a toll. The students became restless and difficult to control, and Mrs. Levison decided to give them a break. Released in the gym, the students were wild, chasing each other, climbing the basketball goals, shooting rubber bands, and running up and down the stairs. Even with every seventh grade teacher present, we couldn't control their pent-up energy. We agreed it would be foolish to administer the rest of the test and expect the scores to have any validity. About that time, Mr. Rollins appeared and requested a chance to speak before the students were dismissed. His presence had a calming effect, and without the usual scuffling about seats, the students sat down. I assumed that the topic of his discussion would be the tests. It was, however, on a more personal level.

"The subject of my talk today is pollution," he said without preamble. "Specifically, classroom pollution. There have been complaints that body odor and foot odor are a real problem. It is everyone's responsibility to bathe every day, use deodorant, and wear clean clothes so that you don't offend others. The janitors do a good job of seeing that our school is clean when we arrive in the morning. We should all do our part in keeping ourselves clean also."

With that, he turned on his heel and left the gym. We teachers eyed each other, wondering why he had picked such a time as this to bring up a problem that had been endemic since the school year began. He had barely left the gym when many of the kids turned to whoever sat next to them and, holding their nose, yelled, "Whew! You stink!" and other rude observations.

On that intellectually high plane, school was dismissed.

We set aside time to complete the tests the following morning. When we arrived at the gym, however, we saw that someone had broken in during the night and turned over the desks, scattering them all over the gym, smashing some in the process. Chalk scribbling decorated those that were not damaged. By the time the gym had been put back in order, the period set aside for the test had evaporated. As this was the last day before Easter holidays began, Mr. Rollins decided that the final two hours of the test would have to be given when school reopened.

Since the student desks from my room were still in the gym, I spent the day traveling with my students from one room to another—with all the confusion that entailed. I moved from Mrs. Brenner's room to Pearlie Brantley's room to Mrs. Hadley's room while their respective classes were occupied elsewhere. At lunch break, I tore my pants and had to recruit Mr. Bibbs to watch my fifth period while I rushed home to change. And so it went for the rest of the day. Trying to teach a roomful of restless students in unfamiliar surroundings without my books and displays at hand was futile.

The good news at the end of the school day was that the students had left for the Easter holidays and that nothing else could possibly go wrong. I headed for my room, empty now of everything but my desk and chair. I sat a moment savoring the quiet, then took from a drawer the stack of neglected paperwork that I hoped to finish before heading home. I had barely begun when there was a knock at the door. I looked up and saw two girls standing there. I recognized one of them, Gloria Hampton, one of my fifth-period students, but I didn't know the other. Gloria was white, dumpy, not a troublemaker, neither was she very bright. I didn't know the other student.

"Yes?" I asked. "What is it?"

"Mr. Breckwit, my friend Wilma and I, we missed the school bus," Gloria said as they came into the room, "and we don't have no way to get home. Can you take us?"

I all but groaned aloud. Good-bye to catching up on paperwork. I nodded, shoved back my chair none too gently, put away the papers, and followed them out the door.

After many detours due to work on the roads, we finally arrived at Gloria's house in a run-down neighborhood. Her friend lived several blocks away. Neither apologized for the inconvenience they had caused me. Both thanked me casually, as if delivering them home was included in a teacher's job description.

My mother invited me to come home Saturday and stay through dinner Easter Sunday. I really needed the break and some relaxation. It was wonderful to laze through Saturday afternoon fishing with my brother. Bill and I got our parents' permission to borrow their boat, and we headed for their boathouse at the yacht club on Lake Ferguson. There, the always amiable Willie Smith filled the boat's gas tank, packed our cooler with ice, and sent us on our way.

Bill had turned eighteen just a couple of weeks before. Even though we were physically similar—same height, same blond hair and blue eyes—in many ways we were complete opposites. I had always been a social person who enjoyed being in the limelight. Bill exhibited a quiet leadership that, to the casual observer, could be deceiving. He never wanted to be president of an organization, but he was the one who made it run. He took people at their word, and because of this he had been taken advantage of on more than one occasion. And on more than one occasion, when I had chastened him for being too trusting, he'd replied with a shrug: "You don't have to worry about me. You know our mama didn't raise any stupid children."

It was a perfect day on the lake—deep blue sky reflecting in the water, enough of a breeze to temper the sun's heat. We cruised down to the main sandbar and took a swim. Then it was time to see if we could catch some bream. We baited our hooks and set to work. We were patient but also lucky, and between the two of us we made a good catch. As I was about to bait my hook again, Bill looked at me over his shoulder.

"What time is it getting to be?" he asked.

"My watch says a quarter to five," I answered.

"I guess we better head back," Bill said. "I need time to clean up before I take Jackie to the movie."

Jackie Shepherd and Bill were inseparable. They had been introduced by one of Bill's friends, who dated Jackie's sister, and the four of them double-dated on a regular basis. Jackie was quiet, like Bill. They seemed made for each other.

"What are you guys going to see?" I asked.

"*Love Story.* I thought we'd go to the Fountain Terrace and get something to drink afterwards."

"Sounds good," I answered. "Your double-dating reminds me how Dick Peterson and I used to double-date all the time. Movies, dancing—the senior prom. I wonder how Dick is doing in 'Nam. Well, at least he's an officer and not crawling through cane fields like those poor grunts we see in the newsreels. He's in a different kind of war than the one I'm fighting."

Bill raised his eyebrows. "Is that what you call Leland? A war zone?"

"You're damn right," I nodded.

"And you're going back to Lincoln to teach next year!"

I shook my head. "I haven't told Mom and Dad yet—I wanted to tell them in person that I've been accepted at Ole Miss for graduate school. Barring my military deferment being revoked, I'm heading back to school."

"Hey! That's great! You realize we'll both be at Ole Miss next year?"

"You've got a while before you have to worry about military service or what you want to do with your life. My advice is to stay in school. By the time you graduate the war will probably be over."

"This discussion sounds like what our parents must have gone through during World War II," Bill mused. "We aren't the first generation to have our lives screwed up by world politics; and, we won't be the last."

It was dusk as we pulled up anchor and set out for home. The angle of the sun's rays on the water splintered by our wake reminded us that dusk comes quickly at this time of year, and we lost no time in returning to the boathouse. Gathering our catch of bream, we shared some with Willie after he'd helped us secure the boat, then sped back to the house.

Easter Sunday was a beautiful, cloudless day in the Delta. The weather was still cool enough to wear a jacket without sweltering. How restful it was to sit in a pew with other members of the church and listen to Dr. Golding preach instead of being in charge of thirty unruly students. Dr. Golding didn't once have to tell anyone in the congregation to shut up. When he said sing hymns, we sang, and when he said to pray, we prayed. When the service ended, the churchgoers left in an orderly manner—no poking, jabbing, tripping each other up. I'd almost forgotten that people could assemble peaceably and show respect for each other.

Mom had put a roast in the oven before we went to church, and by the time we got back the house was filled with delicious aromas. She cooked some rice and gravy and green beans to go with the salad she'd cut up that morning. For dessert she treated us to some of her strawberry shortcake—always a winner.

While Dad did the dishes after that great meal, Bill and I gathered pecans from the tree in the backyard. Soon after that, Aunt Katherine came by for a visit; then Bill and I walked down to Greenway Park to see what was going on there.

That night I called the Stein house to see if Sally was home for her spring break. She was.

"Sally. David. Thank goodness you're home. How about a burger and a beer?"

"Let's do it to it," she quickly responded.

I picked her up, and we headed for Strazi's taproom. Small talk prevailed in the car as I made a beeline for our destination.

Sally waited until our pitcher of beer was served before she asked, "Is it getting better at Lincoln?"

"No! If anything it's gotten worse," I responded without hesitation. I then proceeded to use Sally as a sounding board for everything that I had bottled up inside.

She listened patiently until I finished venting, then commented, "I guess the powers that be couldn't have screwed it up much worse if they'd tried."

I took a sip of beer and ate a french fry as I measured my thoughts. "I'm sure that there are people up the ladder who have decided that if there's enough confusion, we'll go back to the old status quo. So what do we do—destroy a generation so that the status quo can rock along? But enough of this! Let's get out of here and go sit on the levee and enjoy each other's company." We did.

The incomplete Otis-Lennon exams still awaited us when Lincoln Attendance Center opened on Monday. Since the janitors had returned all the student desks to the respective homerooms, we had no choice but to give the remainder of the test in our classrooms. Mrs. Levison timed the test over the public-address system. One segment involved her reading a story to the participants and then giving them questions to answer about what they had heard.

As was expected, some of the white students complained that they couldn't understand Mrs. Levison's diction, which resulted in her having to repeat almost every section. What was supposed to be a thirty-two-minute exercise dragged from 9:30 until noon. About midway through the marathon, Pearlie watched my class while I went to Greenville to deposit my check in my very anemic account before the bank closed. Mission accomplished, but my punishment for leaving the school premises on school time to take care of personal business was that I ran over a nail coming back from Greenville. I was greeted with a flat when school let out that afternoon.

The next morning I arrived at school relieved that my seventh graders had completed the pesky test. Today I could once again take over my room and resume the job for which I was hired. I'd spent a lot of time preparing today's lesson, trying to teach at my class's level about the flowering of Western culture during the twelfth century. I was fascinated with the emphasis on reason as opposed to theology, which had dominated previous centuries, and hoped I could bring to life the distrust with which early church fathers had viewed what they considered an attack on man's salvation.

Alas, as I passed Mr. Rollins's office on my way into the school building, he motioned me into his office.

"I'm sorry, David," he said, "but we've had to take over your room to use for the eighth graders to take their test. You can use Tommy Seaton's room. I hope we can wrap everything up today."

"You and me both," I responded through clenched teeth, knowing from experience that this maneuver would try my patience to the utmost as well as use up most of the first period. By the time my homeroom and I had trailed from one end of the first-floor hall to Tommy's room at the opposite end, with the class going through the usual arguments and scuffling about who was to sit where and why, my enthusiasm for Western culture's twelfth-century florescence had dampened markedly.

34

In contrast to the violence in the schools and outside in the street which March had brought, April came in gently. Flower-scented breezes wafted through the open windows at Lincoln, girls donned spring outfits, and both races seemed to want to take a deep breath before returning to the business of hating each other. As if to reinforce this release from tension, I found a note attached to one of Mildred Kimber's test papers:

> love is every
> where right

I didn't pay much attention to this announcement, thinking it was the musings of a bored student. On her homework assignment the next week, a second note appeared:

> is Mildred in Love
> yest or no

I circled "yest."

Though I didn't make any overt acknowledgment of the two communiqués, I began to pay more attention to Mildred's behavior. I became aware that she seemed more settled, less a participant in the normal shenanigans of the students around her. She had a dreamy attitude, as if she'd been given a sedative. One day in the teachers' lounge I mentioned this change to Michelle, who also taught Mildred.

"You've noticed it too?" She raised her eyebrows. "I didn't think men were known for their ability to observe subtle changes like that."

"With symptoms as marked as hers, you'd have to be blind and dumb not to notice," I replied.

Michelle smiled and nodded. "She actually made a respectable grade on a test, and she's behaving a lot better in class. What do you think is going on?"

"I have to confess that I had a little help with my observations," I admitted. I told her of the two notes I'd received.

"I should have known you weren't relying just on male intuition. Anyway," she hurried on before I could reply, "let's hope it's contagious and they all get it."

A few days later, I gave a chapter quiz on which Mildred made an 80—the first passing mark I'd given her the entire year! The next week I gave a quiz, and Mildred made her first-ever 100. It was a toss-up as to whose morale was higher—hers or mine. Still, I refrained from commenting for fear I might jinx a good trend.

She must have been disappointed that I hadn't mentioned her changed behavior and better grades, for she wrote me a note telling of her infatuation:

Dear Mr. Beckwith
I am in love with a very sweet boy. And he in love with me. I love him very much. If you love a girl hard I love a boy you are in love I no I am I like you but—not as hard as I love my sweet how I love him very very much chack it

> With love
> Your Mildred

I thanked her for the note and told her how pleased I was about her friendship. I was careful to call it "friendship," not a "love affair."

The next day, as I was straightening my desk to get ready to go to lunch, who should show up but a smiling Mildred with a tall, gawky black boy in tow. They stood facing me across the desk.

"Mr. Blekwith," Mildred said shyly, "this is Willie."

Willie had an Afro and wore a clean but rumpled blue shirt and pants, and regarded me with an uneasy expression in his dark, wide-spaced eyes. He looked sixteen years old at the most. I wondered what pressure she had used to drag him to this meeting. I felt like a father whose daughter had brought a fiancée for inspection and approval so that he could ask for her hand in marriage.

"Well, Willie," I said as I held out my hand, "it's a pleasure to meet you. Mildred has told me what a fine person you are."

Mildred beamed. Willie tentatively took my extended hand, as if unsure what he was supposed to do with it. I wondered if this was the first time he'd shaken hands with a white adult.

"So, you're in the seventh grade," I continued brightly, retrieving my hand.

"Yessir," Willie stammered.

There was a pause.

"And I bet you're a good student," I rattled on, trying to keep the pause from extending itself indefinitely. "So, what's your favorite subject?"

He shuffled his feet. "Ah dunno," he managed.

Another pause.

"Well, I better finish getting my desk cleared up before fifth period gets here," I said. "It's been nice to meet you."

Head bent, he nodded.

Mildred continued to beam as she led Willie to the door. She seemed satisfied that she had taken care of the necessary social amenities.

They'd scarcely left when Michelle stopped by my room on her way to the cafeteria. "Was that who I think it was?" she asked.

"Yeah, that's Willie," I nodded. "A real conversationalist." I told her of his stimulating comments.

Michelle frowned. "You don't think they're serious, do you?"

"Yep. I get the feeling that this is the first time either of them has been attracted to someone of the opposite sex, and they're convinced they're meant for each other."

"They're children!" Michelle groaned.

"You know that, and I know that, but you'd have a hard time convincing them," I answered.

The next day I found a note on my desk.

Dear D. B.

How are you find I holp Willie say hollo I love him so much Mr David if you love a girl like I love Willie you are in love. We are going to be marry Sunday what are you going to give me I will let you see him tomorrow

Love
Love Mildred & Willie

They did indeed get married, and, despite urging from all of their teachers to stay in school and finish their education, they dropped out. Willie got a job earning $1.60 an hour loading trucks at the chemical plant. How could two people survive on that? To a great extent, school had been uninteresting and irrelevant to them before they met. Now that they were together, school had no place in their lives. They were convinced that life would be beautiful. I wondered how long it would take for them to wake up to reality. Mildred had asked in her note what I was going to give them for their wedding. The most important thing they needed, but which I could not give, was wisdom.

~

The introduction of white students into Lincoln's formerly all-black student body did not noticeably improve academic achievement. European history did, however, carry more interest for the whites because of their ability to identify with the Anglo-European backgrounds. In addition, white students appeared to have a longer attention span and would finish classroom assignments fifteen to thirty minutes before black students. The quality of work was not discernibly better, though.

On one occasion I gave a pop quiz to my morning classes. During lunch period, after overhearing students talk in the hall, I could tell that questions and answers on the test had circulated to members of my afternoon classes. Instead of giving the identical test to the later classes, I asked the same questions but in reverse order. When I graded the tests, a third of the class had answered the questions exactly as they were given to the morning students. The rampant cheating and claims of innocence when caught continued to baffle me.

As the time for six-week exams approached, I decided that the tests would contain no question that had not been used on a previous exam. I thought this would make studying a simple task, since I had returned test papers to be used as a study guide.

"Surely, this will inspire students to try to do well on the exams and use that as a mechanism to pull up their otherwise dismal grades," I told Mrs. Hadley.

She eyed me dubiously. "I hope you didn't bet any money on it."

Instead of being grateful to me for helping them improve their grades, the students demanded that I tell them exactly which of the old questions I planned to use. When I refused, it was as if I had deprived them of their God-given right to achieve success with no effort on their part. The results in my 7C class were dismal: for white students there was one A, one B, three C's, one D, and one F; for blacks students there were no A's, one B, three C's, one D, and twenty-five F's. My other classes followed the same pattern. Disheartened, I mentioned the fact in the teachers' lounge and found that these grades were typical.

∼

By mid-April, Lincoln School was back on the track of having academic class schedules play second fiddle to sporting events. One week, Friday classes were dismissed at 10:30 to attend a basketball tournament. Those students who couldn't afford to attend were held in study halls. The next week, school was dismissed at 2:00 for a basketball game—another wasted afternoon.

Grousing among the teaching staff was at an all-time high, and morale sank to its lowest level ever. Pointing fingers at the administration became the favorite pastime in the teachers' lounge. The complaints were many: conduct in the classrooms is deplorable; the amount of time devoted to non-academic events is inexcusable; the school has no organization; no one is in charge; kids roam the halls during class periods and talk back to teachers in class. The accusations went on and on.

At the end of the six-week grading period, report cards were given out. As I expected, all the students maintained that they deserved better than the grade they had received. After the report cards had been distributed, Mr. Rollins called a special meeting of the faculty in the library after school. Attendance was almost 100 percent.

"Thanks for coming after what has been an exhausting and disappointing six weeks," he began. "There are a lot of frayed nerves, justifiably so, and everyone has been inconvenienced." He paced back and forth, deep in thought, as if wondering how much he should say to the mixed black/white audience. Then he stopped in the middle of the room and faced all of us. "Our office has heard rumors of a mass exodus of whites from the public school system for the upcoming year. That would be a disaster, and many of us hope it will not happen. Our office has had numerous complaints—that the school is disorganized, that teachers do not stay in their classrooms properly supervising the children, that corporal punishment should be abolished. We are trying to address these complaints, and have decided that from now on, corporal punishment will be delivered only by Mr. Bibbs or myself. As to the first two complaints, we are doing our best to bring order out of chaos. For teachers to leave their classrooms unattended is unacceptable."

He let that sink in for a few moments, then pulled from his shirt pocket a piece of paper.

"I'd like to read a paraphrase of 1 Corinthians 13, with which you doubtless are familiar. It would do us all good to take its message to heart."

Though I teach with the skill of the finest teacher,
And have not understanding,
I am become only a clever speaker and a charming entertainer.
And though I understand all techniques and methods,
And though I have much training, so that I may feel
Quite competent, but have no understanding of the
Ways my pupils think . . . it is not enough.

And if I spend hours in lesson preparations,
And become tense and nervous with strain,
But have no understanding of the problems of my pupils . . .
It is still not enough.

The understanding teacher is patient, very kind;
Is not shocked when young people bring her confidences;
Does not gossip; is not easily discouraged.
Does not behave herself in ways that are unworthy,
But is *at all times* a living example to her students
Of the Good Way of life of which she speaks.

Understanding never fails,
But whether there be materials, they shall become obsolete,
Whether there be methods, they shall be outmoded;
Whether there be techniques, they shall be abandoned;

For we know only a little, and can pass on to our children
Only a little; but when we have understanding, then all
Our efforts will become creative, and our influence will
Live forever in the lives of our pupils.

When I was a child, I spoke with immaturity,
My emotions were uncontrolled, and I behaved childishly.
But now that I am an adult, I must face life as it is,
With courage and with understanding.
And now abideth Skill, Devotion, and Understanding . . .
These three, and the greatest of these is Understanding.

Elouise D. Rivinius

35

After Mr. Rollins read the poem and made his plea for understanding and tolerance, I resolved to try, from now on, to practice both. Easier said than done. The following day, I tried to lead a class discussion about what the world would be like in the year 2000. Just as my students had begun to really participate and enjoy the discussion, Johnny Hampton got up from his seat and headed for the wastebasket to throw away a piece of paper. He tossed it over his left shoulder, it missed, and he picked it up and tried again. This time he succeeded. On the way back to his seat, he danced a little jig to celebrate his success. By now his antics had not only disrupted the concentration of the class but had also deflected interest in pursuing the discussion. Giggles, hoots, and clapping broke out. I found myself grinding my teeth in frustration.

"Well, Johnny," I said levelly, "since you seem to enjoy dancing so much, come up to the front and dance for the whole class."

"I don't want to," he grumbled.

"Then I suggest you go to Mr. Rollins's office instead of interrupting my class."

Johnny refused the punishment Mr. Rollins offered and chose instead to go home.

Two days later he changed his mind and returned to school to receive his punishment. Just as Mr. Rollins arrived at my class to deal with Johnny,

Charles Robinson jumped out of his chair and struck Dorothy Myers, who was collecting homework. Johnny had to wait while Mr. Rollins dealt with Charles. After Johnny had received a couple of licks, he started to cry. Then, after Mr. Rollins left, both Johnny and Charles sulked for the rest of the period. When the bell rang and students made for the door, Johnny walked by my desk and made a swipe with his hand, sending all my books and papers to the floor. Before I could say a word, he was out the door. So much for tolerance and understanding!

$\sim$

By early May, racial tension had escalated dramatically. There were constant fights on the playground, most of them serious enough to require adult intervention. The tension was especially noticeable among the girls. Since we were no longer allowed to use corporal punishment, I began to make those who misbehaved write a one-hundred-word essay on the subject of misbehaving. The first two girls in my classroom who were sentenced to write an essay on behavior were white.

How I Should Behave In Class
    First of all I should learn how to keep my big mouth shut and second only talking when I'm asked to speak or when I answering a question, not my neighbor has ask me but the teacher. I should have my mine on nothing else but history class. Having good behavior is not just being nice to the teacher it's also co-operating with him (her). By co-operating with the teacher I mean paying attention to him and not something else. When speaking of behavior this just doesn't mean being nice to someone or something like that it means to conduct oneself in a proper way or to act in a self-satisfied way.
    By: Miss Catheryn Marie Fratesi
    She knows all about behavior know that she's looked it up

What I will not do in History Class in 100 word or more
    While Mr. Beckwith is out of the room I will not talk about him. I will not eat candy nor gum in the room. I will not talk when Mr. Beckwith is in the room. I will behave myself in history. I will do everything he say do. I will away sit quite. I will always act in good. I will nevery hollow across the room at Cathy. And I get in to the room i will not

asked to be excuse. I will never chew gum. I will never pop Mr. Beckwith with an rubber.

This is 118 word

The End

I guess I should have felt encouraged that even though they didn't make use of their knowledge, they did know the difference between good and bad behavior.

One afternoon after school, a brawl started in the bus parking lot. I was in my room putting things away for the day when an urgent announcement came over the loudspeaker from Mr. Bibbs: "All male staff members report to the bus parking lot immediately. There's trouble."

I left my room and ran to the lot. Some of my colleagues had arrived at the scene before me. They were already busy trying to part black and white combatants who seemed to be slugging it out everywhere. Two of the brawlers were the same two girls who had written me an essay on behavior only a week before. As fast as the teachers separated some participants, others entered the fray. No weapons were involved, only flailing fists and feet, but the ferocity and determination of both sides was such that we couldn't gain control. Suddenly, I heard the scream of sirens, and we were joined by members of the Leland Police Department. The police had no better success. There were too many students and too few of us, and emotions were running high. The brawl was finally halted when the police sprayed Mace into the crowd. I didn't take a direct hit, but I felt my eyes sting as I got a bit of the drift. I was not prepared for this aspect of the teacher's role. Mr. Cain and I sat on the curb when it was finally over to try to let the adrenalin subside. The combatants were herded onto buses which drove quickly away before trouble could spark again.

Mr. Rollins spent the next day in an unsuccessful attempt to find the instigators of the melee. Finally, just before school was dismissed, he made an announcement over the loudspeaker.

"This is a warning," he said in a very forceful voice. "If any Lincoln student is involved either as an instigator or a participant in a future brawl of this nature, you will be suspended from school for two weeks. This kind of behavior will not be tolerated."

My students thought Mr. Rollins was way out of line, that a brawl wasn't all that serious. After all, no one got seriously hurt.

"It sounds like you didn't understand what Mr. Rollins said," I broke in. "I thought he made it very clear that if a student participates in a brawl in any way, that student will be suspended. No exceptions, no excuses, no extenuating circumstances. If you are involved, then you are gone. If you wish to attend Lincoln, you must distance yourself from any disturbance. That is Mr. Rollins's policy. I agree with him. I will not be able to go to him and plead your case. It will be over for you. This is not a democracy. It's his way or the highway."

When I finished, there were groans, moans, and objections that I ignored. Their attitude was that they were not the ones out of bounds—we were. The faculty was grossly unfair.

The following day, I returned to my room after lunch to find desks piled on top of each other, the seat of my chair coated in chalk, and "Go to hell!" scribbled in red crayon on the blackboard. This was retribution for the stern lecture I had delivered the day before. I was never able to apprehend the culprits, and I was furious not only at the destruction which went unpunished but also about the time wasted in cleaning up the mess.

The violence in the schools coincided with my classes' study of religions of the world. From the Crusades to the Holocaust, differences over religious beliefs had caused more deaths than disputes over land, water rights, and inheritances. Most of my seventh graders' knowledge of religious topics was limited to the local version they had been exposed to through their families. Not only were they unfamiliar with other faiths, but in most cases they had never even heard of them.

The study of religions of the world gave me the opportunity to try to improve my students' limited reading ability, expose them to the moralistic messages that might lessen racial tension, and develop the diverse racial and social groups into a cohesive unit. I set aside time during homeroom for the students to read a passage of their choice from the Bible or an alternative inspirational source. The reading would be followed by a song that they could choose from some worn paperback songbooks I'd managed to retrieve from the trash at the Methodist church in Greenville.

Once the novelty of this had worn off, retaining the class's attention was hampered by the limited reading ability of the daily leader. Readings were diverse. Some were from a Bible I kept in the room. Other readings came from fundamentalist publications in local churches that they had brought from home. We had readings from mainline Protestant publications, but many were from churches such as the Mormon, Christian Science, Bethel African Methodist Episcopal, Mount Zion Primitive Baptist, and Mennonite. The one selection everyone knew was the Lord's Prayer. Songs ranged from "Amazing Grace" to "Are You Sleeping, Brother John?"

One morning Stanley Gildart read a passage from Psalms and then led the class in the hymn "The Old Rugged Cross." This was the morning after the day I'd given the class a test on the Muslim religion. After the class took the test, I collected the papers and put them in my desk drawer for safekeeping until I had time to grade them. Just then, Mrs. Hadley stopped at my door and beckoned to me to step into the hall. She reminded me of a meeting in the teachers' lounge after lunch. In passing, I mentioned that Stanley had just finished leading the class in the day's inspirational reading. She rolled her eyes. "He could use it," she said as she hurried off.

As I stepped back into the room, there was Stanley at my desk; the drawer was open, and he was rifling through the test papers to find his so he could change some of his answers. Obviously, my focus on ethics was unsuccessful.

"Cheating gets you an automatic zero, Stanley," I said after class.

"I know that," he nodded, "only please, Mr. Beck, don't tell anybody the reason for the zero."

That wasn't my only occasion to wonder about absorption levels in class talks about religions of the world. In the midst of our class discussion about the Muslim faith, Mary Bishop raised her hand.

"Mr. Beck, can Muslim men have babies?"

Topics that seemed to stimulate the most enthusiasm were Lucifer's expulsion from heaven and the story of Noah's ark. When I stated that a group of archaeologists had recently reported that they might have discovered the ark on a mountain, their interest waned. I got the same reaction when I attempted to broach the subject of the German legend about Faust, the man who sold his soul to the Devil in exchange for knowledge and power. The class decided that both stories were so far-fetched that I must have made them up. I would never be worthy competition for Reverend Ike Eikerenkoetter, the flamboyant radio evangelist who wrote *Thinkanomics and the Science of Living.*

In a last-ditch effort to rekindle interest, I gave the students an assignment. They were to write a report on a religion that we had studied. These reports were to be presented to the class. The reports were remarkably bad, resulting in a really, really low level of attention, which led in turn to discipline problems. The solution? I became the one to report about different religions around the world. Another lecture! The morale of the class was fine; mine was down around my ankles.

In discussing the structure of the Roman Catholic Church, I thought I was making progress until I gave a pop quiz. A no-brainer true/false question was: "The monks married the nuns and raised little priests."

Three-fourths of the students marked it "true."

All I could do was shake my head and groan.

36

April showers bring May flowers, the saying goes. May Day, once an important holiday but now all but ignored, was the harbinger of the end of the school year and the beginning of the extended summer vacation. It was the month for graduations, and for some, the end of school careers. For others it would be only a temporary hiatus before going to college. I couldn't believe that almost a whole year had passed since I had graduated from the University of Mississippi.

For Lincoln Attendance Center it was a final opportunity to end the turbulent school year on a positive note. Or, just another month to continue the bickering, confusion, and hatred that had been the hallmark of the 1969–70 school year. Leland had gained a lot of unwanted national publicity. All the fallacies in the hastily organized, patchwork system created by a judge in the cloistered confines of his office became more evident by the week. The new social order did not work, because legislating human relations was not possible.

"Dago!"

"Nigger!"

"Redneck!"

"Burr head!"

Name-calling was common. Students became progressively more aggressive and brazen. As I watched a track meet one day while talking to two students, Charles Robinson asked me for a dollar to buy some beer.

My blistering negative reply all but knocked him back on his heels.

At the same track meet, as I was having a pleasant discussion with two of our white teachers, Mr. and Mrs. Webb, some black students from Dean started misbehaving in the stands. When Mr. Webb attempted to correct one of them, the boys started a fight with him. His wife intervened, only to be told by one of the students to "Go to hell!" As I tried to control that student, the others broke free and disappeared into the crowd.

～

Brawls became commonplace—not only among the boys, but also the girls. A group of black girls formed an "organization" (more commonly known as a gang) and strong-armed those girls who did not want to join. The members traveled in a pack around town. White students, being greatly outnumbered and without clear-cut leadership, tried to avoid dangerous situations, but they weren't always successful.

Students who wouldn't ordinarily have been troublemakers took advantage of this environment to show their darker sides. At the end of the first week of May, I was lecturing to my class when I heard a loud noise coming from a classroom further down the hall. I hurried to investigate the fracas, which came from Michelle's room. When I entered the room, I saw two black girls slugging it out while screaming at each other. Michelle, with her back up against the blackboard like a caged animal, was yelling "Stop it! Stop it!" The fight continued as if she weren't there. The rest of the students were backed up against the windows on one side of the room and the wall on the other. As I entered the fray and tried to control the brawlers, one of them grabbed the other's hair with one hand and yanked her head back. With the other hand she raked my arm with her long fingernails. As I tried to get my arm away from her I splattered blood on Michelle's blouse, which terrified her even more.

Then the unexpected happened. Charles Robinson, the boy I had written off in my mind as a lost cause, sprang from the pack of students huddled at the windows and grabbed one of the girls. Another student took heart from his action and grabbed the other. Stepping over upturned desks, I led Michelle away from the melee. By then, Mrs. Hadley had heard the commotion and alerted Mr. Rollins, who soon arrived and took the two combatants to his office. With the help of the students, Michelle and I put the room back in order. Our hearts were still pounding when we sat in two empty desks to regain our composure. The students were mute.

Michelle took a couple of deep breaths, then turned and looked at me. "I'll be all right now. Thank God you were close by."

She turned to Charles. "You were great. Thanks so much."

He beamed at her praise.

She glanced down at the front of her blood-stained blouse and grimaced. "What a mess. I'm afraid it won't come out."

"Someday one of us ought to write a book about this year." I gave her an oblique look. "Want to collaborate?"

She shook her head and gazed out of the window. "I'll want to forget this year as soon as I can, not write about it."

Realizing I'd better see what mayhem was going on in my own room, I pushed myself to my feet. "Back to the salt mines," I said. "I hope I've still got a class and that they're in their seats."

Her "Thanks again" followed me out the door.

More trouble came at lunch. This time it was a fight on the playground, where two boys were engaged in a slugfest in the quadrangle. Teacher Bill Hayes grabbed one, I grabbed the other until Mr. Bibbs came to take charge. A third conflict that day broke out in the bus parking lot when the black girls in the "organization" began battling those who had chosen not to join. Every male teacher available ran to the bus lot. As we entered the fray, we heard police sirens, slamming car doors, and police whistles. The next thing I knew, my eyes had that now-familiar stinging sensation. A haze rose over the lot as Mace permeated the air. There was a thundering sound of fleeing footsteps, and suddenly the bus area was empty. Adults in the neighborhood had heard the disturbance and came to investigate, and their shouting and gesticulating made the police's job even more complicated.

The bus brawl made both regional and national news, again giving Leland negative media coverage. The perpetrators who had initiated the fracas were hard to identify among the innocent bystanders who were drawn into the violence.

Mr. Rollins called an emergency faculty meeting the next afternoon to discuss how to suppress the racism that was most prevalent in the ninth grade students. He asked for suggestions about what could be done to lessen tensions.

"There have been racial problems since the 1600s," Tommy Seaton said. "How can we be expected to solve this with one semester of integrated schools?"

Murmurs of agreement resounded.

"Time. It's going to take time," someone else contributed.

"Another problem we have," Mr. Rollins went on, "is that some of the black students are cutting their last-period class and leaving the campus. If last-period delinquencies are detected, effective immediately the penalty is suspension until a parent-student conference with me or Mr. Bibbs can be arranged."

At the end of the meeting, Mr. Rollins asked us to give him the names of any students whom we thought might be mentally disturbed.

I heard a snicker behind me and turned to see an embarrassed Michelle covering her mouth with her hand. She looked at me and whispered, "I'll just copy my whole grade book and turn it in."

Her whisper was louder than she'd intended, and there were muffled laughs of agreement to her suggestion. Mr. Rollins tried, but did not succeed, in looking disapprovingly at Michelle.

Mr. Bibbs and I exited the meeting together. "The minds of some of these kids, black or white, aren't colorful enough to be classified as disturbed," he murmured as we started down the hall.

"Speaking of colorful," I rejoined, "I guess you heard about Mrs. Levison's remark to Mary Bishop the other day?"

"No, I missed that," he answered.

"You know the white girl Gail McCool?"

He nodded.

"She ran out of Mrs. Hadley's class crying that Mary had called her an ugly little fat whitey," I said. "When Mrs. Levison heard about it, she called Mary down to her office and told her, 'Although Gail may outweigh you physically, she outweighs you mentally by an even wider margin. If your IQ results were basketball scores, you wouldn't even be in the game.'"

"What was Mary's response?" Mr. Bibbs asked.

"A blank. To make a point with someone, you need to be sure they've got the intelligence to understand it. Maybe you've got to expect a certain amount of jealousy to develop when one student has a 72 IQ and the other has 110, even if the 72 doesn't have enough sense to know the difference."

He nodded knowingly. "You remember that expression 'My mama didn't raise no fools?' Well, I'm afraid Mary's mama did."

～

As May progressed, the racial discord intensified at the previously all-white Dean. Black thugs began blocking entryways to the classrooms, forcing the white students to brush up against them in order to enter. This was used as an excuse to start fights. Watching the news on TV that night, I learned that Dean was considered a kettle about to boil over. Many of the white teachers walked out of their classrooms. The black kids took over the school. Students who didn't want to go to class milled about in the halls.

John Ward, Dean's principal, didn't know what to do. He didn't discipline the students; he didn't back his staff. Many teachers walked off the job. Since there weren't enough substitutes to replace them, some classes had no teacher at all. Mr. Ward seemed to believe that the situation was so bad that it couldn't get worse and would have to improve. Things at Dean didn't improve, though; in fact, they finally deteriorated to the point that the only way to maintain order was to allow only a portion of the student body to attend school on any particular day.

In the teachers' lounge at Lincoln we discussed the chaos at Dean. Mrs. Little reminded us of Mr. Rollins's advice to Mr. Ward back at the beginning of the semester: clamp down on the troublemakers the minute they start. "Mr. Ward didn't pay attention," she said. "Now, since they got away with the small things at the beginning, the thugs are getting away with the bigger things and the situation is out of control."

"By comparison to Dean, we look pretty good," I said.

"We lost some battles, but at Dean they've lost the war," Mrs. Hadley added.

Unable to resist a little dig at Mrs. Hadley, I knitted my brow in a puzzled frown. "Wasn't that where you wanted to work when you first came here?"

Her eyes narrowed. "You and your big mouth!"

37

As the semester finally wound down, the time neared for final exams. I was caught up in a tug-of-war of emotions. At the beginning of the last six weeks I had finally gotten the guts to tell Mr. Rollins that I was going to graduate school. Instead of trying to give me a guilt trip, he was very understanding. As word of my plans circulated around the school, some of my colleagues teased me about abandoning them in their time of need. I heard comments like "Well, when the going gets tough, the tough get going—out of here!"

On one occasion, a playful Bill Hayes embarrassed me in the teachers' lounge by getting down on one knee in front of me. "Please, Massa David, take me wid' you. I promises to be good," he pleaded in his best Stepinfetchit imitation. Appreciative guffaws accompanied applause.

That encouraged Pearlie to pretend to swoon in my lap, proclaiming, "Now, Romeo, I have no reason to live!"

Mrs. Levison knew that these and other taunts, despite being couched in jest, did sometimes sting me. She stopped me in the hall one morning.

"Don't let the jabs of the other teachers get to you," she advised. "They mean well. I understand your decision. If you were one of my children, which you really have become, I'd encourage you to be all that you can be. Don't let what others say deter you."

I thanked her for her thoughtfulness. "Their comments did bother me," I confessed, "but what you say means more to me than their criticism."

Even though her words didn't completely assuage my feelings of guilt, I felt better when we parted. In spite of telling myself that Lincoln was just a job, I knew that wasn't true. I would leave part of myself here.

Our days now were spent almost entirely on review, which bored the students. A rumor circulated that the black girls in the "organization" were planning a fight against the white girls on the last day of school. Mr. Bibbs called me aside and told me to be on my toes, because in black schools the last day was called "Grudge Day," the day when revenge was taken for any injustices—whether real or perceived—that had occurred during the school year.

At a faculty meeting, Mr. Rollins told us that report cards would be given out in the gym instead of the homerooms so that he and Mr. Bibbs would be there to deal with any last-minute problems. "I've also decided that, on the last day, we will dismiss the town students fifteen minutes before the bus students," he said. "This will avoid any confrontation between the two groups and will also minimize the possibility that problems between white and black parents will arise."

Teachers spent time in those waning days before exams trying to determine which students in our homerooms would return to Lincoln in the fall. The preregistration card was a simple one-sided form asking for name, address, phone, and birth date. As usual, it took half the period to get the cards filled out and collected. All the black students in my homeroom said they would return in September. Three of the white students said they would return, two said they would not, and three had not answered.

I decided to try one last wonderful, innovative idea on my Lincoln students before I disappeared over the horizon. That was to let them ask each other questions that they thought were important for the final exam. They, too, thought this was an exceptionally good idea. Alas, the questions nearly always missed the important points and concentrated on trivia. The respondents then either all tried to answer the questions at once by shouting out answers, or used the time as an excuse to be disruptive. This novel idea, like my others, failed. The following day, I surrendered. I went through the book and told them the questions I would be asking. Once again, every question on the final exam would come from a previous test.

After lunch that day, the student body was summoned to the gym by Mr. Rollins. "My purpose for bringing you here is to explain the summer school program," he began. "When you get your final report card, some of you will see 'summer school recommended' on it. This notice means that your teachers think that some of your skills may be deficient and that summer school would bring them up to where they ought to be."

He paused amid murmurings and quizzical looks from some of those present. Then he continued: "Summer school is a voluntary program—I cannot force you to be present. It will be in your best interest, if you get such a notice, that you do attend. The term starts June 7 and ends July 12; classes last until noon. Buses will run for those who need transportation. If you have any questions, your homeroom teacher will answer them."

When we returned to homeroom, a sea of questions swamped me—as usual, all at one time. "How we going to know if we need summer school?" Five times, I went through an explanation of how yearly averages are derived and how they are used as a guide to decide whom to recommend for summer school. Each explanation elicited a fresh barrage of questions. Mercifully, the bell rescued me. Why do the simplest concepts turn complicated?

Exams started the next day, Friday. As usual, the students didn't take exams seriously, and I spent a lot of time policing and threatening. After grading the papers, I found that most of the class failed in spite of the fact that I had told them what questions I was going to ask. Was I talking to myself?

Monday, when exams continued, I told the students in 7C that this was their final chance to improve their grades. On a whim I decided that a bribe was in order. "If you concentrate on the exam, do not disturb students around you, and do your level best to succeed, I will add ten points to your test paper," I announced.

To my astonishment, my idea worked. I had only one disciplinary problem during the whole period. They concentrated on the test, and behaved as they had never done before. I tried the tactic again on 7E that afternoon. Again there was dramatic change in behavior. Why hadn't I thought of this before?

Complete victory was not to be mine, however. In spite of the fact that the exam consisted of one hundred multiple-choice questions, ninety-eight of which had been used on previous tests, I knew that some students in my lower classes would assume that failure was inevitable, would rush through the exam, and then, with time on their hands, would cause mischief. To deter this, I suggested that anyone finishing the questions early could enhance their test paper with appropriate drawings or sayings. Perhaps they misunderstood my use of "appropriate."

Only thing I dislike about you, you don't ever let anyone go to get water.

Mr Beckwith is a real nice teacher if he is white

Dear Mr. Beckwith I have enjoyed being with you this year, and I think you Are a wonderful person. even tho you have been mean some days in a week.

> Ed Allen Good luck to you the fellow year

Dear Mr. Beckwith,
   I have enjoyed being with you this semester. You are real nice except for a few times you got mean. But I guess that's what teachers are for.
> Sincerely, Cindy
> (P.S. good luck to your future)

Mr Beckwith you are a nice teacher but when I ask you can I do something I can't Do it. I guess you think I'm like the others but I'm not.

> Irma

You have been a wonderful teacher to me, Even though I have had you only for 1 Semester. I like to come to your class.

Mr. Beckwith a nice good man. Please don't take no point off my paper

> Sign by: Michael O'Reilly

Dear Mr. Beckwith,
   I have enjoyed having you this semester. You are real nice person. I hope you have a real nice summer. May all the years to come be ful of you for you.
> May God bless you always.
> A 7E brat,
> Cathy F
> P.S Sorry about the hard times I gave you.

Dear Mr. Beckwith,
   I have enjoyed spending this second semester with you. My grades

have improved a great deal from the first semester. Coach Glascow was a big shot and I didn't learn to much under him. I wish you luck in your future years.

Sign: a nutty students

P.S. I don't think those 22 licks from Mrs. Hadley did my and good!

Dear Mr. Beckwith,

I have not learned much in History the whole year. Not just in your room. I thank you for what you tried to teach me. I have enjoyed being in your room. I probably did not do well on this paper because I had to go to church. We have been having a revival at Glendale Baptist Church and I want you to come.

Mr. Beckwith is a nice onist man he is understanding he is friendly he is kind he is trust Worthy and also loyal. P.S. I enjoyed your teaching Mr. Beckwith

The last two questions on the exam were meant to be another small bonus. There was no right or wrong answer.

Question 99

(1) I have enjoyed this semester at Lincoln.

(2) Lincoln is no different from any other school I have attended.

(3) I have hated this semester at Lincoln.

Of the white students responding, 11 indicated that they liked it, 8 found it no different from any other school they had attended, and 9 hated it. Most of those who hated it were girls. Of the black students, 75 liked it, 39 saw no difference, and 7 expressed a dislike.

Question 100

Mr. Beckwith is:

(1) a real stinker

(2) a heavenly being

(3) a mean louse

(4) a brilliant, understanding teacher.

My personal poll resulted in 14 real stinkers, 14 heavenly beings, 17 louses, and 105 brilliant, understanding teachers.

I'm not sure my college statistics teacher would have considered this a valid sampling technique, but it added two points to each test score.

On Tuesday, since the students were not required to attend school, we assembled final records. Charles Robinson paid me a visit, pleading with me to overlook his past indiscretions and bad grades and pass him to eighth grade. When I refused, his attitude abruptly changed and he vowed to get even. By the end of the day, I had finished my work. What a relief to have it all behind me.

Fifteen students in my homeroom were not promoted to eighth grade unless they attended summer school. Only eight of them signed up to attend. Two of my female black students would not get their final accounting from me, since they had never bothered to return their report cards from the previous six weeks.

That night, vandals struck the school, breaking 140 windows. Every window in the Home Economics department and half of those in the library were smashed. For some unknown reason, only one window in my homeroom was destroyed. The rock was still on the floor the next morning. Police arrested two black third grade students; because of their age, the boys were released to their parents.

Early the next day, in broad daylight, black students entered the school, smashed light fixtures, and knocked down doors. That night, thugs broke into Mrs. Levison's office, using a crowbar to pry the lock and the doorknob off of her door. They tore open her filing cabinets, tossed papers and files from one end of her office to the other, and filled her telephone with shaving cream. The vandals destroyed all the record books, promotion sheets, and grade books that the teachers had completed and returned to Mrs. Levison, and stole the keys to all the classrooms. Before report cards could be handed out the next day, the promotion data had to be reassembled from the records that could be located. We were all numb from shock at this vicious, senseless attack.

That afternoon, Mr. Levison made an unexpected visit to my classroom. I was sitting at my desk, musing about the sad end to the year.

"David, I've brought you your final check." He handed it to me across my desk, then stuck his hands in his pockets and walked a few paces toward the window. "I don't know what's going to happen tomorrow when report cards are handed out. We may see more vandalism from people disappointed in their grades." He shook his head. "So much senseless waste."

Then he stopped and faced me. "I don't need to tell you, my friend, that you're a perfect target and scapegoat for anything and everything. Don't tell anyone I gave you your check early. I'm holding everyone else's until tomorrow." He smiled. "You've been an asset to the school. I'm going to miss not having you around." He held out his hand, and I grasped it for a few moments.

"Thanks. That means a lot to me," I said. "I've changed in many ways— for the better, I hope. If I weren't going on to graduate school, I'd consider coming back to see how things turn out." We looked at each other. "I'm going to miss you and all the others. It's been one hell of a year, hasn't it?"

"It certainly has," he nodded. "Well, good luck. I know you'll do fine."

As I watched him leave, I thought back to the first time we'd met when I had come to my first faculty meeting. It seemed so long ago. I *had* grown up.

Later that afternoon, Mr. Bibbs came by my room. "Couldn't talk you into staying, I guess," he said as he walked toward my desk. "Given a little more time, I'd have made a real teacher out of you. The raw material is there."

"You guys are making it tough for me to leave." I smiled. "Man, you're the best. A real pro. I wish I could be like you."

"Well, if I can't make a teacher out of you, maybe I can make you into a beer drinker. I'll treat you to a couple after we're through with work—as a thank-you for a job well done." He shrugged. "And because I like you."

"Mr. Bigham said he didn't want us to be seen in a juke joint."

"Screw that hypocrite. He's history," Mr. Bibbs said with a grin.

"Will I be welcomed in a black juke joint?" I asked.

"People have always wondered about me—the nigger in the woodpile because of my light complexion. We'll make them wonder more. You'll be my nigger in the woodpile."

Just then, Mr. Rollins stuck his head in the door. "I heard that, niggers. I'd go with you, but I've got a baby at home. Drink one for me. We deserve it. We survived, which is more than I can say for Bigham and Ward. Just remember this," he said, looking at me, "one of these days, when you're some kind of big shot, don't forget your roots."

With a wave of his hand, he was gone.

38

The next day the gym was buzzing with energy. Teachers had handed out report cards, which had elicited bragging on the part of those who'd been promoted and groans from those who'd be returning for summer school. Any gloom was short lived, however. Soon there was the usual chasing each other around the gym or up and down the bleachers. Mr. Rollins and Mr. Bibbs stood ready to head off any serious outbreak of rowdiness, but for the most part this exuberance was due to being through with school. Final results were of secondary importance to the fact that school was out! Students yelled good-byes to those they wouldn't see until fall; others told of vacation plans.

"Hey, J. D., whatcha doin' this summer?"

"I'm just hangin' out. What you gonna do?"

"I'm gonna go see my grandmother. You gotta go to summer school?"

"Nah. I'll be working. I got a job at the railroad yard."

Some of the white parents, afraid to send their children alone to pick up their report card, had also come to the gym. Vertis Ethridge's parents came with her. They seemed to enjoy glaring at me, but at this point I didn't care. One plus about not coming back in the fall would be not having to endure the Vertises of this world. Brenda McGary tried every argument and tactic, including tears, to talk me into giving her a report card. I had told her numerous times that she would not receive the card because she had never returned it to me after the second six weeks. Furthermore, until she paid all the fines she owed, there would be no report card.

Several students asked me again why I wrote "summer school recommended" or "summer school required" on their report card. Wearily, and for the umpteenth time, I explained that "summer school recommended" or "summer school required" did indeed mean they had to attend summer school and make passing grades to be promoted to eighth grade.

When the distribution of report cards was complete, we dismissed the town students but held the bus students for another fifteen minutes; then, they were gone.

While the adrenalin evaporated, I went back to my empty classroom and sat at my desk. I needed a few moments in the quiet just one last time. As I stared out over the desks, I saw the faces of the many who had passed through—the good students, the bad, and the indifferent. Had I touched any of them in a meaningful way? Or was I just one more teacher to them? A tap on the door broke into my reflection.

"May I come in?" It was Mrs. Levison.

"Certainly!" I rose from my chair. "You're always welcome."

"I'll never get used to seeing someone else behind your desk," she said, walking toward me.

"Sitting here in peace over the last few minutes, I realized that this has become home. I'm going to miss all the teachers and the staff. But I'm especially going to miss you." I frowned, suddenly filled with ambivalence. "Should I stay?"

She shook her head. "No, David. You've got a life to live. You're young. Finish your schooling, or do your duty in the armed services before you meet some young lady who wants you to get married and have a family. I just hope we don't lose touch."

Tears came to my eyes as she opened her arms and we embraced. Not black and white, not older and younger, not experienced and inexperienced; just two people who liked and respected each other. As we separated, there were tears in her eyes too. We didn't need more talk—the hug said it all.

After she left, I walked to the window. My gaze traveled across the yard where grass struggled to survive, on to the oak tree shading the sidewalk, then to the street where students had marched, chanting slogans and shaking their fists. So much had happened. My interview with Mr. Bigham seemed like an aeon ago. Never again would I read with indifference newspaper articles about school unrest, or academic excellence, or teacher walkouts. I had been in the trenches.

"I've come to say good-bye."

As I turned to see Michelle walking toward me, I realized again that she was everything a man could want in a woman. Beautiful, smart, good company. I couldn't think of anything negative about her—except that our timing was off. Mrs. Levison's advice that I finish my education before settling down was good, but singularly difficult to view dispassionately.

She came to stand beside me at the window. I examined her profile, trying not to dwell on the line of her cheek, the perfect chin as she gazed at the scene I'd surveyed moments before. She was frowning.

"What's the matter?" I asked.

"I just told Mr. Rollins that I've decided not to come back in the fall."

"Really? I thought you were set on staying. What changed your mind?"

She turned and faced me. "I'm just not willing to put up with all the disruption: having to be a policeman most of the time instead of a teacher, the friction between the black and white teachers as well as the students. I feel ineffective here. I guess I don't have the missionary zeal that's necessary to cope with the daily clashes. And with you gone, I won't have anybody I can really talk to." She smiled. "We did have some good talks, didn't we? I always felt so at home with you. I knew that whatever I confided in you wouldn't go any further."

"Yes," I nodded. "I'll miss that! But I can hardly urge you to stay when I'm leaving."

"You've got a good reason for leaving. I feel like I'm abandoning a sinking ship."

"Don't beat up on yourself. You did a good job," I countered.

"Thanks. I did try." She pushed herself from the windowsill and we looked at each other, reluctant to let go. I pulled her to me and we held each other, not caring that someone passing might see us. She lifted her face, and we kissed for the last time.

"Good-bye," she murmured. "I wish things could have been different."

As I watched her walk away, I felt that part of me was leaving. "Michelle," I said hoarsely. She turned to face me. "This doesn't have to be the end. You know my parents' address in Greenville. When you get settled you could write me in care of them—let me know how to reach you. You might even find a job in Oxford. We could go to some Ole Miss football games, and I know a great pizza place—as good as Lillo's."

"My, oh my. You'll be a carefree student again."

I shook my head. "Not after having sat on the other side of the desk for a year," I countered. "I wish we'd known each other at Ole Miss."

"That might not have worked," she suggested. "We were different people then—just teenagers." She smiled. "I'm glad it worked now."

There was nothing left to say. I had trouble swallowing as I watched her go out of the door.

Musing about what might have been, I gathered the last of my belongings from my desk, took one final look around the classroom. It was so still. I smiled as I thought back to the energy and noise generated by thirty restless children. I had so often longed for peace and quiet. Now, I missed their bustle and high spirits.

A last good-bye awaited me. I walked down the hall to Mr. Rollins's office. He sat with his feet propped up on his desk, his tie loosened. He looked over his shoulder at me as I entered.

"I was hoping you'd stop by before you left the building," he said. He swung his feet to the floor and turned to face me.

"You knew I would." I frowned. "You don't just walk out on friends without saying good-bye."

"One hell of a year wasn't it?" he said. "But we took everything they threw at us, and here we are." He shook his fist in the air. "We survived phase one—too bad you won't be a part of phase two."

"I thought I just wanted to pass time for a year. But, damn it, you're not making leaving any easier. I feel like I ought to be coming back. You know—I think I may have reached some of them."

"One thing I know—you'll never be the same. You've changed some of these kids; we've also changed you. Good luck. You're gonna do fine. When you've grown up, let me know what you turn out to be."

"I'll do that," I promised. "Meanwhile, I've got a date."

"Michelle?" he asked.

My eyebrows rose. "You know about Michelle and me?"

"I may be black, but that doesn't mean I'm blind and stupid," he retorted.

"Oh," I said.

My inadequate response made him grin. "Don't worry. It's not that obvious. She's a good teacher," he said, "not to mention a good-looker," he added with a wink.

"Do you want to hear about my date, or don't you?"

"Sure. Lay it on me."

"I'm off to lunch with Mrs. Hadley and Pearlie."

He laughed. "Mrs. Hadley. She was a piece of work when she first came here. But I've really gotten to like her. I'm glad we had you both. We're better for it."

He stood up, and we shook hands for the final time.

I walked out of the building toward the teachers' parking lot, where I loaded my old Rambler with the world globe and the other flotsam and jetsam I'd brought to school during the year. As I slid under the steering wheel I couldn't shake off an unexplainable sadness. *What the hell's the matter with you? You aren't going to miss that ramshackle building or the misbehavior of the kids. It's been traumatic and an unsettling experience, and you should be glad to be out.* Instead, I wondered who would be teaching my seventh graders next year. Would that teacher be careful of the ones that needed to be encouraged, mindful of the hardships many of these children faced?

As I drove away and Lincoln Attendance Center receded into the distance, I flipped on radio station WDDT, hoping for distraction. Johnny Cash was singing:

No, the circle won't be broken,
By and by, Lord, by and by . . .
("Daddy Sang Bass," Carl Perkins)

Epilogue

More than thirty years have passed since my year at Lincoln. Thanks in part to my favorable lottery number in the draft, I was able to finish my MBA without interruption. Subsequently, I embarked on a career with two of Wall Street's largest firms—an experience that has now spanned my working career. I never completely left teaching. For many years I was an adjunct finance professor for several colleges, and occasionally I've guest-lectured in secondary schools. All in all, I've made several thousand public presentations. My teaching experience at Lincoln prepared me for the future, leaving behind the guy who once nervously fumbled to find enough to say to make it until the bell rang each day.

In 2003, feeling nostalgic about that chaotic year and tumultuous era, I went back to the town of Leland to discover what changes had taken place in the old stomping ground. I parked in the visitors' parking lot and made my way to the front of the building. Though the sign by the entrance announced Leland Middle School, the engraving in the concrete over the front door still said Lincoln Attendance Center. The building is dedicated to the long deceased A. B. Levison, which means nothing to many newcomers. As I entered the building, I could still hear Mr. Levison's voice and picture him as he was when I saw him at the first faculty meeting: erect, welcoming, a smile on his face as he held out his hand to welcome this white neophyte.

In the principal's office, I paused to look into what used to be Mrs. Levison's domain where she worked miracles with rebellious students. A nicely dressed black receptionist greeted me. She was attractive, younger than I.

"I used to teach here," I told her after I'd introduced myself. "I wonder if I could speak with the principal for a few minutes."

"Have a seat," she said. "I'll go and ask her."

As I waited, the familiar surroundings triggered thoughts of Michelle. We hadn't kept the promise to stay in touch. I had written her in care of her parents, and when I had no reply I'd made a phone call. Her mother told me that she had forwarded my letter to Michelle in Ft. Walton Beach, Florida. "She's teaching in a high school there," her mother explained. "I'm sure you'll be hearing from her shortly."

When no reply came, I was very disappointed. In time, however, I wondered if we would have been compatible over the long haul, or if we had been two people caught up in a sea of social change, clinging to each other to keep from drowning. Probably she had married and was raising a family, as I was. I wished her well.

The principal soon appeared at the door. She was also black. "Do come in," she smiled graciously. "I would love to talk with you."

Seated opposite her at her desk, I seemed to be in a time warp. Mr. Rollins should be sitting in her seat.

"How long ago were you here?" she asked, "and what did you teach?"

I told her it was the year that integration had been mandated by the U.S. Supreme Court. "It wasn't an easy year," I concluded.

She nodded. "So I've heard. Many changes have taken place since then."

I began to ask her about those I knew. I started with Mr. Rollins.

She shook her head sadly. "I knew him. Ted was such a fine man. He became the first black principal at the Greenville High School—my alma mater. He died too young of a terminal illness. He was only sixty-four when he passed. He has been greatly missed."

I shook my head. "What a shame. He was one of a kind. I got to know him well during my stint here," I said, "and admired him so much."

She told me that the Levisons had both passed but that their legacy lived on in the person of their daughter, who became an educator in the Delta.

"I am truly saddened to hear these stories. They were all the salt of the earth. I wish I knew just how to express my feelings," I responded.

"I know what you're trying to say. Sometimes there just aren't words to express what we want to say. Mrs. Levison was only fifty-nine when she died in 1974. She became the guidance counselor at Dean after Heno Head left. When Mrs. Levison died she had been ill for some time. I think she had cancer. Mr. Levison only lived for a couple more years after she died, but he was more than ten years older than she was. He died of cancer as well," she nodded sympathetically.

"What ever happened to Virgil Bigham?" I asked next.

"As I'm sure you recall, Mr. Bigham left Leland the year you worked at Lincoln and became the superintendent of schools in Pontotoc. I guess he had Delta mud between his toes, however. He returned to Leland to retire in 1972."

"Dodging a few mudpies in the meantime," I said cryptically.

She only smiled.

"What about Mr. Woolly?" I asked.

"I'm pretty sure the Woollys retired to Florida. Oh, by the way, speaking of superintendents, one of your colleagues, Ilean Kelly, is now our school superintendent. Her married name is Richards. She started at Lincoln the same year you did. Taught history at the high school."

Of the other people I mentioned, there were some she had never heard of, while others had moved from the area. I told her about the local blues legend, Boogaloo Ames, having once tried to teach me piano. That brought a big smile to her face. "His funeral filled the E. E. Bass auditorium in Greenville, and all but one of his pallbearers was white."

When I asked about Mr. Bibbs, she nodded. "He's very much alive. Several years ago, he was promoted to being the first black principal of Dean High School." She shrugged. "He later left education—why, I never knew—and then spent his remaining working career as the owner of a concrete contracting company." She smiled. "Mr. Bibbs's management skills are legendary, even today."

"I'd like to see him, if that's possible," I said.

"I'm sure he'd be glad to see you too. I'll give you his phone number." She looked up his number and wrote it on a piece of paper for me.

I thanked her for her time and information. "You've been most helpful."

Later that day, I phoned Mr. Bibbs at his home, and he urged me to come and visit. I arrived at his one-story, attractive brick house and found that, though older, he was still the pragmatic, mentally tough person I'd known when we were together at Lincoln. He invited me into his sitting room, which overlooked a garden where, he said, his wife routinely worked miracles. Mr. Bibbs said that he had a brown thumb and could probably even kill weeds. His wife was currently attending an all-day flower festival.

He offered me iced tea, and we sat for what seemed like fifteen minutes but was actually two hours, renewing old ties. We talked about values, personal discipline, the necessity of a good education in today's ever more complex world. We also reviewed the turbulent times we'd been through at Lincoln. "The confusion didn't end with the '69–'70 school year," he said. "The following year was a difficult one. Lincoln was partially destroyed by fire—of unknown origin. Walkouts continued. Many people, black and white, said things they later regretted. The turmoil of the sixties wasn't confined to the South, though the South bore the brunt of the criticism for the race discrepancies," he said.

"Did many of the whites leave the schools?" I asked.

He nodded. "Many did, but not all of them. Too often, blacks with limited means, ability, and influence were the primary force in the public schools. More than anyone else they had a vested interest in making positive things happen. Unfortunately, they just didn't know how to manipulate the system. Community support for their efforts was either nonexistent or misdirected." He shook his head. "The problems haven't vanished over the past thirty years, but the system has endured."

"What's it like today?" I asked.

"Blacks and whites have learned not only to coexist but to respect each other. Today, students choose the 'Teacher of the Year' based not on race but on merit. The system has managed to produce people who make a meaningful contribution to society."

He sipped his tea and then set down his glass. "Back in 1969, no one would have believed that a little more than three decades later, the president of the United States, George W. Bush, would appoint a black man to his cabinet. Roderick Paige, the first African American to serve as U.S. secretary of education, was raised in poverty in Jim Crow Mississippi. His early exposure to education was through a dilapidated segregated 'separate but equal' schoolhouse that often didn't have enough textbooks for all the students. He not only completed college but went on to earn a doctorate. He became the president's adviser on problems that educators face."

I nodded. "Remember what a stir it caused when James Meredith integrated Ole Miss? Well, I just saw an article in the paper saying that his son, Joseph, was chosen as the top doctoral student at the Ole Miss business school."

"As our students would have said, 'Who'd a thunk it!'" Mr. Bibbs said.

I smiled. "That sounds familiar."

"Remember Charles Murray?" he asked.

"I'll never forget the day we had that showdown with him at the library. If you hadn't intervened I'm not sure what would have happened next. What prison is he in now?"

"I'm sure you would have handled the situation—you usually did. But he's not in prison. He's a sergeant with the Leland Police Department. He was officer of the year two years ago."

"Good for him. Sometimes you never know. Just think: Charles, the exemplary public servant. Certainly a far cry from pseudo-respectable white citizen Byron De La, who we all knew was nothing more than a out-of-control cold-blooded murderer," I countered.

"Those of us in the black community sure were glad to see him finally get what he had coming. It was worth the wait."

"Most of us in the white community thought the same thing. We were just afraid to take a stand. I think it's ironic that the *Clarion-Ledger*, long a defender of segregation, did the investigative reporting that finally reopened the Medgar Evers case and led to Beckwith's conviction. It was also a testament to changing times that Byron was convicted not in a federal court but by the assistant district attorney of Hinds County in the same state court system that Byron taunted and thought he was immune from," I reflected.

"We both know it was not the same court," Mr. Bibbs reminded me. "He finally got convicted by a real jury of his peers. There's a lot of people who're glad the mean SOB finally died in prison. He should have spent most of his life there. David, I guess I won't live long enough to see one homogeneous community instead of separate black and white communities, but hopefully you will. De La's conviction certainly brought us closer to that day."

I pushed myself to my feet. "It's been wonderful to touch base with you again. I heard at the school that you're a successful businessman. That didn't surprise me. I can't imagine any endeavor at which you wouldn't be successful. You're one of a kind. It's been a privilege to know you."

He patted me on the back as he walked me to the door. "Give yourself some credit, too. You were more of an influence in that school than you realized. You remember Eddie Watts?"

"Eddie Watts?" I frowned, dredging back through the thirty years for a clue. Then I smiled. "Eddie! Of course! What's happened to him? I hope it's good."

Mr. Bibbs nodded.

"Very good! You took an interest in him when everybody else had given up. You'd be proud to see him now. He went on to finish high school. He and his 'mentor,' Shirley Foster, got married. You remember how good he was at fixing things? Now he's the owner of a car repair shop. He has a thriving business—most of his customers are white—and Shirley keeps the books. They're upstanding members of their community and have two children, both of whom are in college."

I shook my head in amazement. "That gangling fifteen-year-old boy looked like a real loser. All he needed was a chance."

Mr. Bibbs nodded. "And somebody like you to give it to him."

Appendix 1
Internal Staff Memorandum
for Leland Schools

LELAND CONSOLIDATED SCHOOLS
Leland, Mississippi
January 21, 1970

Under orders of the U.S. District Court Leland Consolidated School District is now required to reorganize as follows:

All students in grades 1, 2, 3, and grades 10, 11, and 12 will attend Dean Attendance Center and all students in grades 4, 5, 6, 7, 8, and 9 will attend Lincoln Center. Teachers will, in most cases, be assigned to the center housing the grade they have been teaching.

In order to carry out this court order it will be necessary to suspend classes for all students from the end of school today, January 21, until Monday, February 2.

STUDENTS FOLLOW THIS SCHEDULE

Friday, January 23—All 7, 8, 9 grade students report to Lincoln Attendance Center gymnasium at 8:30 a.m. for pre-registration. All buses will run and you should be at school approximately an hour. You will be given further instructions at this meeting. All students in grades 10, 11, and 12 report to Dean Attendance Center auditorium for pre-registration at

8:30 a.m. All buses will run and you should be at school approximately an hour. You will be given further instructions at this meeting.

Monday, January 26—All students in grades 1, 2, and 3 meet in the auditorium at Dean Attendance Center at 8:30 a.m. for pre-registration. All buses will run and you will be at school approximately one hour.

All students in grades 4, 5, and 6 meet in the gymnasium at Lincoln Attendance Center at 8:30 for pre-registration. All buses will run and you will be at school approximately one hour.

ALL STUDENTS RIDE THEIR SAME BUSES
UNTIL FURTHER NOTIFIED

John F. Woolly
Assistant Superintendent

Appendix 2
National States' Rights
Party Newsletter

IN MIXED SCHOOLS

The U.S. Juvenile Delinquency Subcommittee had released its latest find-ings. During the past two years the crime rate in intergrated [*sic*] schools has jumped up by 2,600 per cent. They found that the duties of a teacher "has been reduced to a level of keeping discipline."

A study of violent crime INSIDE building and grounds of some 110 in-tegrated schools revealed 26 murders, 81 rapes, 680 aggravated assaults and 14,102 larcenies. Teachers often have to carry guns to protect themselves and walkie-talkies to call for help. One city spends $500,000 a year for 170 spe-cial armed guards to patrol halls in mixed schools.

One of the most shocking aspects of this violent trend is that schools offi-cials often "HUSH UP" the violence to keep the parents from withdrawing their children. Newspapers co-operate with school officials and do not pub-lish the news, even students often do not hear all the details of what happens in their own school.

It is almost unbelievable that liberals continue to express wonder at why white people don't want their children to attend mixed schools. We simply want our children to receive a decent education and not be thrown into a den worse than a reform school. It is simply self-defense for the rights of Whites that we fight against school mixing.

Most of those so-called "LIMOUSINE LIBERALS" are in the upper bracket and live far away from the Blacks. If they exist in expensive high rise downtown apartments, their own children go to private schools. It is easy for them to tell the poor White working class that our children "GAIN SO MUCH SOCIAL ENRICHMENT" by associating with Blacks in Mixed schools.

These liberals owe their high living to the labor of the White working man. We are not about to stand idly by and allow these smirking snobs to toss our innocent little children to schools festering with mild and mangy black savages.

We urge all who keep the White race from being a victim of these warped and fuzzy minder [sic] creeps to join the NSRP today. Let's put a stop once and for all to those who work to destroy our scared children.

The following report appeared in the Washington Daily News for October 2, 1969. Washington's public schools were described on the Hill as terrifying blackboard jungles of rape, gang beatings, extortion, dope and senseless vandalism.

This grim picture was outlined by D.C. school and city officials who testified before a D.C. Senate subcommittee on Public Health Education and Welfare, headed by Sen. William B. Spond (D., Va.)

Anacostia Principle [sic] Russ Lombardi told the panal [sic] of one case in which some youths brought sawed-off shotguns to the school. Lombardi also described a gun duel on the school front steps where one youth, not a student, leveled his .45 cal. pistol at this enemies. The enemy left but returned later with sawed-off shotguns.

Another witness said he found a bloodied hypodermic needle on the school lawn obviously dropped by one student who had just taken a shot of heroin.

"There is no question the use of narcotics in school buildings has increased," Charles T. Duncan, the city's acting public safety director told the committee. "This is indicated by the greater number of arrests that have been made for narcotic violations on school premises."

One witness told of a gang of youths who blocked a bridge leading to an elementary school in Southeast Washington. The gang, using threats of beating the younger children, extracted toll charges from the children when they tried to walk to school.

The slaying of Norman Clifford, assistant principal of Cardoza High School who was shot by teenagers who were attempting to rob the school bank last year, has made the teachers more fearful about accosting outsiders in the halls or playgrounds.

Acting School Supt. Benjamin Henley testified that between the first of Sept. and the first of Jan. $133,637 worth of items have been stolen from the D.C. schools. During the past year the vandals smashed 43,695 window panes costing $477,271 to replace them, he said.

To solve the problem, Henley said, the chief need is for resources—"RE-SOURCES TO PROVIDE QUICK COMMUNICATION BETWEEN THE SCHOOL AND POLICE."

Some of the school administrators say the only way to discourage the senseless school destruction is to turn the schools into fortresses.

HOW VIOLENCE IN SCHOOLS IS RISING

A senate studt [*sic*] of 110 school districts show this increase in school crimes—

	1968	1969
Homicides	15	26
Forcible rapes	51	81
Robberies	396	1,508
Aggravated assaults	475	680
Burglaries and larcenies	7,604	14,102
Weapon offences	419	1,089
Narcotics violations	73	854
Drunkeness	370	1,035
Assaults on teachers	25	1,801

A Legal Chartered Organization. The Leland Chapter of the Americans for the Preservation of the White Race. The Leland Chapter was organized and chartered a year ago and it has a membership of 500.

Appendix 3
Letter by National States' Rights
Party National Chairman J. E. Stoner

In carr[y]ing on the struggle for White Christian America and the preservation of our White race, we long ago had to determine whether we were right or wrong. There is no such thing as being half right or half wrong when the existance of our White race is being determined. In this racial civil war, we are either 100% wrong or 100% right. Since God created the White race superior to all other races and created white people in his image, it is our right and our right [*sic*] to live. We must not allow the Jews to murder our White race by pumping the animal jungle blood of Africa into the veins of God's specially created White race.

Since our efforts to preserve the White race are 199% right, we can correctly be described as white racists. We are proud to be totally and completely for the right and extremely against all enemies of our White people.

At a time when the survival of our Race is being determined, moderation is treason to the White race. Our Lord Jesus Christ condemns moderates and wants no part of the lukewarm cowards who have no backbone. Read what our Lord says in the Bible. In Revelation 3:14–16 our Lord says, "And unto the angel of the church of the Laodiceans write; These things saith the Amen, the faithful and true witness, the beginning of the creation of God; I know thy works, that thou wert neither cold or hot. So then because thou art lukewarm, and neither hot or cold, I will spew thee out of my mouth."

It is thus clear that the Son of God is against the lukewarm, otherwise known as moderates. We can only win victory for White Christian America with the strong, not the lukewarm who are unwilling to take a clear cut stand for what is right and against what is wrong. The National States Rights Party is a White organization that wants nothing to do with the lukewarm. We are happy that the Son of God approves of our rejection of lukewarm methods.

When it comes to the racials [sic] civil war in America, we Whites are right. And our Jew and Negro enemies are wrong. There is no middle ground. We of the NSRP are determined to force all members of the White race to choose sides. They must either stand up and be counted as White and on the White side, or go over and jion [sic] the Jews and Black savsges [sic] and declare themselves to be enemies of the White race for as long as they live. Of course, when they jion the camp of the black beasts, we won't have to worry about them any more because the black terrorists will cut them up and kill them. Remember, the blacks hate every person with a White skin and they hate White race mixers more than they hate White racists. The Negroes only have contempt for Whites who are so degenerate as to betray their own kind and join the Black camp.

The sentimental fools and other race mixers with White skins are now caught in a crossfire between White patriots and the Black ape radicals. The middle ground between the White and Black forces if [sic] disappearing at a rapid rate and leaving the White skinned race mixers in an untenable position. Regardless of whether they want to choose half right and half wrong, [they] are, more and more every day, being forced to choose between the rightousness [sic] of White racism on God's side and the evil of the Jews and Negroes with their Satanic Black degeneracy on the other side.

By the time that the racial crisis in America comes to a head, all Whites will be forced to choose sides. That is good. A[s] more Whites are forces to choose sides, they will choose the White side. That will guarantee victory to the White race in America.